My Best Teachers Were Saints

My Best Teachers
Were Saints

*What Every Educator Can Learn
from the Heroes of the Church*

Susan H. Swetnam

LOYOLA PRESS.
A JESUIT MINISTRY
Chicago

LOYOLA PRESS.
A JESUIT MINISTRY

3441 N. Ashland Avenue
Chicago, Illinois 60657
(800) 621-1008
www.loyolapress.com

Text from Bob Dufford's song, "Be Not Afraid," quoted on p. 69 is from hymnal *Breaking Bread*, © 1975, 1978, Robert J. Dufford, SJ, and OCP Publications, 5536 NE Hassalo, Portland, OR 97213. All rights reserved. Used with permission.

Text on p. 97 from Benjamin Britten's cantata, SAINT NICOLAS, © Copyright 1948 by Boosey & Co., Ltd. Reprinted by permission.

Unless otherwise noted, Scripture quotations are taken from the *New American Bible with Revised New Testament and Psalms*, copyright © 1991, 1986, 1970 Confraternity of Christian Doctrine, Inc., Washington, DC. Used with permission. All rights reserved. No portion of the *New American Bible* may be reprinted without permission in writing from the copyright holder.

Scripture quotations marked "NRSV" are taken from the New Revised Standard Version Bible: Catholic Edition, copyright © 1993 and 1989 by the Division of Christian Education of the National Council of the Churches of Christ in the U.S.A. Used by permission. All rights reserved.

Cover design: Anni Betts
Interior design: Kathryn Seckman Kirsch

Library of Congress Cataloging-in-Publication Data
Swetnam, Susan Hendricks.
    My best teachers were saints / Susan H. Swetnam.
        p.   cm.
    Includes bibliographical references and index.
    ISBN-13: 978-0-8294-2329-7 (alk. paper)
    ISBN-10: 0-8294-2329-X (alk. paper)
    1. Christian saints—Biography. 2. Teaching. 3. Education. I. Title.
    BX393.S94 2006
    282.092'2—dc22
    [B]

                                            2006035559

Printed in the United States of America
    08 09 10 11 Versa 10 9 8 7 6 5 4 3

To my first mentors at the University of Delaware:

JERRY C. BEASLEY

D. HEYWARD BROCK

ANNA JANNEY DE ARMOND

JOSEPH HUSZTI

EDWARD ROSENBERRY

And to my late husband, FORD SWETNAM,
one of the best teachers that the world has ever seen.

Table of Contents

July

August

September

October

November

December

Introduction

The concept of mentoring—in which a seasoned practitioner consults with and oversees the work of a less experienced person—has received a great deal of attention lately in education circles. It has long been standard practice to mentor absolute beginners: every elementary and secondary school teacher can remember student teaching, and many colleges and universities designate faculty members to visit new teaching assistants' classes and to hold advisory conferences. Today, many institutions have expanded mentoring, assigning experienced teachers to work with new faculty members in their first years of employment. Additionally, mentors can be designated to work with those whose evaluations suggest the need for improvement. Formal and informal brown-bag lunches, in-service meetings, and after-hours sessions also invite teachers to draw on more experienced colleagues. We can learn a great deal from those who have been teaching for a long time, and these are lessons about the reality of interaction with students that no textbook, no educational theory class can provide. Mentors can offer stories about the times they have been frustrated or surprised; they can offer suggestions and inspirations gained from long experience; they can open new teachers' eyes to wider perspectives.

Beyond these physically present mentors, most of us who are teachers, no matter how experienced, also rely on absent mentors through our memories of our own past best teachers. We use their methods; we model their classroom and evaluation styles. We steal their exercises and insights into particular subject matter. Sometimes we even catch ourselves sounding like them or using their gestures. "What would X do in this situation?" we ask ourselves, when we are at our wits' end. These internal mentors can save our professional lives, and our sanity.

After one difficult day a few years ago in my own teaching career, when I had solved a problem by doing what I guessed a beloved mentor of mine would have done, I caught myself thanking her out loud as I drove home. For several months, I'd been reading my way through *Butler's Lives of the Saints* daily as a sort of morning meditation, and it suddenly struck me that such psychological summoning of my mentor was a kind of veneration, a grateful invoking of someone on whom, to paraphrase the Catholic liturgy, I'd "relied for help."

As I thought about that insight over the next few days, I realized that I'd also been drawing practical inspiration from my morning readings, that some of the literal saints recognized by the Catholic Church had been very, very helpful to me in my teaching life as well as my spiritual one. This book has grown from that recognition. Its basic premise is that reflecting on the lives of the saints as mentors has a great deal to offer all teachers. One doesn't have to be Catholic to appreciate the rich paradigms that saints' lives offer; one doesn't have to believe, even, that all of the personalities chronicled actually existed. One simply has to believe in the power of stories.

Lest teachers shake their heads at this point and complain that they are expected to be saints enough already—working long hours for little pay, encumbered with extra duties, held to impossibly high standards—let me offer the reassurance that *saints* doesn't mean "perfect people." In fact, one of the most attractive things about saints' stories has always been that many of them chronicle complicated, vexed *human* lives, much like ours. Some saints were anything but saintly in their early years. Others, even while leading lives regarded as holy, are reported to have been headstrong, impatient, or just plain prickly. Some got angry; some flailed around before finding their callings; some lost heart temporarily. Nor were their paths easy, with angel choruses showing them the right things to do. The stories of many saints show them facing challenges that echo teachers' daily challenges.

Like us, saints are depicted as often having to deal with recalcitrant and difficult people (including peers). Their stories record that saints faced self-doubt and dry spells in their own inspiration or became too full of themselves; they reached moments when they recognized that their once-helpful paradigms had to change. But all of them found ways to rekindle vocation, and all persevered in doing the work they were meant to do.

The idea of drawing on saints as human models is a very old one, for the Catholic Church has always considered saints as different in degree, not kind, from the ordinary faithful. Saints are, Jacques Douillet has written, "those who march in front and give the example." In the very earliest years of the church, they were simply people who, after their deaths, were venerated by Christians. Saints included martyrs and other holy people whose names had been recorded (canonized) so that others would remember them. Said to be sitting in the presence of Christ, they were believed to be able to intercede directly for the faithful. At first, saints were chosen by local acclaim, their cults centered on their tombs and relics. The centralized church didn't get involved until the Middle Ages, when the increasing power of the papacy lent prestige to a pope's authorization of a saint. During the reign of Innocent III (1198–1216), more formal procedures for canonization were established. The process was further consolidated in 1634, when Pope Urban VIII declared that it was the pope's responsibility alone to designate saints, although those honored previously were grandfathered in. Urban VIII systematized a process of investigation requiring written records, evidence of miracles, or other documentation. The procedure was formulated definitively in the 1917 Code of Canon Law, then reformed in 1983 by Pope John Paul II, who changed the previously trial-like inquiry (which involved a formal devil's advocate who presented unfavorable facts about the nominee) to a more streamlined process. Under John Paul II, 484 new saints were added to the calendar, many from parts of the world that previously had been underrepresented: Asia, North and South America, Africa.

Today a holy person becomes a saint in three stages. First, the person is declared *venerable*, which means that the saint can be venerated in a particular place or by a particular congregation. To earn this designation, the church collects all of the person's writings and evidence from witnesses about his or her life and miracles, and makes minute inquiries. The evidence is sent to Rome and considered by judges. If the person is found to be a martyr or to be noted for the "heroism of his virtue," the pope designates him *blessed*. In order for the person to become a full-fledged saint, ongoing documentation must be provided, including evidence of further miracles. Once the pope formally canonizes the person by proclamation in Rome, the designation is irrevocable.

Catholic tradition continues to honors saints on their feast days, and religious art depicting them hangs in many churches. Many Catholics still associate particular saints with particular occupations, life stages, difficulties, and ailments, and they pray to those saints for specific help in appropriate circumstances. People who "hearingly and unconditionally respond[ed] to God's call" and "led a life of ever-increasing union and conformity with Christ," saints are thought to be close enough to Christ to intercede for their followers. "Friends in heaven," the *New Catholic Encyclopedia* calls them.

As the twenty-first century begins, thousands of men and women have been honored as blesseds or saints. No one knows how many saints have been venerated during the history of the church, given the lack of early records about locally recognized saints and irresolvable confusion about whether or not some early saints with the same or similar names were the same person. The latest edition of the Roman Martyrology alone, which is limited to premodern saints, includes 6,500. The earliest extant calendar of saints dates from the fourth century; by the Middle Ages, many calendars and martyrologies were available, including Jacobus de Voragine's *The Golden Legend*, a best seller in thirteenth-century century Europe, which has continued to stay in print and interest scholars.

During the Reformation, Protestants derided veneration of the saints as idolatry and the stuff of legend. In response, the Bollandists, a group of Jesuits, began in the early seventeenth century a rigorous investigation into the lives of saints that sought to distinguish reliable information from unreliable. Their ongoing research has resulted in the publication of more than sixty volumes. A multivolume calendar of the lives of about 1,500 saints for English readers was compiled by Reverend Alban Butler and published in London between 1756 and 1759. This work, revised and brought up-to-date by Herbert J. Thurston in the early twentieth century, then again by Thurston in cooperation with Donald Atwater in 1956, was reprinted in a manageable four-volume format in the 1980s and 1990s. The 1996 edition of this work—which blends the inspirational, the amazing, and the frankly bizarre—is my own favorite early morning read. Saints have become so popular in recent years ("They're the new angels," someone said to me as I prepared this book) that many works about them are currently in print. One of the most widely available is *The Oxford Dictionary of the Saints*, which has recently been updated (2004) to include a broader range of saints, including some of John Paul II's canonizations.

From the myriad of extant saints, the work that follows selects a limited number whose lives and works have particular relevance for teachers, including teachers in secular elementary and middle schools, high schools, colleges and universities, as well as parochial school teachers, religious education personnel, and catechists. In the following pages, the reader will find some saints who were literally teachers, such as St. John Bosco and St. Jean-Baptiste de La Salle (the patron saint of teachers), and others whose challenges and achievements, though they were not educators, apply to teachers' work.

This book introduces fifty-two saints—one for each week of the year—in the order of the dates of their feast days. These feasts were traditionally assigned to the day of the saint's death, but some feasts have been given alternate dates on the church calendar in modern times, and some saints have more than one feast day. While most of the saints in this book are discussed on their current feast days, attentive readers will note that others appear on their former or alternate feast days. My rationale for these decisions was to include as many of the most compelling saints for teachers as possible. These fifty-two represent a broad range of periods, nationalities, and types of saints (legendary, historical, martyrs, virgins, religious leaders). Each entry includes two components: a biographical sketch of the saint's life, and a reflective essay suggesting how that saint's career might apply to teachers. As readers work through this compilation, they will doubtless think of other things that might be said about these saints, and those familiar with saints may find themselves wondering why their favorites haven't been included. The answer is, simply, that a book like this cannot be comprehensive, either on the level of each individual entry or on the level of the catalog as a whole. If readers begin to muse about saints for themselves, though, this book has served its purpose.

To help readers learn more about the saints whom they find particularly interesting, I've included bibliographies of suggested readings. These are not intended as comprehensive scholarly bibliographies but as lists of works that I found particularly helpful and/or provocative as I investigated each saint. I've also included page references for the 2004 edition of the *Oxford Dictionary of Saints* and for the 1996 edition of *Butler's Lives of the Saints*, since these should be easy for readers to access. My own research for this book was conducted in the spring and summer of 2005 in the libraries of Gonzaga University, Spokane, Washington; The Catholic University of America and Georgetown University, Washington, DC; and Loyola University and

DePaul University, Chicago, Illinois. I am grateful to the Idaho State University Office of Research for funds supporting this work. I am also grateful to the Loyola Press staff, especially Jim and Barbara Campbell Jeanette Graham, and Vinita Wright for their faith in this book and their assistance in its preparation.

Over the past thirty years, I've taught high school students, under-graduates, and graduate students; I've worked in public humanities programming and in workshops for children and for creative writers. I find it shocking, really—as must all longtime teachers—to imagine how many human beings have sat in my various kinds of classes. In so many ways, though, the most satisfying kind of teaching for me has always been working with teachers. In pedagogy classes, in-services, and summer institutes, we form what I believe are the most impor-tant of communities, united in the most noble of purposes. We learn from each other in these settings, and from all the mentors who are sitting beside us in spirit in these rooms. By contrast, in the everyday classroom it's easy to feel isolated, alone with problems no one else has ever faced, devoid of inspiration and of help. I hope that this book, as it invites teachers to move through a year in the company of others, will help to counter such loneliness. We must remember that we are not alone as we seek to inspire and instruct others, and to be examples ourselves. For, as saints' lives illustrate, men and women whose lives are celebrated as holy—mentors of the best kind—have walked these paths before.

1

The Healing Power
of Meaningful Work

St. Elizabeth Ann Seton

1774–1821 ~ USA ~ Feast: January 4

Elizabeth Ann Seton was America's first native-born saint, founder of the Sisters of Charity. She was born into colonial New York aristocracy in 1774, daughter of Richard Bayley, a physician who served as first health officer of the city of New York. Elizabeth's mother died three years after her birth, and her father married a woman who did not take warmly to Elizabeth. Because the marriage was stormy, Elizabeth lived for a time with her uncle in New Rochelle, New York, taking comfort in contemplation of nature and in her devout Episcopalian faith. At twenty, the vivacious, beautiful Elizabeth married William Magee Seton, the son of another prominent New York family. The couple lived in fashionable Wall Street, with Alexander Hamilton as a neighbor. Elizabeth Seton was active in charitable works, and she bore five children.

Around the turn of the nineteenth century, difficulties began to come to the Setons. When William's father died, Elizabeth became mother to that family's children as well as her own. Then William began to manifest symptoms of the tuberculosis that had afflicted other members of his family. During the financial downturn of 1800, the Setons declared bankruptcy and moved to a smaller house. Elizabeth is reported to have been calm during these changes; besides providing love and stability for her family, she also helped her father tend victims of a yellow fever epidemic, during which Dr. Bayley himself died. In 1803, William's condition worsened, and the couple went to Italy for a change of climate. When they arrived, however, they were quarantined in cold, damp conditions because William was already ill. William began to hemorrhage, and he died two weeks later. Elizabeth Seton was left a widow at age twenty-nine in a strange country. William's business associates Antonio and Amabilia Filicchi befriended her, and she began discussing religion and attending church with them. By the time she sailed for home a year later, she was emotionally and spiritually committed to Catholicism.

When Seton returned to New York, however, she encountered great opposition to her new faith. Her minister had warned her before the voyage against the seductions of "the splendid and sumptuous worship of Italy," and he and her friends and relatives were shocked when she returned attracted to Catholicism, "an immigrant religion, whose congregation was composed of the city's lowest elements." Full of "tears and sighs," Seton tried to pray at her old Episcopal church but found herself drawn to a nearby Catholic Church instead. Deciding finally that her conversion was "[God's] affair now," she formally became Catholic on March 14, 1805. Friends began calling her "poor deluded Mrs. Seton"; their criticism became harsher when two of Elizabeth's sisters-in-law, Cecilia and Harriet Seton, converted to Catholicism. Elizabeth rebelled against pity and censure (writing tartly that she was being treated as a child who did not know what was good for her) and turned her efforts to attempting to found a Catholic school in New York.

After anti-Catholic prejudice repeatedly blocked her efforts, Seton was invited to Baltimore by Father Louis William Dubourg. In 1808 she and three of her daughters opened a school there; soon, other women joined them. A year later, a former sea captain purchased land near Emmitsburg (the home of Mt. St. Mary's College) for a convent. Seton and her newly organized Sisters of St. Joseph (later American

Sisters of Charity) took up their work first in a small stone house, then in The White House, a larger building that allowed them to run a substantial school, the first staffed by nuns in the United States. Both boarders and day pupils began to arrive in 1810; the school grew to include as many needy girls and paying pupils as it could hold. Seton dreamed of religious education for all children, and the order expanded to establish the first Catholic orphanage in the country in Philadelphia in 1814 and an orphanage in New York in 1817.

Though her order prospered, Seton suffered many trials: one daughter's death from tuberculosis and another's from a tumor; the deaths of her beloved sisters-in-law, who joined Seton's order; the death of nineteen members of her household over ten years, mostly from tuberculosis. Still, new candidates kept coming, and Elizabeth Seton embraced her role as "mother," leading her order, inspiring her students, and advising young people until her own death of tuberculosis in 1821. Her surviving daughter, Catherine, became a Sister of Charity in 1846 and spent more than forty years ministering to prisoners in New York.

Today, Sisters of Charity across the United States and Canada devote themselves to teaching and serving the poor. When Elizabeth Ann Seton was canonized by Pope Paul VI in 1975, one thousand members of her order were present. She is popularly considered a patron of Catholic schools.

Accepting a Life of Service

Although teachers can draw inspiration from saints who were not educators by profession, it seems appropriate to begin this book with a saint who found her calling squarely—one might say *exemplarily*—in education. Elizabeth Ann Seton was a natural teacher, with "a passion for babies." She eagerly embraced teaching after her widowhood, though she could have lived on the charity of her friends. Alongside her duties as mother superior, she visited classrooms regularly and taught religion and perhaps music and French. She also instructed through copious correspondence with former pupils, parents, and friends. All of her work was distinguished by loving attention. One visitor to the school commented on her "manner of looking upon twenty people in a room with a look of affection and interest, showing an interest for all and a concern in all their concerns."

As a mother herself, though, Seton knew that discipline was essential to learning, and her school was orderly. Days were strictly organized, with time for worship, adoration, study, and recreation interwoven with class periods. Teachers kept watch over their students' behavior and sent Mother Seton weekly reports; if a student acquired a "bad point," she had to balance it with two "good points" by month's end. Discipline was enforced during both school and recreation; girls who went walking always traveled in groups, attended by a nun in front and a nun behind. Secure in the orderly days under Seton's "maternal tenderness," students found their time at the school very happy. "St. Joseph's the blest abode of innocence and virtue how I Long to see it," one former pupil wrote.

Elizabeth Seton was such a natural educator that some who encountered her at St. Joseph's must have assumed that she'd always lived a humble life of service to others. This wasn't true, however. Though Seton had always been altruistic and thoughtful, as a young woman she had been a belle moving at the top of New York society, the wife of a man who doted on her, a wealthy woman with beautiful children. Everyone must have envied her. Then, one by one, her comforts disappeared: first the money, then her beloved father and father-in-law, then, in the greatest blow of all, her husband. It is difficult to imagine how disoriented, how vulnerable she must have felt. Even after she became a Sister of St. Joseph, the blows multiplied, her children and her beloved friends dying until only her two sons and one daughter remained, all living physically distant from her. That she did feel sometimes like Job, despite her joy in faith, is suggested in one of her letters: "Here I go, like iron or rock, day after day, as he pleases and how he pleases; but to be sure, when my time comes, I shall be very glad."

As Elizabeth Seton's children and friends were stripped away, she was left with her work to give her life meaning, and she performed it with ever-increasing vigor, arranging for expansion missions, formalizing the order's charter, and redoubling her correspondence. Even in her last years, a biographer has written, "a host of events . . . enlisted the attention of Elizabeth Seton, aroused her sympathies, or required her energy." This focus on work in the absence of family might strike us today as somewhat pathetic, even as we grant the nobility of her particular calling. She must have been so lonely, we might assume, as her duties became her life. Pop psychology might even suggest that she was using work to avoid dealing with her pain. *Workaholic* is a term of derision today; men and women too devoted to their professions are presented in the media as objects of pity, unfulfilled and wrongheaded betrayers of human bonds. Self-help books chime in here, suggesting that it is dangerous to put too much weight on what we do for a living, rather than "who we are."

Those arguments would have made little sense to Elizabeth Seton. The details of her biography and her letters confirm that for Mother Seton, work was a joy, not a chore. Rather than a second-rate compensation for real life, it *was* real life. Yes, her life now was in a different key than during her marriage, but it was no less fulfilling. For she was performing work that God meant her to do. And as she poured herself out for others, she actually felt her human bonds growing. "I am a Mother encompassed by many children of different dispositions—not equally amiable or congenial—but bound to love, instruct, and provide for the happiness of all, to give an example of cheerfulness, peace, [and] resignation," she explained to a friend. She took comfort that her example was contagious, describing the tranquility of the school and grounds, "the solitude of our mountains . . . skipping children over the woods which in spring are covered with wild flowers . . . all . . . quiet . . . each helping the other with a look of good will which must indeed be seen to be believed."

Left adrift, Elizabeth Seton did not surrender to self-pity. She didn't rely on others to care for her. Instead, she listened to the call to vocation, and she reinvented herself, taking up a life of service that must have made her former existence, though still beloved, look small. Of all the possibilities, she chose *teaching* as the best way to live out her new faith, and teaching made her life significant beyond the family circle.

And so, she is a central mentor for educators, reminding us of how potentially fulfilling the calling we have chosen can become. Our spouses, our families, our friends—of course they also define us. Of course we shouldn't spend all evenings, all weekends, working. But there's no shame in admitting that we are to a large extent defined by what we do for a living, when that job is teaching. For we labor in the same vineyard as Elizabeth Seton, and our work ensures that we, too, will matter, despite what our lives beyond the classroom might bring.

For Further Reading

Joseph I. Dirvin, *Mrs. Seton, Foundress of the American Sisters of Charity* (New York: Farrar, Strauss and Giroux, 1962).

Boniface Hanley, "Elizabeth Ann Seton," in *With Minds of Their Own: Eight Women Who Made a Difference* (Notre Dame, IN: Ave Maria Press, 1991), 67–96.

Betty Ann McNeill, D.C., "Biography of Elizabeth Ann Seton." www.emmitsburg.net/setonshrine/bio.htm.

Annabelle M. Melville, *Elizabeth Bayley Seton, 1774–1821* (New York: Scribner, 1951).

David Hugh Farmer, ed., *The Oxford Dictionary of Saints* (New York: Oxford University Press, 2004), 473–74.

2

Blessed Andre Bessette

1845–1937 ~ Canada ~ Feast: January 6

Blessed Andre Bessette was born Alfred Bessette in 1845 in a small French-Canadian village near Montreal. One of ten children, he lost both his father (in a logging accident) and his mother (to tuberculosis) when he was young. Without the money required to enter an apprenticeship, Bessette cheerfully supported himself by whatever work offered itself: he was alternately a shoemaker, a baker, a farmhand, a blacksmith, a day laborer, a mill and factory worker. When he was in his late teens and early twenties, he crossed the border to work in the United States. Early on, he developed a particular devotion to St. Joseph and attempted "as much as possible to imitate the toilsome and prayerful life of his patron saint."

When he was twenty-three, Bessette returned to Canada to live with relatives, impressing a local priest with his devotion to God and St. Joseph. Although the young man could not read and write and he suffered from chronic stomach problems, the priest listened when he said that he felt a religious calling and told him that his lack of education did not matter. Some brothers, the priest said, served as lay brothers, devoting themselves to manual labor in imitation of St. Joseph. In 1870, when Bessette was twenty-five, this priest sent him to the Congregation of the Holy Cross with a note saying that he was "sending . . . a saint." At first the Brothers were dubious, and even began action to dismiss Bessette due to his health problems and illiteracy.

7

Bessette succeeded in becoming Brother Andre, however, and went to serve in the order's Notre Dame College in Montreal, a school for boys. There he was assigned a multitude of practical duties. He kept the linens, served in the infirmary, worked as a janitor, was responsible for ringing the bells, worked in the garden, delivered the mail, and ran errands. Principally, though, he was the porter/doorkeeper (he joked that "at the end of my novitiate, my superiors showed me the door, and I stayed there for forty years—without leaving"). Always on call, he was responsible for greeting visitors, taking messages to those within, and standing watch. He lived in a tiny room adjacent to the door, sleeping by choice on a plank bed only sixteen inches wide, and when he went to the chapel for his frequent prayers, he always stood where he could hear the doorbell.

Brother Andre thus lived a humble, useful life, widely beloved by both the boys and his brothers in the order. After a few years, though, he began to attract notice for a more startling gift: healing. Brother Andre began anointing the sick with St. Joseph's oil (oil that had been consecrated before a statue of St. Joseph) and telling them to hold a St. Joseph's medal and pray; miraculous cures were reported. Soon, so many sick people were coming to the convent looking for Brother Andre that his superiors began complaining that the work of the college was being disrupted and the boys put in danger of contagion. "This is not a hospital! Keep the sick people away!" one said.

Brother Andre moved his ministry across the street to a bus shelter. Though he faced accusations of quackery, the Archbishop of Montreal allowed his ministry to continue, remarking that if the work were human and flawed, it "would collapse of itself. If it is of God, it will last." Last it did, for Brother Andre was soon seeing hundreds of people every day. He insisted that the cures came not from him but from God, that St. Joseph "was using him in the same way that an electrical generator makes use of a wire." Always humble, he liked to say that he was only St. Joseph's "little dog." Petitioners' prayers and unconditional faith in St. Joseph were what cured them, he insisted. Even though Andre could not cure everyone (he remarked that some people did not have enough faith, while others were not meant to be cured on earth), he became a byword for healing. One estimate suggests that he helped ten thousand people over twenty-seven years.

Brother Andre's reputation spread, and his time became completely absorbed by sick people, some of whom had to wait in line for several days to see him. In the midst of these labors, he took up the second of his great tasks, insisting that a shrine to St. Joseph be erected on Mont Royal above the monastery. A lay friend bought land in the place that Brother Andre reported St. Joseph had chosen for his oratory, and the archbishop approved the project in 1904, stipulating only that the order not go into debt for the construction. Andre spent 1908 to 1909 erecting a small wooden shelter, funded by small donations and the money that he made cutting boys' hair. Over time the shelter was roofed and enlarged, and a road was built up the mountain. A crypt was constructed in 1915; a basilica begun in 1924. Though the grand church was not finished until thirty years after Brother Andre's death, he always expressed confidence in its completion. At one point, Andre took a statue of St. Joseph to the unroofed, unfinished basilica, proclaiming his trust that St. Joseph would "see to" his own enclosure if he desired it.

In old age, Brother Andre became irascible with hypochondriacs and people with minor illnesses who sought his aid frivolously, but he wept in regret for those episodes and asked his fellow monks to pray for his conversion. When he died in January 1937, his body was displayed in his shrine, and three hundred thousand people came to honor him. Pilgrims still seek cures there, in the "Lourdes of Canada," honoring this humble servant of God and St. Joseph.

RESPECTING ONE ANOTHER'S GIFTS

Support staff, they are commonly called, and every organization that includes teachers also includes them. They are school and parish secretaries, janitors, cafeteria workers, and bus drivers.

As teachers, we may be tempted to consider ourselves somewhat above them. Our institution's mission, after all—the work of imparting knowledge and skills, perhaps of fostering faith—depends on us. We have talent and a calling; we've received extended education; we possess specialized skills. If a secretary or a bus driver quits, we might miss the person, but that spot is not difficult to fill. We, on the other hand, are unique.

At Notre Dame College, Brother Andre served as support staff but, as his story makes clear, he was hardly replaceable. While he cheerfully performed the most mundane tasks—sweeping the floors, greeting visitors, taking messages, cutting hair—he was also perfecting his devotion to St. Joseph, a devotion that before long bore abundant fruit. The joke on the teaching brothers and on the superiors was that illiterate Brother Andre turned out to be the most inspirational teacher of all. His cures taught faith and revealed God's power; his insistence that a basilica *would* arise someday taught patience and the effectiveness of prayer. This humble man was the holiest of all, and he inspired hundreds of thousands of people.

How life would change if we'd remember Brother Andre when we encounter the workers who keep our organizations going! Rather than snapping at a secretary when she doesn't get our copying done on time, we'd remember the multitude of little responsibilities that she faces every day. We'd imagine her life when she's not at work: her spirituality, and the good that she does. We'd think of her as a person rather than a tool, and we'd be kind.

Now and then, we can even see such behavior modeled. I used to work with a man, a respected full professor, who sometimes put out the mail when the secretaries were overwhelmed, sometimes made the office coffee, while those below him in the teaching hierarchy thought such jobs beneath their dignity. If someone complimented him on this work, he would shrug and say that these things needed to be done. We were all workers here. That's what Brother Andre's cooperative, humble spirit looks like, I think.

And, while the Brother Andres around us might not be working miracle cures or building basilicas, there might very well be holy teachers among them. One of my parish friends, a young mother, tells me that the bus driver who transports her five-year-old to parochial kindergarten is the most influential person in the child's life right now. Her son is the last to be dropped off, and the driver and the child have time to talk. Sometimes, she says, as when the boy has had an argument with a playmate and is feeling sad, the bus driver takes a longer way home so that he can hear the child out. The boy repeats what the bus driver says at dinner, and the advice is always good and dependable. So is the friendship between them.

We teachers would do well to build a daily habit of respect for those who perform the humble work of our organization. Like Brother Andre, they may be treated as someone's "little dog," but, as someone remarked of him, they may be even now barking "so loud that the whole world will hear," even if we cannot. We *are* all workers here, all entitled to dignity. Who can guess what we might build together if we remembered that?

For Further Reading

Real Boudreau, *Brother André, CSC, The Apostle of Saint Joseph* (New York: Benziger Brothers, 1938).

C. Bernard Ruffin, *The Life of Brother André: The Miracle Worker of St. Joseph* (Huntington, IN: Our Sunday Visitor, 1988).

3

St. Ita of Killeedy

Died c. 570 - Ireland - Feast: January 15

Ita (birth name Deirdre) was a chieftain's daughter in sixth-century Ireland who declined to marry, devoting herself instead to the education of young boys. In her convent school, she won renown as "the second Brigid." Ita adored children; it is reported that the infant Jesus appeared to her in visions, and that she composed Gaelic lullabies for him. These are unabashedly maternal: "Jesukin," one of the most famous says, is "Next to my heart thro' every night," a "nursling . . . on my breast."

While Ita was still a very young nun, the monk Erc brought her the royal infant who became St. Brendan the Navigator, whom Erc ("like one of the Magi") had claimed from his parents. For five years, Ita nurtured and taught Brendan; then the child went off to monastic study. Brendan became famous for founding monasteries, for his missionary voyages, and for the book narrating them, which became "the primary travelogue of the middle ages." Brendan's career as a navigator began badly, however, for he set out in a very small ship that kept getting blown in a circle, and he was forced to abandon his voyage. Back home, he stagnated for five years, "his soul . . . restless and his quest unfulfilled," until he consulted the practical Ita. "God gave you common sense and intelligence," she is reported to have told him. "Cooperate with Him, and get a bigger ship with a serviceable rudder!"

Brendan took her advice, and, on his next voyage—in a large oak ship, with a crew of sixty—he traveled far. Some evidence suggests that he reached Newfoundland and Florida. One legend even equates him with the Mesoamerican Quetzalcoatl. He returned to become a bishop, to found additional monasteries and a university, to serve as a judge and a navigational consultant; he may have taken another voyage to the Mediterranean and Palestine. As Brendan's adventuresome life evolved, Ita remained quietly in her convent school for decades, "prudent in word and work, sweet and winning in her address, but constant of mind and firm of purpose." Brendan returned often, we are told, to seek her advice, and he is her most famous student, but Ita is called "foster mother of the saints of Erin" not simply for him, but also for other boys whom she mentored long after he had left her care.

After helping bring up generations of boys, Ita died in 570. She is commemorated in an Irish church that bears her name, and also at St. Brendan's church, where a stained-glass window shows her gently watching over the toddler Brendan and an angel, who play together at her feet.

Nurturing, Then Letting Go

Sweet Ita, denying herself literal motherhood to mother the sons of strangers! Gentle Ita, who "loved much fosterage," seeing her "Jesukin" in the upturned baby faces around her! All of us teachers who get attached to our charges can claim kinship with her. It is so difficult to let them go, after a class, a year, several years, these students whom we come to believe are *ours*. They're mostly merry as they leave us, voyaging out to some new country of their own. We would be sorry if they were not excited and ready for new adventures; if they instead clung to us, that would mean that we had failed.

Still, our hearts miss them, and it is always a joyful day when an e-mail or card arrives, or former students show up at our door, remembering us as we remember them. We're always proud of our students when they tell us about the grand things that they're doing, but it's especially gratifying when they return to ask our advice or tell us that they've successfully invoked our voice in a crisis. Such moments remind us of the worth of what we do, and it's wonderful when we have a student like Brendan to reassure us again and again, in person, that our tutelage continues to matter.

Even if we have former students who periodically stay in touch, however, most of our lives will consist of long stretches when we never hear from students with whom we were close. It's tempting to feel a little stodgy and neglected, then, as we remain in our classrooms, year after year, ministering to successive generations whom we cannot help but love, though they will leave us, too. It's tempting to wonder if we've worked in vain. Like all parents, we stay behind as our children make their own independent lives, and it often seems that our hearts yearn toward them more than theirs to us.

Ita must have felt that yearning, too, quiet in her convent walls, as she turned to a new crop of "Jesukins," knowing that in time she would have to open her hands and let them go, too. But she did it, again and again, drawing on an infinite well of love, spending herself as Christ was spent. What could have comforted her but the knowledge that she had loved her boys, taught them, nurtured them as well as she possibly could, that each generation was as important as the last, that her vocation was to be God's instrument?

She has so much to teach us, gentle Ita, performing work that stretched the boundaries of the wider world, while remaining inside her convent walls.

For Further Reading

Mary Ryan D'Arcy, *The Saints of Ireland: A Chronological Account of the Lives and Works of Ireland's Saints and Missionaries at Home and Abroad* (St. Paul, MN: The Irish American Cultural Institute, 1974).

George Aloysius Little, *Brendan the Navigator, An Interpretation by Dr. George A. Little* (Dublin: H. M. Gill and Son, 1945).

Vincent J. O'Malley, "Ita of Killeedy and Brendan the Navigator," in *Saintly Companions: A Cross-reference of Sainted Relationships* (New York: Alba House, 1995), 167–69.

Robert T. Reilly, *Irish Saints* (New York: Vision Books, 1964).

Paul Burns, ed., *Butler's Lives of the Saints* (Collegeville, MN: Liturgical Press, 1996), 1:96–97.

Oxford, 265–66.

4

The Value of

Challenging Our Students

St. Francis de Sales

1567–1622 ~ France ~ Feast: January 24

D evout, articulate, hardworking, and intellectually brilliant, St. Francis de Sales was an evangelical bishop and a renowned spiritual advisor. Francis was born to an aristocratic family, the son of a diplomat, in Savoy in 1567. He studied at the University College of Clermont in Paris (where family connections exposed him to the highest levels of French society), then earned a law degree from the University of Padua. Though his father wanted him to marry well and advance his family, Francis was determined to follow his strong sense of vocation, and he became a priest in 1593. "He took up his duties with an ardour which never abated," Butler reports, preaching in an accessible style and ministering to the poor.

A year later, Francis de Sales undertook a mission to reconvert Protestants in Chablais near Lake Geneva, traveling only with his cousin. At first, the work went slowly and was physically demanding and dangerous; he was attacked by wolves and by assassins. Slowly, though, de Sales began making inroads by writing tracts, which he slipped under doors, and by befriending children. When his bishop visited the area a few years later, many people had returned to Catholicism. Deeply impressed, the prelate chose Francis as his successor, and he became Bishop of Geneva in 1602. He was distinguished by the economy of his household, his charity, his preaching, and his zeal.

Francis de Sales corresponded extensively with those who sought his spiritual direction. His advice was noted both for its kindness and for its firmness. His most famous disciple was the young widow St. Jane Frances de Chantal. Sales met Chantal in Dijon in 1604; she immediately recognized him, it is said, having seen him in a vision. Chantal had already decided to devote herself to a life of chastity and good works, but she still dressed stylishly. The story goes that one night soon after they met, Sales turned to her and asked if she had really determined to stay unmarried. "Yes," she said, surprised at the question. "Then why don't you lower your colors?" he asked. Chastened, Chantal recognized that she was sending a mixed message, and she immediately reformed her appearance as a sign of her absolute commitment to her new vocation. The two became close, lifelong friends and correspondents, and in 1610 they founded the Order of the Visitation of Holy Mary, supervised by de Chantal under Sales' direction, establishing eighty-six convents.

In addition to hundreds of letters, Francis de Sales produced several books. The best known are *Treatise of the Love of God*, which instructs readers to "love without measure," as God loves, and *Introduction to a Devout Life*, a manual of spiritual guidance, which de Sales assembled from notes that he had written to a cousin who placed herself under his spiritual direction.

Francis de Sales died young, at fifty-six in 1622, after having preached extensively in France during the winter of 1662 at the request of Louis XIII. He was beatified just forty years later, then canonized in 1665 and declared a doctor of the church in 1877. He is the patron saint of writers and journalists.

Putting Students on the Spot, with Love

"I don't like to put my students on the spot," said the young teacher whom I was observing. I had just told him, as gently as possible, that I thought he should ask his students more challenging questions and probe their vague remarks in discussion. He was handing them conclusions, protecting them from difficult thinking. "Why not allow them to take risks?" I asked.

He wasn't buying my advice. "I don't think it's fair to ask students to go out on a limb," he said, drawing himself up with some pride. "I'm not that kind of teacher. I believe in empowering students, not intimidating them."

Then I couldn't help but smile, remembering the two best—yes, "empowering," even—moments in my own school career. Both had involved teachers whom I loved, teachers who with all gentleness had deliberately put me *way* out on limbs. The first happened in an undergraduate sophomore literature survey. We had just read John Milton's seventeenth-century pastoral elegy "Lycidas," and the class was floundering. No wonder: pastoral elegies follow dense and difficult poetic conventions of form, content, and sequence of topics. "Why would a poet choose such a stylized genre to write about something as personal as a close friend's death?" one of my classmates had asked.

My teacher did not answer that question. Instead, she turned to *me*, in that room of forty students. "Susan," she said, not aggressively, but in a tone that allowed no demur. "What do you think of this poem? Do you think it's a good poem?"

I took a very deep breath, consulted my instinct, and decided to trust it. "Yes," I said, "it is a very good poem." And then I heard myself talking about why strict form could be helpful: it gave the poet a framework useful in chaotic states like grief; it linked the poem to other poems written in other periods in that same form, and thus universalized its message. I was eighteen then, and I didn't use quite those words, but I said things like that . . . things that I hadn't known that I knew until I heard them coming out of *my* mouth. My teacher nodded and for a millisecond looked directly into my eyes with a quiet smile, then turned back to the rest of the class . . . then discussion started. I didn't say much else for the rest of that hour, however, for I was sitting transfixed, radiant with my teacher's approval. My life changed that morning.

Something similar happened when I was a graduate student, in a seminar on the eighteenth-century novel. There were only ten of us around the table that night, discussing a famous critic's book about the writers we'd been reading that semester. The critic's bias was clear, I had thought as I prepared for class; he praised those novelists whose fiction supported his thesis and argued that others were lesser writers. My favorite writer of the class, Henry Fielding, was the one this critic liked least, and I was bristling after reading the assignment. I came to class ready to speak up.

My chance came so quickly that it dazzled me, with the first real question of the evening. "Okay, Susan," my teacher said, "what do you think of the discussion of Fielding in the reading for tonight?" For a moment, bold as I had mentally been in defending Fielding in the privacy of my mind, I doubted myself. The author of this study was one of the most famous literary critics of the eighteenth-century novel, after all. Our teacher—a very famous scholar himself, and a man whom I adored—had *chosen* this book for us to read—it was the only secondary source he had required us to buy. Of course, I thought suddenly, this argument couldn't be wrong. Of course I was being presumptuous, with my little one-year-of-graduate-study background, to think of challenging it.

Once again, though, something in me insisted that I had to trust my instinct, and I heard myself saying that I thought the critic's thesis had blinded him to Fielding's merits. "Good for you!" my teacher said. "How about the rest of you?"—and I sat, glowing and dazed again, as the discussion danced around me.

How sad for students when their teachers do not selectively invite them onto such limbs. Yes, it is risky to ask challenging questions in any teaching situation, secular or sacred, elementary or advanced. If a student can't answer, that student can feel betrayed or put on the spot, and both she and the teacher can look bad. It's important to remember, though, that challenges don't have to be aggressively designed to embarrass people, and that students aren't necessarily such sensitive souls that we don't dare disturb their comfort. Sometimes, if we "directors" (whether spiritual or secular) want students to break through to a new level of understanding, putting them on the spot might be just what they need.

St. Francis de Sales understood this. While reassuring those who sought his spiritual direction that he loved them, he did not hesitate to challenge them. "Then why don't you lower your colors?" he asked Jane Frances de Chantal—and she realized that, though he was criticizing her, he would not have been inviting her to give herself fully to her new life if he had not assumed that she could do so. De Sales' *Introduction to a Devout Life* is imbued with similar attempts to move readers beyond their comfort zones. He counsels, for instance, that it is not enough to physically give up "dangerous things": one must stop even *caring* for them internally if one is to make spiritual progress. Although in Sales' lifetime he was criticized for being too gentle with sinners, such evidence shows that with those in whom he saw great potential, he could be demanding, indeed—"the medicine of life," as he termed spiritual directors who asked hard questions.

How I wish that people like that young teacher whom I observed could have worked with Francis de Sales, or with one of my own beloved teachers! All of these people recognized that it's a tragedy to protect students from ever stretching because they might be embarrassed; to never confront them is a shame. For true empowerment, as these wise ones knew, isn't fostered by safety. Rather, people begin to glimpse their own potential only when, surprised, they discover themselves rising to challenges—especially when those challenges are posed by careful, loving, and, yes, *demanding* mentors who will settle for only the best for those in their care.

For Further Reading

Michael De la Bedoyere, *Francis de Sales* (New York: Harper and Brothers, 1960).

Francis de Sales, *Introduction to the Devout Life*, ed. John K. Ryan (New York: Image Books, 1972).

Wendy M. Wright and Joseph F. Power, eds., *Francis de Sales, Jane de Chantal: Letters of Spiritual Direction*, trans. Pérrone Marie Thibert (New York: Paulist Press, 1988).

Butler's, 1:195–201.

Oxford, 206.

5

Hard Work . . .
and Miracles

St. John Bosco

1815–1888 ~ Italy ~ Feast: January 31

St. John Bosco was born in 1815 in northern Italy to a devout family of peasant farmers. His father died when he was two, and his widowed mother, Margaret, a paragon of faith, raised her three sons to work hard and to love God. "God always sees you," she told young John, a lesson that he later passed on to his own "family." Bosco always had a sense of vocation. When he was nine years old, he dreamed of being at the head of an unruly group of cursing boys. The Virgin Mary appeared to him and said "There is your field . . . it's there you must labor." In the dream, the boys became wild animals, then were changed to lambs.

As a youth, Bosco began holding religious services for other children. In the way that he conducted them, he anticipated his later insistence that instruction must be tempered with play. These services began with recitation of the rosary, hymns, and a sermon; then the young Bosco entertained the assembled children with acrobatics and tricks. He insisted that if children did not come to the first part of the celebration, they couldn't see the entertainment. His vocation was soon officially recognized. One day on the road, he spoke with a priest, Don Colosso, who saw his worth and who supported his seminary training. He was ordained in 1841, and, after a short period as a parish priest, went to Turin for further study.

When Bosco arrived in 1846, Turin was a city full of social problems. With booming industrialization, its population had grown to

136,000 from 40,000 a century before. Workers, especially young men, flocked there for employment, but many did not find reliable work. They lived in crowded slums. Adult criminals and child delinquents roamed the streets. Don Bosco went with fellow priests to minister to prisoners, and he found himself drawn to unfortunate boys like those whom he had glimpsed in his dream. Soon he was holding religious observances—catechism lessons and worship coupled with recreation—in the streets and the fields for Turin's strays, and his kind attention soon drew hundreds of street boys to his care.

Bosco continued holding "festive oratory" services for "his boys" after he accepted a post as chaplain to an orphanage founded by a wealthy woman. While he seems to have easily managed to find the energy and time for his flock, even while hearing the confessions of four hundred children, finding a place to gather became a problem. After the noise of three hundred street boys at sport became so great that the orphanage was disrupted, John was told that his charges were no longer welcome on the grounds. He moved the gatherings to houses, but neighbors complained. He tried a field, but the sheer number of boys' feet wore out the grass, and he lost that venue, too. Police came to all of his oratory meetings to keep watch.

Finally, the saint leased and eventually bought a shed, then a house, then expanded the house. He began taking in boarders, and he began training more educated boys to teach the street children. His mother moved in with him to help with the work. After a few years, Bosco resigned his job at the orphanage. "My whole life . . . is bound up with the care of these lads, and nothing or nobody shall turn me aside from the path which God has clearly shown me," he told the orphanage owner. He started vocational training for the boys, eventually supervising tailors', bookbinders', shoemakers', carpenters', and printers' shops on his property. Within a few years, he was working with five hundred boys, including 150 boarders. He slept fewer than five hours a night.

Bosco was especially famous and beloved as a confessor; he could see into the souls of those who came to him. It was reported that sometimes his kind glance caused those who had not planned on confessing to fall on their knees before him. An optimistic realist about human psychology, the saint insisted that people learned best with encouragement. What punishment was given should be as light as possible, suited to the sinner and the sin, and always assigned lovingly, to help the penitent learn. Don Bosco was an involved, attentive mentor. "You can do nothing with" children, he once told a cardinal, "unless you win their confidence and their love." Boys should be "surrounded, as much as possible, with a loving supervision and assistance during recreation, in class, and in their work," he advised fellow teachers. When young people "are encouraged by kindly admonition, and as soon as they show signs of forgetting their duty they are charitably reminded of it and recalled to better sentiments," he said, they would truly learn to do God's will.

Early in his work, Bosco began trying to recruit promising boys as priests, but the first four boys who worked under his direction eventually left him. Undeterred and patient, he succeeded in interesting another small group of boys in his program; these formed the nucleus of his Salesian Order, which was approved in 1869 and established its Rule in 1874. During his lifetime, about 250 houses of his Society were founded, and by 1910 it had nearly four thousand members. Through his life, Don Bosco produced more than one hundred books to aid in teaching and learning. Fittingly, given his emphasis on recreation, among them were plays (including one designed to teach the metric system!). He also instituted field trips, "autumn excursions" in which boys and instructors traveled around the countryside holding holy observances as they enjoyed the fresh air. He was deeply beloved by teachers and students alike.

Besides his work with boys, Bosco built two churches in Turin; he ministered to citizens at large during a cholera epidemic, and he supervised the founding of an order of Salesian nuns. An indefatigable worker, he died in 1888, and was canonized in 1934. Pope Pius XI said of him, "In his life the supernatural almost became the natural and the extraordinary ordinary."

Teaching as Joyous Self-Sacrifice

As I've been working on this book, I've had to explain over and over to initially dubious colleagues that I'm *not* arguing that teachers should be martyrs. Saints are varied, interesting, and even humorous, I've insisted, and so are the examples they provide. Asking teachers to troop meekly to immolation is not the point, and I'd be the last to so troop myself.

In the case of St. John Bosco, admittedly, that assurance requires some qualification. Don Bosco was not an immolated, tortured-on-the-wheel kind of saint; he was a lively, energetically proactive presence who lived very much in this world. Still, his example does remind teachers that sacrifice is inevitably part of our profession, if we take that profession seriously.

One thing that Bosco sacrificed was his public dignity. Working with "marginal" students (or those frankly on the other side of the margin, as his juvenile delinquents were), he was obliged to lose face sometimes. Then as now, some difficult students refused to cooperate, playing their idealistic teachers for all they were worth (in Bosco's case, they absconded with bedding, with coats, and with shoes). During oratory meetings, the boys' rowdy behavior brought him into public disrepute. Students who had seemed most promising let him down repeatedly, and he must have heard, at least in his own head, voices mocking his hopes.

Unrelentingly high standards also had to be sacrificed. Even after Bosco assembled a group of young clerics, their behavior was "by no means ideal." "Many could not manage to get up in the morning because they were too fond of their beds," Bosco recalled. "Others did not go down to take their classes. . . . They prayed when they were with the boys but never did any spiritual reading or meditation as required by the masters of spiritual life."

Perhaps the greatest sacrifice that Don Bosco made—and insisted that his teachers make—was to offer students an incredible amount of personal attention. What we would today call *individualized instruction*—which, as all teachers know, is extremely time-consuming—was at the heart of his system. "He was always ready to hear confessions." Giving "a rare example of constancy, sacrifice, and admirable patience, . . . he worked like a martyr," one biographer writes. Bosco supplemented formal confession with regular applications of a *parola all'orecchio*, a whispered, individualized word in a particular boy's ear. Tailored to each boy's need and temperament, coming at exactly opportune moments, these councils of advice, encouragement, and admonition were the result of constant attention and constant memory of individual boys' circumstances.

Don Bosco also emphasized that more formal student conferences should be occasions of intense faculty focus. Quick, preoccupied meetings did little, he suggested to his Salesians. When a teacher worked individually with a student, Bosco said, he should be unhurried, attentive, as if that meeting were the only thing he had to do that day. He could not simply lecture and prescribe. He had to listen carefully and to respond thoughtfully. He had to consider the larger interests of the student and to become completely absorbed in that conference. Bosco acknowledged that such attention could be difficult, because his priests were busy. In fact, he noted that he expected them to have more to do than the time seemed to allow. Still, he would have no teachers too busy for essential, individualized student contact.

The key to gaining students' confidence and inspiring them to do their best work, Bosco wrote, was to let them know that the teacher cared deeply about them, demonstrating that one had "great confidence" in each student by patiently giving second, third, and fourth chances. The teacher's mission also meant that it was necessary to expend a great deal of energy. "The things we do seem to us hard and full of labour," he commiserated with his auditors in a homily.

Still, Don Bosco contended that there was a compelling reason for all of this sacrifice. "All these things . . . will seem more endurable and easier when done for the salvation of a brother," he proclaimed in the same sermon. Such a sense of altruism can help us still, today, to keep our own spirits up through the very hard work of teaching. "What is nobler than to rule minds or to mould the character of the young?" Don Bosco himself proclaimed. Teachers, he said, were "imitat[ing] the Lord" when they "neglect[ed] nothing on behalf of [their] brethren."

Don Bosco's own commitment bore fruit to an astounding degree. "Everybody was convinced of being beloved by him," one student who became a priest wrote of Don Bosco. Thus "anxiety and preoccupation vanished." "It will never be possible," another student added, "to convey any idea of the amount of energy which a look or a word of Don Bosco could convey to our souls."

Few of us will ever face so daunting a clientele as Don Bosco did; few of us will ever have to work so hard. But his life reminds us that self-sacrifice does come with our job—and has the potential to work miracles.

For Further Reading

F. A. Forbes, *St. John Bosco: The Friend of Youth* (Rockford, IL: TAN Books, 2001).

Edna Beyer Phelan, *Don Bosco: A Spritual Portrait* (Garden City, NY: Doubleday, 1963).

Lancelot Sheppard, *Don Bosco* (Westminster, MD: Newman Press, 1957).

Butler's, 1:208–12.

Oxford, 71–72.

6

To Call
All of Them by Name

St. Blaise

Died c. 315 ~ Armenia ~ Feast: February 3

Little is known about the historical St. Blaise. He is reported to have been bishop of Sebastia in Armenia and to have been martyred during persecutions instigated by the region's governor, Licinius, around 315. Blaise was the well-educated son of a wealthy Christian physician and his wife; he became bishop as a young man.

When Licinius began to persecute Christians, Blaise was sent by divine command into hiding in a mountain cave. There he lived alone except for the company of wild beasts, which did not fear or attack him but came daily for his blessing. "They waited patiently outside his cave until he had finished his devotions," reads one account. Wild birds, which he knew individually, brought him his food, and he healed sick and wounded animals, taking time with each as he would have with human sufferers in his episcopal care.

One day, however, hunters who were seeking beasts for the amphitheater discovered Blaise. Though "greatly astonished" at the sight of the saint surrounded by prayerful beasts, they bound him and took him back to the governor. On the way, Blaise pitied draft horses and stopped to bless them. When the group encountered a peasant woman who was distraught because a wolf had taken her only pig, Blaise called the wolf and ordered it to release its prey. The wolf obeyed, and the pig was restored, uninjured. They also met a woman whose son was dying of a fish bone stuck in his throat, and Blaise cured him by touching his throat and dislodging the bone.

Once in the capital city, Blaise was scourged and imprisoned without food, but the woman whose pig he had saved brought meat (the pig itself, in some versions of the story) and candles for light. He was then tortured by having his flesh torn by wool combs; then he was beheaded.

Blaise is the patron saint of wild animals, beasts of burden, and (bizarrely, in the tradition that often associates saints with the instruments of torture used on them) wool combers. He is invoked for throat troubles, and on his feast day candles are held in the shape of a cross to the throats of sufferers. Water blessed in his name is given to sick cattle and humans. He was a very popular saint in the Middle Ages. Elaborate English festivals honoring him, which featured shepherds and shepherdesses, were reported in the eighteenth century. Bavarian farmers still bring their draft horses to be blessed at his feast.

Calming Wild Beasts—and Unruly Children

Is there any teacher who, having heard the story of St. Blaise, wouldn't identify with a patron saint of wild beasts? Is there any teacher who wouldn't long for his secrets? Just imagine: no more ripping, tearing, yowling, rending each other . . . just quiet upturned faces waiting (waiting!) in expectation of a blessing. "Drop the pig," he says, and the wolf drops it. It's amazing . . . it's improbable, to say the least.

I know a teacher, however, who is an heir to St. Blaise. For more than thirty years she has taught sixth grade in parochial school, a grade level in which children can be especially beastlike as their hormones kick in. Her classes are renowned for their good-humored civility, though, and for their enthusiasm for learning. Her students regularly score highest in the city on state standardized tests, and they volunteer for community service eagerly. She is invited every year to high school and college graduations and weddings of her former students, and she receives many thank-you notes. Parents of her students worship her. In her classes, sullen or flighty young beasts become cooperative human beings. Her skill has always seemed miraculous to me.

Recently, though, after I spent a few hours in her classroom, I realized that her secret was finite, attainable—and very Blaise-like. Simply put, my friend Susan understands the power of the gaze. During those hours, when Susan turned to a student, she was fully engaged, truly focused, as she looked into the student's eyes and said the student's name. She was not intimidating; she wasn't using the trick that all of us runners know: stop, look hard in the dog's eyes, say its name, and snap your fingers, freezing it in its tracks. She was kindly, totally interested, and she listened. That child became, for that moment, the focus of her life. He wasn't a generic sixth grader, any more than a particular draft horse would have been a generic beast of burden to Blaise as he noticed its sufferings and blessed it.

Undivided human attention is incredibly powerful. It brings the soul of the gazer into direct contact with the soul of the subject. You might even say that it reminds people that they are real and, thus, that their actions and thoughts influence others beyond themselves. A medieval painting of Blaise and the wolf shows him looking deeply into the creature's eyes as it drops the pig, embarrassed by its own conduct. The day that I observed Susan and her students, I saw her constantly reminding those restless twelve-year-olds that they were real, too. Her gaze said that someone was noticing them because they *mattered.* Someone cared what they were doing, how they felt. Someone expected the best of them because they were capable of the best. And so they rose to the occasion.

We can't get lazy, Blaise reminds us. We can't think of our students as a herd, a pack, or they'll start acting that way. Instead, we have to be brave and look them in the eye, extending our energy, our notice, our compassion. We have to call them each by name, every day.

For Further Reading

Christina Hole, "Saint Blaise," in *Saints in Folklore* (New York: M. Barrows. 1965), 59–67.

Butler's, 1:239.

Oxford, 63.

7

The Real Work
of Interruptions

St. Scholastica

Died c. 543 ~ Italy ~ Feast: February 10

Scholastica was the sister (traditionally the twin) of St. Benedict, "the father of western monasticism." The little that we know about her life comes from the *Dialogues* of St. Gregory the Great, who became pope in 590, about fifty years after she died. Gregory probably learned of Scholastica during his own monastic experience. Gregory reports that Scholastica devoted herself to God as her brother did; she founded an abbey of nuns in Plombariola, near Benedict's Monte Cassino monastery, and served as abbess under his direction. Though Scholastica and Benedict loved and respected each other deeply, they saw each other only once a year, at a house outside of both monasteries. These were joyful meetings, where the two consulted on spiritual matters and praised God.

Their last meeting, around 543, was the most distinctive, as Gregory tells it. Scholastica may have intuited that she and her brother were having their final conversation in this world, for she begged Benedict to stay and converse until daybreak. Firm in his allegiance to his Rule, Benedict insisted that he had to leave. Then Scholastica bowed her head and asked God to grant her wish. Immediately, a thunderstorm arose with such violence that Benedict could not go out of doors. He exclaimed, "May God forgive you, sister. What have you done?"

Scholastica was nonplussed. "I asked a favor of you, and you refused it," she said. "I asked it of God, and he has granted it." At that, Benedict conceded. "It is not often that great saints have been given little lessons in charity by their sisters," John Coulson writes, but Scholastica prevailed. Benedict stayed until morning, and they talked of heaven and of the bliss of salvation.

Three days after this meeting, Scholastica died. Benedict was praying alone in his cell at the time and, full of joy, saw her soul ascending to heaven as a dove. He had her body brought to the tomb in which he planned to be buried. "So it happened to these two, whose minds had ever been united in the Lord, that even in the grave their bodies were not separated," remarks Gregory. Scholastica is the patron of Benedictine nunneries.

MAKING TIME FOR STUDENTS

It was not a telephone message that I was glad to retrieve. "I'm so sorry to bother you," my former student said on the recording. "But I really need your help. I'm *desperate* for your help."

She had just begun a new class that she'd always wanted to teach at her junior high school, a creative writing class. She'd spent all summer planning and dreaming about the shape that this course would take. But now, just a month into the school year, she realized that her plan wasn't working. She'd expected delighted students discovering their voices, and what she had was a disaster. Her students acted up in class and were rarely prepared. Their papers were trite and terrible, and she had overheard students in the hallways mocking the assignments. "I'd really like you to look at my syllabus and some of my lesson plans and assignments," she said. "Actually, I'd love for you to come to a couple of classes, if you could, and tell me, frankly, what you see going on. If you could find the time, it would be a miracle."

"That's right," I told my late husband, Ford. "It sure would be." My own semester was so busy that I hadn't written for a week. Besides teaching, I was supervising two independent study students and a new teaching assistant, chairing a committee and serving on two others, and planning a book discussion that I'd promised (in a moment of madness) to present at a public library. I was already feeling guilty about neglecting my own students. And I was supposed to help her with hers?

What turned me to responsibility was not a God-sent thunderstorm, but Ford, characteristically extending the benefit of a doubt to a student. "I think that you ought to think about it, Susan," he said. "She was a really good graduate student, and she's been teaching for three years now. She wouldn't bother you for nothing. She trusts you. She loves you."

And so I grudgingly called my former student, grudgingly drove to a coffee shop to meet her late one afternoon, and grudgingly carved out a few mornings to go and observe her classes. Before long, I remembered how much I'd liked her and had admired her intelligence and her spirit. Once I stopped grudging, it was easy enough for me, with all of the miles under my wheels, to suggest where she might be going wrong and how she might revise her practice. Her classes got better in a hurry. All she had really needed was an experienced eye for a short time, and, instead of finding the extra work to be a drain on my energy, I discovered that it gave me renewed pleasure in teaching.

It's chastening to discover that what you have in common with one of your favorite saints—Benedict, in my case—is a flaw, an unfortunate episode of stubborn, uncharitable reluctance. It's sobering to discover that you almost spurned a chance to use your particular gifts to help someone who takes you as a model. God intervened to save Benedict from long-term regret. When Scholastica had asked him to violate his own rule, he must have felt put out; perhaps he got on a mental high horse ("Doesn't she know that I have work to do, prayers still to say tonight, monks who may need me right now?"). Then, after God took the decision out of his hands, Benedict must have felt the gentle wave of an inevitable, wiser course wash over him. They had talked about heaven, all night long, and that must have comforted his sister at the end.

Like Benedict in this story, it's so easy for us teachers to get caught up in our own importance, our focus on here-and-now work. In such moods, ad hoc requests for help can come as annoying interruptions. The story of Scholastica and Benedict's last meeting suggests, though, that "interruptions" can be our real work. Scholastica was so gentle, but so determined, and God listened to her. She needed Benedict then, and she was not afraid to insist. When our former students need us, similarly, we have a responsibility to carve out time, somehow, so that we can be open to them. Like it or not, our tutelage doesn't end when they leave our classrooms. Those who consider us mentors, as Scholastica considered Benedict, will always consult us in their minds, even if they don't actually call. When they do, we have an obligation to listen, and that obligation is good for us, for it turns us from our headlong busyness to real-time compassion.

Similarly, we ought to give our own mentors the compliment of asking for their advice when we really need it. I spent many hours when I was a young teacher imagining what my favorite professor would have done in particular situations. I didn't call her, for I was too proud, too stubborn, and I thought that she'd think less of me if she knew that I couldn't figure out problems for myself. Now she's gone, and I really am on my own.

Scholastica was wiser, and we would all do well to remember what her gentle insistence demonstrates: that it's not an imposition to ask for a mentor's help, indeed, that one blesses the mentor in the asking.

For Further Reading

John Coulson, ed., *The Saints: A Concise Biographical Dictionary* (New York: Hawthorne Books, Inc., 1958), 396.

Butler's, 1:292–93.

Oxford, 470.

8

WONDER THAT BREAKS
INTO THE EVERYDAY

Blessed Fra Angelico

c. 1387–1455 ~ Italy ~ Feast: February 18

B lessed Fra Angelico was a Renaissance painter, a Dominican monk whose depictions of sacred subjects have been celebrated by both the Catholic Church and secular art critics. He was born Guido di Pietro around 1387 and entered the Dominican order in 1420 with his brother. After spending his novitiate in Cortona, he returned to the Dominican convent at Fiesole, in the hills above Florence, and took the religious name *John*. Historically, though, he has been better known as Fra Angelico, a title referring to his humble, sweet nature as well as to the beautiful piety reflected in his paintings. This appellation was popularized widely by the art historian Giorgio Vasari in the sixteenth century, but evidence suggests that it was being used for John as early as 1469.

In 1436, John moved with his brother and other monks to the Monastery of St. Marco in Florence, a formerly abandoned convent that had been refurbished by Cosimo de' Medici the Elder, a patron of the Dominicans. John became the monastery's steward and worked as the convent's artist: he painted an image for the high altar of the church, decorated the cloister, and adorned individual cells with frescoes depicting Christ's life and resurrection. Though romantic depictions of Fra Angelico's life suggest that he was "the prototype of the mystic artist rapt in the contemplation of ineffable visions, which he painted in spells of blissful piety," art historians have established that he was actually "a man of the Renaissance," drawing on contemporary techniques and interested in both humanism and the aesthetic principles of Thomas Aquinas.

Besides painting for San Marco, Fra Angelico also completed many commissions for other religious orders and churches. Some of these were in Florence, others in Cortona and Orvieto. When Pope Eugene IV participated in the inaugural ceremonies for the cloister at San Marco, he was so deeply moved by Fra Angelico's paintings that he invited Fra Angelico to Rome to execute commissions for Peter's Basilica and the chapel of the Sacrament in the Vatican. Pope Nicholas V also commissioned paintings by Fra Angelico for his studio. At the time of the painter's death, February, 1455, he was again in Rome, painting for the Roman Dominican friary of Santa Maria Sopra Minerva.

Despite high acclaim during his lifetime, Fra Angelico was a humble man. When Pope Eugene nominated him for Archbishop of Florence, the painter insisted that his prior was more worthy, and that man became St. Antoninus. Fra Angelico could not stop his own posthumous fame from spreading, though; by the sixteenth century, painted depictions of him always showed him with a halo. The art historian Vasari spread the story that Angelico never took up a brush without praying beforehand. San Marco has remained one of the most famous attractions of Florence for art-loving travelers.

Fra Angelico was beatified by John Paul II on February 18, 1984. The pope's homily that day affirmed the church's "profound interest in the progress of culture and art, and . . . the fruitful dialogue with it" and reminded listeners that "art is . . . a path that can lead to Christian perfection." "With his whole life he sang the glory of God, which he carried like a treasure in the depths of his heart and expressed in his art," the pope said of Fra Angelico. "His works are a permanent message of Christianity, and at the same time a deeply human message."

PRESENTING A DEEPLY HUMAN MESSAGE

I love Fra Angelico's paintings. I've been to San Marco, have spent many happy hours there, actually, in the church, the cloister, the dormitories, and the museum. As I write these words, I have a postcard on my desk of my favorite work of his, the famous *Annunciation* that is painted at the top of the dormitory stairs. While I admire the religious content of his work, certainly its technical brilliance and its unearthly beauty, the thing that keeps bringing me back to Fra Angelico is one of the qualities that Pope John Paul mentioned: its "deeply human message." Although I'm not certain exactly what the pope meant by that phrase, I know what I mean: Fra Angelico's capacity to make sacred scenes and figures psychologically recognizable paradigms of human interaction. Figures in Fra Angelico's paintings respond to each other with empathy and interest; as we view them, the sacred becomes something we can understand, and so our own interactions become ennobled.

To me, a brief comparison of three of the artist's *Annunications* illustrates this (the Annunciation was a favorite subject in Florence, and Fra Angelico painted many). In an early version that Fra Angelico produced for the altar at Cortona, the Virgin is very young, with an open face. She sits, leaning forward to understand, quizzical, even. The angel in this picture bends forward, actively gesturing with both hands. He looks into her eyes, on the same level as she is. "Wake up," he seems to be saying with energy to this apparently not-quite-yet comprehending girl. The second *Annunciation* is a late one, painted around 1442, set in a pale interior vault. This Virgin is older, and she seems to have already understood and accepted completely what's going on. She kneels, submissive and calm, eyes lowered, in a position of prayer. This angel, in contrast to the first, stands above her, calm, making no eye contact, looking down in respect, leaning forward ever so slightly, hands in a position of quiet prayer. The third version is my *Annunciation*, the one over the stairs. In this image, Mary has heard the message, but appears stunned, even intimidated by it. She is seated, and she bows her back, her hands crossed lower on her body than in the other images, her face drawn but her eyes open. The first time that I saw this image, I thought that she was an embodiment of clinical shock, her arms warming her core. The angel in this image is the gentlest of them all, attempting to comfort and cheer her. Unlike the others, he smiles, a sweet and reassuring smile. He looks firmly into her eyes (one can almost imagine him saying to her, "stay with me"), and adopts a supremely non-threatening posture, leaning forward slightly, hands crossed, no big loud movements, a gentle, loving presence.

These three *Annunciations*, thus, depict three of Mary's possible immediate psychological responses to the angel's news before she sang the Magnificat. In each of them, the angel responds sensitively, appropriately to the version of Mary before him. These are not stiff, abstract figures, coldly inspirational models beyond human ken. They model human nature, responding and interacting as empathetic humans do, inviting us to imagine ourselves in the scene.

This is all very interesting, a teacher might say, but what's in it for me? A great deal, I think. For we, no less than Fra Angelico, have daily opportunities to help our charges recognize that they, like the characters in his paintings, have a connection to mysteries beyond themselves. Fra Angelico's paintings suggest that the sacred should not be presented as purely otherworldly. His *Annunciations* demonstrate that it's not sacrilege to imagine how Mary felt, just as his paintings in the monks' cells insist that it's not impious to imagine oneself at the Crucifixion. Religious educators can invite their students to put themselves in such scenes—perhaps with the aid of sacred art like his, which makes the ineffable real to human eyes. Discussion of students' reactions could lead them to remember that God has always worked with human raw material, despite its quirkiness. Such scenes remind us that the people to whom all this happened were like us, not perfect people in some ideal "back then." God works with what he has, and what he has is us.

If we teach in secular settings where matters of faith are not discussed, Fra Angelico's vision can still be helpful to us in a self-reflective way, because the astounding interactions he depicts take place in ordinary, daily spaces, much like the spaces in which our lives are lived. In the *Annunciation* on my desk, for instance, Mary sits on a rustic round wooden stool in a simple loggia—an outdoor patio open on two sides; humble wildflowers grow in the lawn behind the angel, and pointed cypress trees climb a steep hill behind a simple board fence, as cypress climb such hills today in Tuscany. Such settings suggest that the divine can suddenly be in our world at even the most apparently mundane times and when we least expect it. For teachers, that means in our classrooms, or the hallway, the parking lot, the gym. We'd better be open to wonder, his paintings remind us, for it is at home in our everyday world.

Fra Angelico's images also insist that people as well as spaces claim kinship with the sacred. In the three *Annunciations*, Mary and the angel are psychologically comprehensible, even in this divine moment. What this implies is that other humans share essential characteristics with her—with angels, even—in their potential for amazement, reverence, fear, and pity. Fra Angelico's work suggests that we need to learn to pay attention to our sacred nature, with all of its interactive capacity for empathy. We need to revere the sacredness of others—even the most apparently earthbound—and to encourage their dignity.

Fra Angelico spent his life looking into human faces, employing them in his art to embody sacred mysteries—celebrating them as tangible connections to the divine. The English poet William Blake also recognized something like this. Though Blake's poem "The Divine Image" was written more than three hundred years after Fra Angelico died, one stanza in particular is likely to have resonated with the monk:

For Mercy has a human heart,
Pity a human face,
And Love, the human form divine,
And Peace, the human dress.

As teachers, let us never forget that mercy, pity, love, and peace—and all of the other virtues—can be a real presence in our mundane world. Even if the divine never breaks literally into our sphere, we need to remember, as Fra Angelico did, that those sacred traits are potentially present all the time, embodied in ourselves and in those around us.

For Further Reading

Giulio Carlo Argan, *Fra Angelico: A Biographical and Critical Study,* trans. James Emmons (Paris: Skira, 1955).

Ferdinand Holböck, *New Saints and Blesseds of the Catholic Church: Blesseds and Saints Canonized by Pope John Paul II during the Years 1979–1983,* trans. Michael J. Miller (San Francisco: Ignatius Press, 2000), 1:112–18.

Oxford, 23–24.

9

"Extreme" Students

St. Dositheus

Died c. 530 ~ Jerusalem ~ Feast: February 23

According to legend, St. Dositheus was a wealthy, wild, and charming young man of the sixth century, page to an army officer. He became curious to see Jerusalem after hearing many stories about the city. Since his superior indulged him as a son, Dositheus soon gained permission to travel there with friends. Visiting Gethsemane, he saw a painting of souls suffering in hell, which struck him with great force, and he wondered aloud what it meant. A woman standing nearby explained judgment and hell to him; when he asked her how to avoid such things, she recommended fasting and prayer.

Her counsel changed Dositheus's life, for, though his comrades laughed at him, he immediately began to abstain from meat, and to pray, and he soon entered a monastery at Gaza. Knowing of Dositheus's sudden conversion, the abbot assigned Dorotheus the Younger as his director, a seasoned monk who "understood the difficulty of extreme swings of fervor" and who would become a saint himself.

The choice was a wise one, for Dositheus did nothing halfway, oscillating between extreme devotion and extreme doubt and depression about his spiritual capacity. He entered the monastery as a glutton (one report suggests that he ate six pounds of bread a day), but Dorotheus led him gently, simply suggesting, every day, that Dositheus try to eat a little less bread than he had the previous day, tapering his consumption to eight ounces or less. Before long, Dositheus "surpassed in virtue the greatest fasters of the monastery." His lively temper also needed moderating. At one point, Dorotheus asked Dositheus to bring him a bottle of wine, then offered it to his pupil. "It is the way of rollicking Goths to drink and shout," he explained, emphasizing that the wine was all that was needed "to make a complete Goth" of Dositheus. While Dositheus took that lesson to heart and began to act in a more seemly way, he retained his almost out-of-control exuberance in the desire to do his monkish duties perfectly. "Look how neatly I've made the beds!" he proclaimed to Dorotheus one day. "Thou art an excellent bed-maker, no doubt," Dorotheus said with a sigh, "but not much of a monk."

At the end of five years, Dositheus was assigned to work in the infirmary, where he served with "incomparable vigilance, charity, and virtue," and was noted for his cheerfulness, which the sick loved. Here, too, he sought to be perfect. Once, when an irritable patient tempted Dositheus "to temper and bad words," Dositheus was overcome by regret and ran to his cell, throwing himself on the floor in an anguish of guilt. He was consoled only when wise Dorotheus came to him to "assure him that God would pardon the little outbreak."

Before long, Dositheus himself became ill, perhaps of tuberculosis. As he grew weaker, he was forced to abandon his hospital work, then his fasting, and he contented himself with continual prayer. When he became too weak for even that, Dorotheus comforted him by telling him not to be anxious, for simply having Christ present in his heart would be enough. In the last moments of Dositheus's life, it was Dorotheus who at first counseled patience to wait for God's time, then gently told him to go in peace and stand before the Trinity, interceding for the community.

The suggestion that the young man might be sainted occasioned a great deal of jealousy in the monastery. "What miracles has he ever done?" monks grumbled. He had led a very ordinary life, they said. Dorotheus told them, however, that there could be no doubt of Dositheus's immediate transportation to heaven, for Dositheus had given up his own will perfectly to God. Many continued to doubt, until one of the order had a dream of deceased community members in heaven. There, among the choir of aged saints, was "a young lay brother, with hair on which the snows of age had not yet fallen, and a hectic color in his cheek." The last detail seemed to confirm that Dorotheus had been right: who could that be but Dositheus, a high-spirited enthusiast, even in heaven.

Nurturing the Perfectionist

We've all encountered them: the students whose exuberance for performing well borders on the obsessive. They are going to do this *perfectly*, they announce, either outright or by their actions. They *live* for this. They are the ones who cringe in class when we suggest, as gently as we can, that their answer isn't perfectly correct (or that another perspective is possible). They are the ones who cry at a B+ or even, as a student of mine once did, incredibly, at an A-. If we offer the slightest suggestion, they take that to mean that they are performing horribly and might as well quit the task, that they are worthless. Other days, when we praise them, they swagger.

Those of us who have established a reputation as wise old hands, people who "under[stand] the difficulty of extreme swings of fervor," find such people assigned to us again and again, as our students, advisees, student teachers. Or they choose us themselves to direct their independent studies, their spiritual quests. *Why me?* we wonder, and we may toy with fantasies of deliberate neglect to insure that this never happens again.

They're draining, these extremists, with their scruples about vocation and competence. They live to please, absorbing our time with questions. They are earnest children, teenagers, or adults always at our desks, lingering after class to talk to us when we just want to go home. They can be new teachers, too, driving us crazy with e-mails and phone calls asking for advice, breaking down into tears when their classes don't go well, asking us if we think they are really cut out for this.

Dositheus was one of them, and Dorotheus was our brother—a very wise brother, indeed. Knowing what he had in his new recruit, Dorotheus was careful to steer Dositheus into a middle course. He moderated by putting his thumb on the side of the scale that was up at the time. If Dositheus was out of control in a prideful way, his teacher qualified that pride, but gently, with a smile, for humor is one of the best ways to encourage healthy distance. If Dositheus was in despair, Dorotheus was gently encouraging. "Let yourself up," he suggested in essence. "You're human, and it's okay. Perfection is not necessary. Do your duty as best you can, and let it be enough." Wisely, he took the whole conversation out of the realm of extremes and counseled gradual progress toward an end that would never be perfectly complete.

Wise teachers can do the same for the enthusiasts entrusted to our care. Though we probably can't avoid grumbling in private sometimes, exhausted by their fervor, we need to remember that the counseling we give these perfectionists is some of the most important teaching we do. Though our charges will probably not join the angel choirs, we can make them more fully human, if we follow Dorotheus. Giving in to self-will, careening from self-castigation to pride, then back again, does not make for a useful or happy life. We can show such intense students that we're all human beings in this together; and they can learn from not simply our words, but also our patience and our tolerance for their failings—and for our own.

For Further Reading

S. Baring-Gould, *The Lives of the Saints*, vol 2 (Edinburgh: J. Grant, 1914), 378–381.

Butler's, 1:403–04.

10

The Brilliant, Tormented Outsider

Blessed Henry Suso

c. 1295–1365 ~ Germany ~ Feast: March 2

Blessed Henry Suso is renowned for his mysticism, which has been the subject of much scholarly study, particularly in the nineteenth and twentieth centuries. He was born around 1295 in Constance, Germany, to a wealthy, ill-matched couple. His father was a worldly, hot-tempered nobleman who loved to hunt and joust; his mother was devout and quiet. Dissatisfied with the boy's temperament, Suso's father sneered that Suso was "more a maid than his sister" and mocked his devotion. Still, the boy persisted in his identification with his mother's character, adopting her surname rather than his father's. When Suso was thirteen, his father allowed him to be placed in a Dominican priory. This admission was probably engineered by a gratuity, since he entered the convent two years earlier than children usually did. Suso later suffered from great scruples of conscience about whether or not he should consider this breach of the usual rules as unethical selling of ecclesiastical preferment.

Despite his early piety, Suso was lukewarm about religion as he began school, restless and given to carelessness. At eighteen, though, he underwent a conversion, and, much to the amazement and derision of his schoolfellows, he withdrew, as a vision had directed him, to "forsake all." Deeply tormented by guilt for his sins and by melancholy, he began extreme devotions, undergoing severe self-imposed penances. He inscribed the letters of the holy name over his heart by pricking himself with a stylus. Besides a hair shirt, he wore a rough leather girdle and a nightshirt studded with nails that dug into his skin, and he padlocked his wrists at night so that he could not scratch bedbugs. He slept on a bare old door with no covering except a coat in winter, and he ate only once a day and drank little. After ten years, when his health began to fail due to his austerities, he was told in a vision to give up his physical penances, and he threw his nail-studded clothing into the Rhine.

Suso then went to Cologne to study with the great German mystic, Meister Eckhart. Though Suso had discarded the outward instruments of his self-castigation, he was still wracked by self-loathing. Patiently and with much effort, Eckhart helped his pupil recover from his guilt and melancholy "and thus set him free from the hell in which he had so long dwelt," as Suso himself wrote in his autobiography. Eckhart emphasized submission of a person's will to God, advising seekers to "flee from oneself, from selfishness and self will, or you will find as little peace in the cell as out of it." Eckhart held that, in the quest to lose oneself in God, few things were as useful as charity. Under Eckhart's guidance, Suso realized that he should stop focusing on his inner torment and turn his energies outward, to serving the world. Rather than continuing his study in Paris, Suso thus returned to Constance and became lector of his former priory. There he met setbacks that tested his new equilibrium, for within a few years he was dismissed from that office, and his first book, an elucidation of Eckhart's mystical theology, drew accusations of heresy. In 1339, during a conflict between the pope and the emperor, the Dominicans chose banishment over collusion with secular power and took up residence outside the city walls. Suso served as prior in exile, helping the order overcome financial crises.

When Suso was about forty years old, he refocused his life to emphasize preaching and pastoral care, especially work with Dominican nuns, whose convents were numerous in the region. He became spiritual advisor to noteworthy women mystics, including Elsbeth Stagel. Suso also became famous for his sermons, which effected many conversions. His trials continued, however: he was accused of fathering an illegitimate child; his sister ran away from her convent; he faced the anger of the male relatives of women whom he received into the convent; he was accused of poisoning a well.

To later generations Suso has been best known as a prolific writer. Using the name *Amandus* and drawing on the chivalric legends that he had heard as a child, he wrote love songs to Mary, Queen of Heaven, which have earned him the titles "the last of the Minnesinger" and "Sweet Suso." Full of lovely images and poetic diction, these devotional verses were very popular in the later Middle Ages. Suso also wrote mystical treatises on theology. His books include *Clock of Wisdom, The Little Book of Eternal Wisdom, The Little Book of Truth,* and his autobiography/biography, *The Life of the Servant.* His pastoral letters to nuns were also collected and published.

Suso died in 1365. His writings were so influential during the next century that one scholar has spoken of "a Suso-Renaissance." He was declared blessed in 1831. Scholars consider him among the most important German mystical philosophers.

Giving the Troubled Genius a Place to Grow

As the previous essay in this book suggests, students reminiscent of St. Dositheus can be annoying, though they have a certain charm. The golden retrievers in our classrooms, they try so hard to please their teachers that they frequently ignore what would really satisfy us, rushing instead to prove themselves with great enthusiasm, then slumping in disappointment when they don't. They're challenging, yes. But they're also sweetly comical, and it's easy for teachers to regard them in a sympathetic light.

There's nothing sweetly comical about the type of student reminiscent of the young Henry Suso. Extraordinarily intelligent, overflowing with potential talents, but rudderless, these students drift in lonely angst. They know that they're "different," as their classmates say, but they find it impossible to heed the advice of one of Suso's former friends: "An ordinary life is the best." They are awkward, often outcast. Others consider them impossibly elitist or just weird; they themselves are afraid that they are failures. They are suffering crises of vocation before their teachers' eyes.

It's painful to watch such students, with "no outlet for [their] genius," as one biographer wrote about the young Suso. They're so obviously unhappy. Some, like Suso, might become what we now call "cutters," mutilating themselves in a modern version of penance. A decade ago, some were among those who dressed in black and affected pale skin. "The dead Michelles," one of my teacher friends called them—with affection, for he had been a gifted drifter in his youth. They might be in the group smoking pot in the parking lot or pouring vodka into orange soda cans. They might simply sit quietly in our classrooms, or stop attending school altogether because they are so depressed. In extreme cases, they can be the tormented, hopeless children who bring guns to school.

We can take comfort, though, in knowing that the Susos we encounter—like the original—*can* break out of their misery, if they receive the right treatment. One of them was my student last semester in an advanced creative writing seminar, and she's a textbook-case grown-up Suso. Jona is over six feet tall, heavily tattooed (some of the art is to cover self-cutting from a less happy period); her hair is a different color each week. She's outspoken, with an unabashed, delightful braying laugh. Like her mother—a nurse who works with me in the local volunteer fire department, a woman who blends kindness and think-for-yourself determination in equal parts—Jona is generous, gentle, and tough. She's an absolutely marvelous creative writer—one of the best in her class last semester, although an undergraduate among graduate students. When students edited in peer groups, everyone wanted to be in Jona's group. Over the course of the semester, my students read their work aloud to each other several times; as Jona rose to give her final reading, her classmates applauded. "You're awesome," another of the undergraduates (more dictionally challenged) said aloud, and they shook their heads with great affection and wonder.

A decade ago, Jona's life was much less happy. Her whole family is gifted, ebullient, frankly eccentric, and she found herself terribly out of place when she came to our small city. It's a community where a "culture of conformity" reigns (to borrow the words of one of my colleagues), where *different* is a pejorative word. Openhearted and open-minded, Jona entered high school, and she was promptly shunned. Other students made fun of her academic gifts as well as her appearance. She said odd, original things in class, and they believed that she was too intense about her studies. One empathetic teacher recognized her nascent talent as a writer and entered her work in a competition, but that attempt at outreach backfired, for Jona was so nervous about the proceedings that she broke down. Another teacher more successfully enlisted her in debate, and in that forum Jona found her revenge on her fellow students, for she competed fiercely, delighting in intimidating her opponents. Still, she remained full of Suso-like self-loathing.

What happened to Jona? Something similar to what happened to Suso, I'd venture: both outgrew adolescence and began to listen to the voices of people who loved them enough to offer the kind of guidance that helped them be true to their own gifts. In Suso's case, that was Meister Eckhart. Eckhart knew what it was to be an eccentric, but he had learned to balance his otherworldliness with action as "a man of the world." Eckhart's advice to Suso was reminiscent of a Zen master's, wise and practical. According to Suso's autobiography, Eckhard told his charge to turn from obsession with himself; Suso had to learn to accept his own nature, the teacher advised, even if it was flawed, and instead to concentrate on what he could do for God and for others. Along the way, Eckhart advised, Suso should practice forgiveness, maintaining "unruffled patience with all men, however brutal or churlish they may be." The unconventional person, Eckhart recognized, would always be unconventional. One simply had to recognize one's own gifts as a privilege, and to invent life in a new dimension.

Something similar happened to Jona. Her family was encouraging through all of her false starts, expressing confidence and pride; she met several teachers who would not give up on her either, though she seemed to have given up on herself. All had patience with her, and they encouraged her to have patience. Time alone has helped considerably. As with Suso, as Jona has grown beyond the stifling confines of her early education, she's discovered a world in which eccentric gifts are valued: a university creative writing program, in her case. To see her flourish in college classes—while her classmates (with their conventional beauty and flabby prose) regard her, awed—is to see a fish discover water.

Writing about the mature Suso's devotional poetry, one commentator remarks, "His interior life seems to have been one great song." Seeing Jona today, I think that most people would envy her composure and her joy. Such outcomes should give us teachers hope when we meet new young Susos, inspiring us to remind them that this misery, too, shall pass. It is for us to demonstrate faith in their genius, and to help them wait also for its fruition.

For Further Reading

James Midgley Clark, "Henry Suso," in *The Great German Mystics: Eckhart, Tauler and Suso* (Oxford: B. Blackwell, 1949), 55–74.

S. M. C. *Henry Suso: Mystic, Saint, and Poet, A Study* (Oxford: Blackfriars, 1947).

Henry Suso, *The Life of Blessed Henry Suso by Himself*, trans. Thomas Francis Knox (London: Burns, Lambert, and Oates, 1865).

Butler's, 1:464–66.

11

St. Thomas Aquinas

c. 1225–1274 ~ Italy
Feast: March 7 (Before 1970, now January 28)

St. Thomas Aquinas was one of the most important Catholic philoso-pher/theologians, noted for his prodigious output and his prayerful devotion to God. He was born around 1225 to a noble Italian family in the castle of Roccasecca, then educated in nearby Monte Casino, St. Benedict's abbey. Sent in 1239 to Naples for further study, Aquinas was a gifted student. He was attracted to and joined the Dominican order, but, because Dominicans were mendicants who took a vow of poverty, his family opposed his wishes and kidnapped him. He was imprisoned in the castle of Monte San Giovanni for two years, where his family attempted to change his mind by sending in a woman of bad character. Aquinas resisted the temptation, and his family finally accepted his decision.

Aquinas studied in Paris and Cologne; his first master was Albert the Great. At first he was so silent that his classmates called him "the dumb Sicilian ox," but after Albert examined him, the master pro-claimed that Aquinas "will yet make his lowing heard to the uttermost parts of the world." After completing his education, Aquinas was called to teach in Paris. There he earned his master's degree, which authorized him to teach anywhere in the world. He wrote biblical commentaries, and he began a major work, *Summa contra Gentiles*, a rational exposi-tion of faith for those who were not Christian.

This work was interrupted when Aquinas was called back to Italy to teach scholars of the papal court and to lecture and preach to others. He began his major work, *Summa Theologiae*, a discussion of faith and God, and continued it after he returned to Paris in 1269. In addition to his preaching and teaching, Aquinas served as advisor to the French King Louis IX. Two stories from this period give some indication of the character he acquired. In one, he was observed kneeling before the altar, when a voice from the cross said, "Thou has written well of me, Thomas; what reward wouldst thou have?" Aquinas is said to have answered, "Nothing but thyself, Lord." The other, a prototypical absentminded professor story, has a distracted Aquinas suddenly banging on a table during lunch with Louis and exclaiming, "That's finished the Manichean heresy!" as he solved a logical problem in his head.

Paris academia was disturbed at the time by controversies between theologians and the university arts faculty, who followed Aristotle and other classical philosophers to conclusions that ecclesiastic authorities believed were subversive to church teaching. The saint attempted to bridge the two, arguing that reason and faith were not contradictory. His books are structured as logical proofs of faith in an almost geometrical sense: they pose a thesis, argue for and against explicitly stated counter-positions, then use logic to reach a conclusion and address objections. An admirer of Aristotle, Aquinas argued that humans were distinguished from animals by their intellect. Since God created both intellect and faith, Aquinas wrote, apparent disparities between them suggested faulty reasoning rather than the error of one or the other. When he taught, he engaged students in debates, encouraging them to use their intellects on problems including the nature of God, the nature of evil, the nature of physical objects, and the purpose of human existence.

Though Aquinas himself managed to skirt ecclesiastical nervousness about the teaching of Aristotle, authorities attempted to censure the universities periodically. In 1272 there was a faculty strike in Paris, and Aquinas was sent to Naples to oversee a school there. A year later, he received a revelation on St. Nicholas's Day and declared that he would not finish his *Summa Theologiae.* "The end of my labours is come," he said. "All that I have written appears to be so much straw after the things that have been revealed to me."

In 1274, on his way to a papal council at Lyon that would attempt to reunite the Greek and Latin churches, Aquinas was taken ill and died. He was canonized in 1323. His twenty volumes of writings— on Aristotle, the Bible, Christian philosophy, the Lord's Prayer, and many other subjects—were perhaps the most important philosophical/ theological texts in medieval and Renaissance Europe. "It is almost impossible for us, at this distance of time, to realize the enormous influence St. Thomas exerted over the minds and theology of his contemporaries and their immediate successors," Butler writes. He was made a doctor of the church in 1567, and his *Summa Theologiae* influenced the Council of Trent. He continues to influence philosophy today. St. Thomas Aquinas is often pictured in art with a book, surrounded by evangelists or Latin doctors of the church listening raptly to his exposition.

Encouraging Students to Think for Themselves

Yes, I'm including St. Thomas Aquinas in the sequence of his original feast day, March 7, rather than his feast since 1970, January 28. I'm fitting him in here because he has to be in this book, and other key saints for teachers fill January.

He must be in this book, for St. Thomas Aquinas is among the most important saints for teachers of both sacred and secular subjects. Aquinas himself hardly distinguished between the two: one learned about faith by reason, he maintained, and reason supported faith. He was interdisciplinary in the highest sense, seeking a truth that spanned apparently uncrossable boundaries.

Whenever we teach by encouraging our students to think for themselves, rather than relying on sheer authority ("Be quiet and believe
me!"), we are following in St. Thomas Aquinas's footsteps. Aquinas's
scholastic method—indeed, the method common in medieval universities, in contradiction to modern assumptions that people in "the dark
ages" blindly and uncritically received truth—forced his students to
reason through problems. In disputatio sessions, a master posed a question that demanded a yes or no answer, then an advanced student was
required to speak for and against both sides, while others listened. The
next day, the master weighed the arguments and presented an answer.
This is critical thinking with a vengeance, a much more rigorous intellectual process than is usually found in modern classrooms—"more
interactive and more risky than the sort we're used to," one modern
commentator writes. Students were required to entertain "dangerous"
arguments, even to practice arguing in their favor, so that they understood both sides of an issue. When they reached a conclusion, thus,
they reached it with their eyes open. Aquinas's books duplicate this
method: he announces a topic with a question, then poses arguments
on both sides and answers them, modeling for his readers the process
his students experienced firsthand.

Whenever we appeal to students' innate curiosity and seek to
heighten it, we are also following Thomas Aquinas. Aquinas accepted
Aristotle's contention in the *Metaphysics* that "all human beings by nature
desire to know." All creatures longed innately to perfect their natures,
he said, and for humans, that meant inquiring. Aquinas argued that
knowing involved seeking out causes, and because God was the first
cause, learning would inevitably lead humans to God. This advocacy
of curiosity was a departure from previous patristic writing. Augustine,
for instance, called curiosity "a vain desire" that encouraged humans
to "proceed to search out the secrets of nature, things outside ourselves,
to know which profits us nothing." For Aquinas, though, "the study of

philosophy is legitimate and praiseworthy in itself." He reconciled faith and the desire to understand the created world.

Aquinas's canonization and his status as a doctor of the church verify that Catholicism and intellectual inquiry are compatible. In its application to an adult religious education classroom, that understanding suggests that historical, revisionist works about church history and biblical contexts may enter the scope of our inquiry and that teachers can include modern, rounded biographies of church figures. This view of intellectual rigor brings us to admit that the canon was shaped in an historical context, and may lead us to investigate other gospels, revelations, and epistles. It might also mean reading about other faiths' contrary positions on theological issues. By bringing in such materials, Aquinas would say, we're not betraying our faith, we're respecting it and those who seek it. His openness is validated in the very best modern Catholic university libraries, which include such books in open stacks.

There is no room for fear in a Thomistic classroom. We cannot hide arguments counter to the positions that we wish students to reach out of fear that the students will be seduced away from the faith; we can't simply hope that students will not think of these arguments or not be introduced to them elsewhere. If we do, and students discover those counterarguments, they are likely to disdain us—rightly, Thomas might say—for we have been treating them as less than rational creatures, denying them their God-given birthright of reasoned exploration. Rather, we must trust that our charges' innate hunger to know the truth and their innate capacity to reason, bolstered by our example, will lead them to truth.

Confidence is at the center of Thomas Aquinas's model, and it is confidence of the highest order, for, as the master himself wrote, God is the source of human beings' rational faculties, and thus is the great "interior" teacher. According to Aquinas, as teachers we are not required to change students' natures, but simply to capitalize on God's handiwork. "One man is said to teach another," Aquinas wrote, "when he proposes by way of signs the same course natural reason would follow of itself. . . . Therefore just as the physician is said to cause health in the patient by working with nature, so a man is said to cause knowledge in another by the operation of the latter's natural reason: this is teaching."

May we have the faith—and the expertise in using our own "natural reason"—to be such teachers.

For Further Reading

Norman Kretzmann and Eleonore Stump, eds., *The Cambridge Companion to Aquinas* (Cambridge: Cambridge University Press, 1993).

Robert McClory, "Thomas Aquinas," in *Faithful Dissenters: Stories of Men and Women Who Loved and Changed the Church* (Maryknoll, NY: Orbis Books, 2000), 139–41.

Jean-Pierre Torrell. *Saint Thomas Aquinas. Volume 1, The Person and His Work*, trans. Robert Royal, rev. ed. (Washington, DC: Catholic University of America Press, 2005).

Butler's, 1:509–13.

Oxford, 503–05.

12

St. Joseph

First century ~ Palestine ~ Feast: March 19

S t. Joseph, the husband of Mary, and Jesus' foster father, has been called "scripture's best supporting actor." Though only limited information about him is presented in the Gospels, his role in Christian thought has greatly expanded, beginning in the Middle Ages and culminating in the nineteenth and twentieth centuries, until he has become one of the most celebrated of the saints.

Joseph appears in the Bible only in accounts of Christ's birth and early childhood, noted as a man who, though humble, was descended from the royal house of David. Matthew writes that Joseph was Mary's betrothed, "a just man and unwilling to put her to shame" (Matthew 1:19, NRSV). When she revealed that she was pregnant, Joseph was told by an angel in a dream about Jesus' true nature and instructed to name the child. In another dream, Matthew reports, an angel told Joseph to flee to Egypt with Mary and Jesus, and to return to Nazareth after Herod died. Joseph also figures in Luke's accounts of the journey to Bethlehem for the census, of Jesus' purification rites, and of Jesus' temporary separation from his family at the age of twelve, when Joseph and Mary found him teaching in the temple. Joseph disappears from both Matthew and Luke before Jesus begins preaching. Mark and John do not discuss Joseph.

During the early centuries of Christianity, apocryphal books told additional stories about Joseph, apparently constructed to answer heretical challenges to Mary's virginity. The second-century

Protoevangelium of James is among the most elaborate. It tells of Mary's birth as a prayed-for child of aged parents and her consecration as a temple virgin. When she was of an age to be married, this book recounts, the high priest brought together worthy widowers as contenders for her hand. Joseph was an old man who had grown sons, but during the meeting the staff which he was carrying burst into bloom. This flowering was taken as a sign that Joseph was to be chosen, though he protested that the disparity between his age and Mary's would subject him to ridicule. After they were betrothed, he went away to work for six months; when he returned, Mary was pregnant. Caught in the dilemma of shedding innocent blood if he exposed her (as an adulteress she and the unborn baby would have been stoned to death), Joseph asked the priest to test her purity with holy water, and she passed the test. The fourth-century *History of Joseph the Carpenter*, similarly, made Joseph an aged widower with grown children, chosen by lot to be Mary's guardian. This account says that he died at age 111, when Jesus was eighteen.

In accordance with these traditions, Christian artists for many centuries depicted Joseph as an old man, a bystander to the great mystery of the Nativity, gentle and selflessly quiet. Many church fathers, including Ambrose and Thomas Aquinas, speculated that Joseph and Mary never consummated their marriage.

During the Middle Ages, however, artists began depicting Joseph as a younger man, and devotion to him began to proliferate. In the fifteenth century, a time of schism, St. Joseph was held up as a model of stewardship by churchmen including St. Bernardino of Siena. Jehan Charlier Gerson, Chancellor of Notre-Dame, emphasized Joseph as simultaneously a simple, hardworking artisan and "head and master of the mother of the head and master of the whole world." Holy women, including St. Bridget of Sweden, experienced celebrated visions of him. Joseph's feast was established by Pope Sixtus IV in 1481. In 1621, Pope

Gregory XV made the celebration a holy day of obligation. During the sixteenth and seventeenth centuries, devotion to Joseph grew; both Ignatius of Loyola and Teresa of Ávila particularly honored him.

By the eighteenth century, Joseph's name had been added to the Litany of the Saints, and many popular and learned works about him were published, emphasizing his steadfast courage, strength, and humility. With the rise of industrialization and the proletarianization of workers, the Catholic Church promoted Joseph as a symbol of the dignity of obedient human labor—an alternative to nascent communism. In his nineteenth-century book *The Hidden Saint*, for instance, Frederick William Faber emphasized Joseph's "promptness of docility" and "immolation of self" in the service of God. Pope Leo XIII explicitly emphasized that workers should "put no trust in the promises of agitators, but turn rather to the example and help of Saint Joseph." In 1870, Joseph was named the patron saint of the Catholic Church, in reflection of his status as "God-appointed protector of Mary."

Joseph's prominence among the saints and his identification with Christian labor continued into the twentieth century. Pius XII established the Association of Italian Workers under St. Joseph's protection in 1955 and decreed May 1 as the Feast of St. Joseph the Worker as an alternative to the Marxist May Day celebration. Several modern saints who performed humble work adopted St. Joseph as patron, including Blessed Andre Bessette and St. Thérèse of Lisieux. St. Joseph is the patron of families, of manual labor (especially carpenters and bursars), and of holy death (because of events related in the apocryphal *History of Joseph the Carpenter* about his own demise). St. Joseph's continued popularity is evinced by the many churches, schools, and hospitals named for him.

Welcoming the Humble, Unsung Tasks

My late husband Ford grew up in the construction trade (his father was a Virginia contractor), and he used to say that the vast majority of the work involved in building something was of the "pick-it-up-and-put-it-over-there" variety. Before and during the work of specialized craftspeople, an army of "hands" move building materials from trucks to the places where they will be needed. They saw and mix and stack and sand; they remove waste bits and pieces; they clean up. There is no one part of a house or bridge or water system to which they can point with pride and say, "I built that," but without the lowly work that they do, no house or bridge or water system would exist.

After long days in our classrooms and offices, with evenings or weekends ahead doomed to preparation, Ford and I would sometimes look at each other and agree, grinning ruefully, that "pick-it-up-and-put-it-over-there" is not a bad description of teaching, either. While teachers do function as skilled craftspeople when we deal directly with students, we also have to be our own "hands." As anyone who has taught knows, lowly preparation work is mostly what we do, time-wise, not star-turn moments in the classroom. Planning class is prep work: all those hours reading, thinking about what we will say and how we will help students practice and encourage them to talk, making lesson plans. Commenting on quizzes and tests and papers is prep work. Writing reports and recommendations, filling out forms (is any teacher's life free of them?), going to meetings that inform us about things we really don't need to know, serving on committees that proliferate work whose value is questionable, speaking with parents, supervising extracurricular activities, and more—all of these constitute the pick-it-up-and-put-it-over-there components of teachers' lives. "You have it so easy," people sometimes say. "You only have to work five hours a day" (or three, for us scandalous college professors). If only they knew.

St. Joseph is a patron saint of "pick-it-up-and-put-it-over there" work, one who can cheer us when we feel mired in the "meaningless" chores connected with teaching. St. Joseph spent his life, after all, in humble support work. As a carpenter, he would have worked on a series of others' projects; no story about him says that he was a particularly sought-after or famous craftsman. With his princely lineage, his subordinate status would have been contrasted unfavorably with his ancestors'. As Mary's husband, he also played a supporting role, protecting a child who was not his, a child who must have frequently baffled him. And yet all of the pictures and the stories depict him as patient with his lot, content to be just "Joseph the worker."

As both biblical and apocryphal accounts of Jesus' birth and childhood verify, though, without Joseph there would have been no New Testament. Without his quiet confidence in dreams, Mary could have been executed with the child in her womb to punish her supposed adultery. Even if Joseph had decided to divorce her "quietly" (Matthew 1:19), she would most likely have perished, homeless, for she could not have resumed her status as a temple virgin or returned to her parents, who, since Mary was a child conceived in old age, would certainly have been dead by that time. Without Joseph's courage to obey the angel and flee to Egypt, the infant Jesus would have died in Herod's pogrom. Without Joseph's steady labor, the child Jesus would not have had food or shelter, a secure home that freed him from anxiety about survival so that he could listen to God's call.

In Joseph's case, thus, humble work was central to God's plan, though Joseph did not know this as he went along. The daily components of carpentering and of fathering a strange, apparently self-willed child must have seemed thankless much of the time. Joseph must have had to perform the same small chores repeatedly, to fight the same battles with his adolescent son. But he persevered, as we must in our own apparently banal, never-finished tasks. Like Joseph, like all "hands," teachers in their behind-the-scenes role can't know how any one piece will contribute to a greater whole, and we are likely to be tempted to do slapdash work. That would be a mistake, however. For a comment that we make on the next-to-last student response that we read late on a Thursday evening might change a student's life; a lesson plan that we make on an ordinary Sunday afternoon when we'd rather be doing something else might turn around a flagging class. Though nineteen of the twenty reports that we write during a given term may indeed never be read carefully, the twentieth could cause an administrator to rethink our program's needs. But only if we write that report, that lesson plan, that comment as if we believe that they are important.

Joseph's life reminds us that humble work is necessary and that unrecognized work can be the fulcrum on which a whole enterprise turns. Grand results come from small steps, invisible to most of the world. When those small steps are not done well, projects limp along, delayed and shoddy, or fail outright. All labor has dignity, Joseph insists to us. We must be patient; we must address even the most apparently mundane aspects of our professional lives with energy and good will, picking it up and putting it over there, time and time again, in the service of a larger cause.

For Further Reading

Donald L. Boisvert, *Sanctity and Male Desire: A Gay Reading of Saints* (Cleveland: Pilgrim Press, 2004), 67–80.

Francis Lad Filas, *Joseph: The Man Closest to Jesus: The Complete Life, Theology and Devotional History of St. Joseph* (Boston: St. Paul Editions, 1962).

Albrecht Koschorke, *The Holy Family and Its Legacy: Religious Imagination from the Gospels to Star Wars*, trans. Thomas Dunlap (New York: Columbia University Press, 2003).

Louise Bourassa Perrotta, *St. Joseph: His Life and His Role in the Church Today* (Huntington, IN: Our Sunday Visitor, 2000).

Butler's, 1:631–33.

Oxford, 288–89.

13

The Gift of
Second Chances

St. Dismas

First century ~ Jerusalem ~ Feast: March 30

Now one of the criminals hanging there reviled Jesus, saying, "Are you not the Messiah? Save yourself and us." The other, however, rebuking him, said in reply, "Have you no fear of God, for you are subject to the same condemnation? And indeed, we have been condemned justly, for the sentence we received corresponds to our crimes, but this man has done nothing criminal." Then he said, "Jesus, remember me when you come into your kingdom." He replied to him, "Amen, I say to you, today you will be with me in Paradise" (Luke 23: 39–43).

This is all that the Bible says about St. Dismas, as the good thief crucified on Christ's right has come to be called (based on the Greek word for "dying" that is used to refer to him in the Gospel of Nicodemus). Dismas had apparently committed a capital crime and was apprehended. Unlike the other thief hanged that day, however, he recognized Christ's divinity, and Christ promised him redemption. Other, noncanonical accounts of Dismas exist, though, and one rounds out his story in a particularly charming way. This is the Arabic "Gospel of the Infancy," which makes Dismas (here named Titus) one of a band of robbers that attacked the holy family many years before the Crucifixion, during the flight to Egypt. As this story goes, Dismas/Titus took pity on the family. When his fellow bandit would not concede mercy, the Good Thief bribed him with forty drachmas, and the family was released unharmed. "The Lord God shall sustain thee with His right hand and give thee remissions of sins," Mary is said to have proclaimed then; the infant Jesus to have prophesied that these two robbers would be crucified with him thirty years later in Jerusalem, and that Titus/Dismas would accompany him to heaven.

Dismas's story has inspired a great deal of discussion about the necessity of baptism and of good works. How could Dismas be saved if he was not baptized? Does that mean that baptism isn't actually required for salvation? Similarly, if good works are important, how could a man who had lived a life of sin, without good works, be saved? The answer, one theologian has suggested, is that Dismas qualifies for "baptism of desire," a doctrine contained both in the *Catechism* and in Vatican II documents. Where baptism is not possible, this doctrine says, a person who seeks God with a sincere heart, repenting of his sins, can be assured of salvation.

Dismas's feast was assigned to March 25 by the *Roman Martyrology* because that was the day when Christ was supposed to have been crucified. Dismas has frequently been depicted in western art and is the patron saint of prisoners, reformed thieves, and funeral directors. His name is sometimes given to prison ministries.

FORGIVING DAILY FOR THE JOY OF IT

I've danced at students' weddings before, but never quite so joyfully as one night last summer, at Jessica's. I'd liked Jessica ever since I got to know her in my Introduction to the English Major course a few years ago. She was smart, she was willing to take chances, and she was impatient with students not as intellectually curious as she was. She had been longing for a teacher to challenge her, and I became that teacher. We had a wonderful semester together.

Until the day I embarrassed her. For some reason, discussion was lagging, and I began to suspect that students hadn't done the necessary preparation. Wishing to show them up a little, I called on Jessica—and she couldn't answer, either. That was the last straw, and I immediately said something not exactly cutting—but pointed enough—about the need to master basic skills before one came to class, about how this whole class wasn't taking the subject matter seriously enough. Then I changed the subject, asking students to freewrite as a spur to discussion. That tactic worked, and I thought that the incident had blown over, until Jessica brushed by me after class, her face set. "I knew the answer," she hissed to me. "I was just thinking. It seemed so obvious; I thought that you were looking for something more." Then she paused and turned her fury on me. "You humiliated me," she said, and stormed out.

I was stunned. I felt terrible. How could I have taken out my frustration on Jessica, the one student who always came through? And so I went to my computer and wrote her an apology (thank goodness for e-mail!). I told her what I've said here, that the whole class session had been frustrating me, and that I had snapped when I shouldn't have. I admitted lack of patience and lack of tact. I asked for her forgiveness.

Luckily for both of us, she gave it to me quickly in word and soon enough in deed, relaxing before my eyes until she was the old Jessica by semester's end. Then she took another class from me (a more advanced one with other students as strong as she was) and we had fun again. I became her advisor. When she was married last summer, she invited me to the wedding.

Forgiveness is breathtaking, and it's particularly relevant to teachers, because, working every day with so many students and colleagues, administrators and parents, we encounter numerous chances to ruffle feathers, and to have our own ruffled. We can be too short, too harsh with others, as I was with Jessica; we can also err the other way, ignoring others when they need attention. We can get lazy and decide that the quality of their work doesn't matter. Though we might vow to always treat others with conscious respect, these things *will* happen to all of us, if we teach for very long, despite our good will. The sheer number of personalities we meet, and the variations of our own moods, make slips inevitable and real injuries likely.

Dismas, thus, should be a great saint for us, because he reminds us that our sins toward others don't necessarily damn us. He reminds us of the possibility of second chances, no matter how badly we've been treated or have treated others. Second chances are always amazing when they are extended to us. *I didn't earn this*, we think, humbled by the grace of the giver, "like the hand of God letting a sinner through the cracks," to quote a line from one of my husband's poems. Forgiveness is also very, very good for us when we extend it to others—not simply for our immortal souls, but also for our psychological peace of mind. I once knew a man who stayed angry at colleagues for something they had done a decade earlier—so angry that he needed medicine to calm himself down. He became insufferable in department meetings, aggrieved, always right in his own mind and bitter in private conversations. He made himself miserable and diminished his effectiveness with students. He never compromised his principles, one might say— once a bad thief, always a bad thief to him, no shilly-shallying—but the grudge had little effect on those whom he condemned, and it did him substantial harm.

Dismas's story reminds us that sometimes we must compromise (or get off our high horses) if we are going to live in a positive way. To me, one of the most evocative aspects of his story is its demonstration (if one grants the premise of baptism of desire) that God can compromise

God's own principles if the case deserves it. "You shall see the face of God and live," says one of my favorite lines in a modern Catholic hymn, Bob Dufford's "Be Not Afraid." If God can bend, forgiving sinners for a lifetime of wrongs, shouldn't we be able to bend to our students, our colleagues, administrators, taxpayers, when they wrong us?

It might even be a good idea to put a copy of a picture of Dismas somewhere where we can catch sight of it—over a desk, by a computer, inside a day planner—to remind us of how important forgiveness is to our work as teachers. For teachers, especially, forgiveness should be a daily task, and a daily joy.

For Further Reading

"Saint Dismas," http://www.catholicexchange.com/church_today/message .asp?sec_id=4&message_id=2578.

"Saint Dismas, Lesson." http://www.catholicexchange.com/church _today/subsectionmsg.asp?subsection_message_id=1045&message_id= 2578&sec_id=4.

Oxford, 145.

Butler's, 1:676–77.

14

IN PRAISE OF

INTELLECTUAL CURIOSITY

St. Isidore of Seville

c. 560–636 ~ Spain ~ Feast: April 4

St. Isidore of Seville, a sixth- / seventh-century archbishop who was one of the greatest scholars of his period, has been called "the Schoolmaster of the Middle Ages." He was born into a noble family around 560 and orphaned young; his education at the Cathedral School in Seville was supervised by his older brother Leander, archbishop of Seville. Leander was a rigorous teacher, and Isidore became learned in many fields. He succeeded Leander as archbishop and served for thirty-six years, until his death.

During his tenure as archbishop of Seville, Isidore presided over important church councils in Spain, and he was active in converting the Visigoths from Arianism, a heresy which claimed that Christ had been human instead of divine. Isidore is best known, though, for his extensive scholarship. Isidore was distinguished for embracing classical, secular knowledge along with theology and biblical studies; his attitude was so inclusively hospitable that it has been called by one biographer "unparalleled in his own period, and never surpassed throughout the Middle Ages." Isidore believed that knowledge was necessary to serve God, and that preserving and celebrating knowledge glorified the God who had given men the gifts to pursue it. Concerned about the intellectual backwardness of his age, he set about transmitting information "so that we might not always grow duller from boorish rusticity." Isidore compiled an encyclopedia of what was believed to be all knowledge in the period, the *Etymologies*, by copying from Greek and Roman writers and church fathers; it was arranged in twenty books, covering topics that included grammar, medicine, God and angels, anatomy and physiology, music, architecture, rhetoric and logic, and mineralogy. He also produced works on biblical numerology, on Christian doctrine and morals, and on Visigoth history. He compiled rules for monks and a dictionary of spiritual allegories. His *Da natura rerum* (On the Nature of Things), a book explaining natural phenomena including the change of seasons, the movement of the sun and moon, tides, weather signs, and meteorology, was written for the king of the Visigoths. Isidore also wrote about law, and his ideas deeply influenced the development of government in Spain.

One of Isidore's greatest concerns was educating priests (he insisted that no one who "did not know his letters" should be one). At the Second Council of Seville in 619 and the Fourth National Council of Toledo in 633, he decreed that every diocese should have a seminary and/or a cathedral school. In keeping with Isidore's own interests, these schools were to teach the liberal arts (particularly rhetoric), medicine, law, Hebrew and Greek, and classical authors, including Aristotle. "It was mainly thanks to him that Spain was a centre of culture when the rest of Europe seemed to be lapsing into barbarianism," Butler writes.

Since Isidore relied only on copying, not on firsthand knowledge, his books are inevitably full of contradictions, blunders, and pseudo-science. Still, commentators agree on the importance of Isidore's writings, for they preserved and transmitted a vast amount of learning in a time when it was not otherwise available. The *Etymologies* continued to be used as a popular schoolbook into the sixteenth century. Isidore's work remains important, too, as a documentation of the state of medieval learning. "To understand Isidore's mental world is nearly to reach the limits of the knowledge of his time," concludes his biographer Ernest Brehaut.

Isidore died in 636, well-known for his charity in addition to his formidable learning. He was declared a doctor of the church in 1722. Because of his encyclopedic knowledge, he has been nominated as the patron saint of the Internet.

OPENING STUDENTS' EYES
BY OUR OWN EXAMPLE

"Widely curious," one of my mentors used to say, was the single most important quality for a teacher, and the quality shared by all good students. If a person knew only his or her own discipline—no matter how well—that person was sadly handicapped. My mentor's own literature classes were dizzying in their breadth and richness; in them, students never just read poems, plays, or novels, but were introduced to music to which the writer or characters would have been listening, to religious and philosophical beliefs that informed their culture, to paintings whose aesthetics paralleled the text's, to the economic and historical context of the times, and even to the architecture that readers would have seen when they looked up from their books. At any given time, this mentor might be reading a work on geology, one on history, two or three biographies, a work of literary criticism or philosophy. He was not above "secular" knowledge, either, for he was a walking encyclopedia of baseball, of Formula One motor racing, and of jazz and bluegrass music.

Students loved his classes, and colleagues and friends loved his conversation. To converse with him was to imagine a world without intellectual boundaries, a world in which unpretentious curiosity was a given. "Why don't you find out?" he would good-naturedly ask his students, when they asked him a question that he could not answer.

He adored people who brought their own informed interests into the conversation, drinking in what they could teach him.

My mentor and Isidore would have gotten along well, for both were intoxicated with learning. Both, too, saw their mission as connecting others to that vast wealth of human achievement, and they trusted that people would be eager to share in this inheritance. Isidore did not assume that the king of the Visigoths was an idiot—he educated him—and he assumed that his priests would be capable of and interested in handling a broad curriculum. My mentor, too, assumed that people were disposed to learn. The quickest way for a student to depress and shock him was not to fail at an assigned task (that could always be corrected, he believed, if the student was willing to work), but to reveal him- or herself to be devoid of curiosity, hostile to learning for learning's sake. I think it's fair to say that, like Isidore, this mentor considered intellectual torpor to be a kind of sacrilege.

Ultimately my mentor regarded torpid students with pity, once his incredulity subsided. They were missing so much. It was sad, he would say, that many of them seemed to come from homes where people did not read, where commentary in *Time* magazine was considered heavy-duty analysis. He remarked on fellow airline passengers who, given a choice of *USA Today* or a real, substantive newspaper—the *New York Times*, the *San Francisco Chronicle*, the *Washington Post*—would always choose the former. They were our students' parents, he would say. They were our students, unless we helped them break through the fog that obscured even their truncated world. We were their only chance to connect with the wealth of human history, of science, of speculation, and of art. And so he would redouble his efforts.

My mentor lived long enough to see the educational system begin to change in ways that make teaching as he did more and more difficult. Today, at every level, we are likely to be held accountable to stereotypical curricula, standardized tests, and outcomes—all of which are possible to list objectively but certainly do not stimulate curiosity and creativity. Students are encouraged from childhood to think vocationally. "I'm in school to be an engineer/an accountant/a speech pathologist," they complain. "Why do I need to learn to write/to learn history/to master algebra?" Considering their education as a linear means to an end, such students are prone to ask a teacher, "What do you want?" They demand to know if material will be on the test, presumably so that they can use brain space only for what they "need" in the narrowest sense. Even liberal arts majors do this, betraying their field's birthright, and—a real tragedy—so do education majors. Even religious education students do it. "How much of this do we really need to know to join the church at Easter?" a woman asked a catechist with whom I am acquainted. It's enough to make Isidore rise from the grave and launch into a lecture about "boorish rusticity."

Lecturing won't help, though, as my mentor knew; all we can do is model wide curiosity ourselves, demonstrating how it enriches the world. All we can do is read, read, read, and experience, experience, experience ourselves, following our interests wherever they take us, bringing our knowledge and enthusiasm to our classes. By so doing, we can suggest that wonder is the desirable norm for a human being, wonder at the riches of human history and science, at the creative productions of the human mind, at theology and comparative religion and church history, at "whatever," as our students say. Some of them will notice, surely, as we noticed our own intellectually curious teachers.

"Have you read all of those books?" freshmen sometimes ask me, viewing the shelves that line my office. I always suspect that the very orderly students, the ones more concerned with producing perfect handwriting on their in-class exams than with content, are appalled by the chaos, for I have too many books for the shelf space, really, and books are stacked on top of books, sideways, crossways, threatening to cascade. The question they want to ask, I suspect, might be something like, "Why would anyone *need* that many books?" But, remembering my mentor and Isidore—and all the books I've read that are *not* in my office—I know that I must respond as if the question were literal, and that there's only one thing that I can say. I smile and scan my shelves, and then I gaze directly into their eyes. "Of course!" I tell them.

For Further Reading

Ernest Brehaut, *An Encyclopedist of the Dark Ages: Isidore of Seville* (New York: Burt Franklin, 1912).

Marie R. Madden, *Political Theory and Law in Medieval Spain* (New York: Fordham University Press, 1930).

Butler's, 2:26–27.

Oxford, 264.

15

THE CALL
TO PROFESSIONALISM

St. Jean-Baptiste de La Salle

1651–1719 ~ France ~ Feast: April 7

Jean-Baptiste de La Salle is the patron saint of teachers. He was born into a wealthy French family in Reims in 1651 and received a classical education. From his youth La Salle wanted to be a priest; he had his head shaved in recognition of entering the priesthood at age ten and became a canon of the cathedral at fifteen, a position that enabled him to pray the Divine Office and assist in the liturgy. Trained in a Parisian seminary, he returned to Reims after his parents died and was ordained in 1678.

Soon after La Salle's ordination, however, he met Adrien Nyel, who was setting up charity schools for boys in Reims. During that period in France, serious education was only for the wealthy; the "Little Schools" that existed for the poor were conducted by ill-educated teachers, brutal in their corporal punishment. Nyel's teachers suffered from the same deficiencies, and La Salle stepped in to help train them, inviting them to meals at his house where he "offered instruction in manners, methods, religion, and tried to provide inspiration." La Salle was appalled at the schoolmasters' ignorance. "If I had thought that the interest I took in the masters out of pure charity would lead me to the necessity of having to live with them, I should have given up," he later wrote, remarking that he thought the men "inferior to [his] valet."

Despite such reservations, advice from his spiritual director and a sense of his own calling led La Salle to devote himself more and more to improving the quality of education for poor boys, and he took over the school. In 1681 the saint invited teachers to live with him and instituted a schedule of regulated life and prayer that included daily pedagogical training. Resentful at the discipline, five teachers soon left, but others came to take their places. Committing himself to education, La Salle resigned his priesthood and sold his goods for famine relief.

Recognizing that teaching at a charity school was "arduous and entirely unremunerative" work that "from a worldly point of view . . . held no attractions whatsoever," La Salle encouraged his teachers to think of their occupation as a vocation. Dedication to God and love of service to students were to be their guiding principles. He constituted his teachers as a religious order, the Institute of Christian Brothers. Insisting that brothers be wholly devoted to teaching, La Salle took the revolutionary step of stipulating that no brother could be a priest.

To professionalize the lay brothers' calling, La Salle provided very practical instruction for the masters themselves through his pedagogical text, *The Conduct of Christian Schools*. Seeking to standardize instructional practice, the work deals with such things as discipline (beware of punishment out of proportion to the offense, he counsels, and of rejecting students' excuses out of hand), the common failings of new teachers (they are likely to waste time, to be partial to certain students, to be too harsh and talkative, to lack conviction), and classroom management (if you want to reestablish order, he says, lower your voice to reduce students' noisiness). Affection and mutual respect should characterize classroom interactions, he urges, for teachers are "ambassadors of God" to their students. He also emphasizes the importance of accountability. At the end of every year, he insists, his teachers must draw up a report on each student's strengths and weaknesses that will follow that student to the next grade.

La Salle also instituted formal teacher training. He established a postulate of fifteen- and sixteen-year-olds who wanted to be teachers, and the group had high admission standards. "It was esteemed an honor to be received among its numbers," one biographer reports. He also established a formal Rule. Masters rose to prepare their lessons each day at six-thirty; then breakfast followed, accompanied by reading from *The Conduct of Christian Schools*; lessons and breaks followed in an orderly sequence. No longer outcasts in a low-status job, his teachers began to embrace their occupation with dedication and satisfaction.

The success of La Salle's methods quickly became apparent (the previously "wild" boys, it is said, were wont to greet the teachers each morning with joy. "Here are the Brothers!" they exclaimed, running out to embrace them). La Salle produced other influential books that spread the influence of his thought, including meditations for teachers, a guide to the "rules for Christian decorum and civility" for boys, and a text on prayer for the brothers. By the time of La Salle's death, in 1719, twenty-two towns in France contained schools founded on his principles. He was canonized in 1900. Today Christian Brothers are particularly active in England and America as well as in France.

TEACHING AS "AN ELITE GUILD . . . A HOLY MINISTRY"

One of the most memorable moments of my career as a teacher trainer began with a sick, defensive rush in my stomach. "Can you stop by the office some time this afternoon?" my chairman asked me, casually, when we passed in the hall. "I have a letter from one of the teachers who was in your in-service last fall that I'd like to talk to you about."

I knew that this couldn't be good. Usually I deal with self-selected folks during in-services—those who apply for weeklong summer institutes and semester-long scholar-in-residence programs. The previous fall, though, I'd been pressured into teaching a two-day "course" during a school break, promising college credit to anyone who attended and wrote a paper. Nearly all of the papers had come in at the last moment, and many were weak. I'd given a lot of low grades.

"This letter," John said across the desk, "is about a C that you gave a student." I knew it, I thought. John and I were longtime friends, but this was going to be a gentle reprimand. "She says that she's been doing in-services like this for years, and that she did exactly the quality of work that she's done before, and that she's never gotten anything less than an A."

As I began to stammer my defense, John broke into a wide grin. "Wait a minute. Stop!" He held up his hand. "Stop, Susan! She's *thanking* you for the C. She wants you to know that she's *glad*. She says that no one else has ever really read what she turned in. This is the first time that someone has actually treated her like a professional. She wants to know when your next in-service is, so that she can sign up."

Jean-Baptiste de La Salle's work is apparently not yet completed. Not only do many taxpayers not take teachers seriously ("You get summers off, and only work six hours a day! Why should we give you a raise?") but some teachers themselves, like the woman in my story, often get accustomed to selling themselves short. *Continuing education? What a nuisance! Evaluations? Innovations? New lesson plans? Come on! I don't make enough money for that.* Sadly, we're still fighting—both within ourselves and with outsiders—the battle for professionalizing our profession.

What can we do about this, those of us who care deeply about teaching? Though we can mount publicity campaigns to try to convince taxpayers that our work should be more valued, though we can publicize our work in parish or diocesan newspapers, all that we can really control is our own sense of professionalism. Fortunately for us, that road has been traveled before. Three hundred years ago,

Jean-Baptiste de La Salle found a way to inspire his teachers with a sense of their own dignity, under circumstances much more dire than those we face.

His strategy was amazingly simple. Rather than hopeful, empty pep talks, he focused on actions. He reasoned that people who behaved as if their work were important would come to believe that it was. And so he *raised* the bar rather than lowering it. His teachers were instructed to lead orderly lives to fortify them for their daily challenges. They were required to plan daily, as if one could not think of teaching without preparation. They were instructed in pedagogy as if teaching were a craft, a technical skill one had to study and at which one could improve—a skill not everyone could develop. Article Five in *The Conduct of Christian Schools*, "Children Who Must and Who Must Not Be Corrected," for example, discusses how to tailor techniques to individual students' learning styles. Providing advice that modern teachers might still find useful, La Salle categorizes particular kinds of students and suggests tactics for disciplining each ("stubborn students" must not be allowed to "mutter" after they return to their seats, for instance, while "gentle children" or newcomers should be "admonish[ed] gently in private"). Attitude change begins with a sense of competence, de La Salle knew, and he provided his teachers with the specific tools they needed to gain that sense, tools for dealing with students, with parents, with administrative tasks. At the same time, he understood—realist that he was—that confidence developed over time, and he provided gentle advice to new teachers about faking it: they should "endeavor to bear [themselves] with an air of assurance and maintain a look of deliberation as if [they] were experienced in teaching."

La Salle also knew that teachers needed to be routinely reinvigorated, and so he incorporated daily in-services into their routine, along with yearly pedagogical retreats. He understood that ongoing self-consciousness about craft was something that all master craftspeople shared (you're already one of his children, actually, if you're reading this book). He reinforced this self-reflection with words on the importance of education. In *Meditations for the Time of Retreat*, he writes that teachers are like the angels in the story of Jacob's ladder, "going up to God to make him aware of the needs of those for whom he had made them responsible and to receive his orders for them," then "coming back down to teach those they were guiding the will of God. . . . You must do the same thing for the children entrusted to your care," he remarks explicitly.

Jean-Baptiste de La Salle's practical advice and his philosophy of teaching can still guide us today. He would be the first to remind us that teaching is *difficult*; it's not for everyone. Colleges of education or religious teacher-training programs should not accept people who have gravitated there because other callings are "too hard"; they should demand the best and brightest. Those of us who supervise new teachers and colleagues, similarly, have a responsibility to ask for quality work. Professionalism ultimately begins at home, though, and we are all responsible for reminding ourselves, every day, that we are members of an elite guild—a "holy . . . ministry"—and for acting like it.

For Further Reading

W. J. Battersby, *De la Salle: A Pioneer of Modern Education* (London: Longmans Green and Company, 1949).

Edward A. Fitzpatrick, *La Salle, Patron of All Teachers* (Milwaukee: Bruce Pub. Co., 1951).

Carl Koch, Ed. *John Baptiste de la Salle: The Sprituality of Christian Education* (Mahwah, NJ: Paulist Press, 2004). (Includes extensive selections from works by La Salle.)

Oxford, 310–11.

16

St. Bernadette of Lourdes

1844–1879 ~ French Basque country ~ Feast: April 16

St. Bernadette of Lourdes, a humble girl whose visions of the Virgin Mary established her native village of Lourdes in southern France as one of the most important pilgrimage sites in Christendom, was born on January 7, 1844. Her birth name was Marie-bernarde Soubirous; she was the oldest of nine children, only four of whom lived. Her father, a miller, was relatively prosperous when she was born. After drought ruined grain crops, however, he was forced to become a day laborer, and the family drifted between temporary shelters. When their poverty made them homeless, a cousin allowed them to live in the twelve-foot-square cellar, a former jail that had been condemned for unsanitary conditions. As a young girl, Bernadette caught cholera and contracted asthma, which would plague her all her life. The family's troubles were compounded by Bernadette's father's arrest for stealing two sacks of flour, and by alcoholism. Many sources, however, attest to the Soubirous' piety and self-respect despite their troubles.

As a girl, Bernadette was sent to work for her former wet nurse; this, her ill health, and the family's poverty kept her from learning to read and write. Her illiteracy prevented her from taking her first communion. In January 1858, she returned home and finally began her education in a free convent-school "paupers' class," seeking to acquire enough literacy and knowledge of the catechism to participate in the Eucharist. She was fourteen, and most of the other children were seven.

Just a month later, on February 11, 1858, Bernadette went to gather firewood with a sister and a friend. Bernadette led them to an eddy formed by a cavelike overhanging rock, called Massabielle, where a small stream joined the River Gave. Bernadette's companions crossed the water to search for wood, and she sat to remove her stockings so that she could join them. Then she felt a wind and saw a beautiful woman holding a rosary and wearing a white dress with a blue sash. Terrified, Bernadette began a rosary. The "lady," as Bernadette called her, smiled and joined in on the recitation. When Bernadette's companions returned, they found her shaken.

The next Sunday, with her mother's reluctant permission, Bernadette heeded an inner call to return to the grotto, bearing holy water in case the apparition was diabolical. When the lady appeared, Bernadette in panic sprinkled all of the water on her, but the more Bernadette sprinkled, the more the lady smiled. A few days later, on Thursday, February 17, the lady spoke to Bernadette, telling her to come to the grotto every day for a fortnight. The lady also advised Bernadette that she promised happiness for Bernadette in the next world, not this one. Adults in attendance that day saw the girl go into a trance, noting her "calm happiness."

So began a series of eighteen additional visions, during which the lady told Bernadette to build a chapel on the site, counseled prayer and penance for Christians, and confided three secrets that Bernadette was forbidden to reveal. No one except Bernadette ever saw the lady. Even skeptics were impressed with her rapturous state during the visions, although local clergy and civil authorities repeatedly subjected her to hostile interrogation. To all her questioners, Bernadette replied simply that she had seen a lady. The visions came almost daily, and observers began to crowd to the grotto. On February 25, the lady instructed Bernadette to "drink at the fountain" in the cave. Bernadette found only a muddy puddle, but she obediently scratched at the grotto floor and drank. When she emerged with her face filthy, the crowd jeered. "The gullible have been well and truly had. Bernadette's real place is in an asylum," wrote a local newspaper. The next day, though, it was clear that the cave had held a hidden spring, for water was flowing freely. On March 1, the first miracle cure took place, and thousands of people began visiting.

With growing evidence that *something* was happening in the grotto, Bernadette's parish priest directed her to ask the lady her name, but the lady only smiled. Only after the fortnight of regular apparitions was past, on March 25, did the lady tell Bernadette "I am the Immaculate Conception," and the girl, who did not understand this phrase (the church had only three years before officially applied this designation to Mary) repeated it on her way home, so that she would not forget it. The priest was astonished. "She could never have made this up," he is reported to have said.

Although Bernadette's visions ended, the cures effected by the spring's water multiplied. A commission of bishops investigated the phenomenon. In 1862, a pastoral Letter proclaimed that Bernadette had indeed seen the Virgin Mary, and a chapel was constructed on the site.

From the time of her earliest visions, Bernadette was harassed by those who wanted to speak with her, take a piece of her clothing, or buy her rosary or prayer book. This attention was painful to the shy, still semiliterate Bernadette, inducing debilitating asthma attacks, but she maintained her dignity, speaking as little as possible, never taking money, and refusing to glorify herself. In 1866, worn out by the attention, Bernadette joined the novitiate of the Sisters of Notre-Dame of Nevers, 300 miles from Lourdes. Her life in the convent was marked by quiet service, humility, and sanctity; she called herself a "broom" that had been used and was now rightly set aside. She did not attend the dedication of the Lourdes basilica in 1876. Always sickly, she died on April 16, 1879, at age thirty-five. She was canonized in 1933. Lourdes is credited with having achieved 4,000 cures by 1908 alone. The spring still produces tens of thousands of gallons of water per week, and millions of pilgrims visit yearly.

Willing to Not Explain Everything

Glowing with the touch of the holy, yet determinedly ordinary; humble, yet defiant, Bernadette stands before us, an enigma. She never articulated what her experience meant (indeed, she never even explicitly called "the lady" the Virgin Mary); she never ventured to guess why she had been chosen. She insisted to the importunate ones who begged her to explain that she could not explain, for she was what she had always been, a simple girl. Though many commentators have attempted to interpret Bernadette—as a prototype of the sanctity of innocence and lowliness, as a clinical example of the power of self-delusion in the service of faith, as a prototype of Christ's passion, as a martyr to official pressure, as a blandly angelic paradigm of obedience—she herself refused to offer any conclusive interpretation.

Sanctified or not, Bernadette must have frustrated the people eager to hear her discuss her experiences. I have to admit that, when I first read the best-selling novel about her, *The Song of Bernadette*, I sympathized just a little with Bernadette's teacher/mother superior, melodramatically villainous character though she is made to be. Just imagine Bernadette in a classroom. Share with others? Not Bernadette. Try to explain, try to reflect, even? Not Bernadette. Respond to invitations to make inferences? Are you kidding? Silence was her primary mode.

So, while we might recommend Bernadette as a model of faith (particularly to meek students), she seems to have little potential as a mentor for teachers. We live by interpretation and inference, after all; our job is to guide students in the process of learning how to explain and reflect, how to reach conclusions—how to make sense, we might say, of the world around them and their own experience (even in religious education classes). Bernadette quietly defied that process.

One might argue, however, that her very challenge to teachers' basic way of proceeding makes her an important mentor saint for us. For Bernadette embodies the limits of rational interpretation. While we can lead our students to confident explanations of many things, her conduct insists that some matters are beyond explanation. She reminds us, in effect, of what we already know: that many questions of faith, questions of cause and effect or interpretation in history or science or economics, questions of human nature or ethics or aesthetic choice or creative process can't be ultimately answered with words, no matter how intently we reflect or analyze or infer. To force ambiguity into a neatly wrapped box is to lie.

And yet how our students crave neatly wrapped boxes! They hate ambiguity. "Tell me," they beg when confronted with problems that have no simple answers. "Explain it to me." If we suggest that an absolute answer is not possible, they may begin to badger us. They may even suggest that we are failing them somehow. They can bring to bear tremendous pressure, as all teachers know. Under that pressure, it's so tempting to say, "Okay, here's my take on that," and watch them write what we've said in their notebooks as if it were gospel truth.

It's easy to see why they insist on encapsulated explanations. If we can explain something, after all, we can confidently possess it. We can check that piece of knowledge off the list. If we rationally understand something, we imagine that the situation is predictable and that we possess some measure of control over it. That's one reason we teach reasoning, why we encourage our students to articulate meaning, after all—so that they will be able to move more confidently around in a world they better understand.

But Bernadette insists that we should not presume to explain something that is beyond human explanation, making it into an easily grasped story. Memoirist Mary Blew has written that to tell a story is to fix an experience into the version told, to change memory to exclude contrary details. If we tell complicated stories too simply to credulous students, we thus might be closing doors rather than opening them, might actually be preventing our students from encountering the world in all of its mystery.

And, ironically, while we might find a Bernadette infuriating in our classroom, we may also be obliged to *be* subversive Bernadettes when dealing with particular subject matter. "Not so fast," we must say to our assurance-seeking students. "That's one way of looking at it," we must reply to those who pose triumphant, too-easy syntheses. Even "I'm not sure" is sometimes an appropriate response from the teacher's podium.

Not only appropriate, but inevitable. For, in a real classroom, our students will inevitably run up against mysteries, and they will turn to us then, hands raised, eyes begging us to make this problem go away. At such times, Bernadette can help us, with her stubborn silence that insisted on ineffable complexity. Our students will almost surely be frustrated if we insist they must learn to live with *not* being sure about everything—what the English poet John Keats called "negative capability." We might even taste a tiny sliver of what Bernadette endured, all her life: the compulsive grasping of human beings who want someone else to hand them answers. But we'll be right.

For Further Reading

Sara Maitland and Wendy Mulford, *Virtuous Magic: Women Saints and Their Meanings* (New York: Continuum, 1999), 22–25.

Thérèse Taylor, *Bernadette of Lourdes: Her Life, Death and Visions* (London: Continuum, 2005).

Franz Werfel, *The Song of Bernadette*, trans. Ludwig Lewisohn (New York: The Viking Press, 1942).

www.CatholicPilgrims.com/lourdes/ba_bernadette_intro.htm.

Oxford, 56–57.

17

From Contemplation
to Action

St. Catherine of Siena

1347–1380 ~ Italy ~ Feast: April 29

S t. Catherine of Siena was a fourteenth-century mystic and activist characterized both by intense devotional piety and "an exceptionally strong will and a very marked individuality." She was born in 1347 to a prosperous dyer, one of more than twenty children, along with a twin who died at birth. When Catherine was six, she had her first mystical experience, a vision of Christ in glory with St. Peter, St. Paul, and St. John. The vision was so lovely that the rapt Catherine wept because her brother woke her.

From then on Catherine determined to devote herself to God, taking a secret vow of virginity when she was seven. Her mother, however, began to groom her for marriage. Catherine reacted in horror, cutting her hair, attempting to spend her time in contemplation, refusing food, and inflicting harsh physical penance on herself. For a time, her family engaged in a contest of wills with her: taking away her room, refusing to let her be alone, and demanding that she socialize with people outside her family. Finally, Catherine called a family council and announced, "Now that by the grace of God I have reached an age of discretion and have more wisdom, know well that in me certain things are so firm that it would be easier to soften a rock than to tear them from my heart." Her amazed father capitulated. "God watch over you sweet daughter," he said. "Now we know with certainty that you are moved not by the whim of youth but by the impulse of divine love. . . . Do as you please and as the holy Spirit instructs you."

Catherine retreated to a cell-like room in her parents' home and lived as a solitary for three years of prayer and penance. She had terrifying visions and periods in which she could not pray; she lost half her body weight. But she also experienced Christ's presence and heard his voice. In 1366, Christ appeared with Mary and angels and gave Catherine a ring (visible to her but not to others), making her his bride. After this experience, Catherine moved out of her solitude into the world—at Christ's demand, she said—becoming a Dominican tertiary at age nineteen.

Catherine sought to give service in hospitals, tending the most desperately ill people by choice, including those in the late stages of cancer; she also worked in prisons and among the poor. Her charity and sanctity soon attracted a devoted group of followers, who called her "Mamma." Catherine's visions continued (some said that she levitated while at church), as did her fasting (she gave up all cooked food except bread and ate only once a day). After local debate about whether she was a fanatical hypocrite, she was called to Florence to defend herself. Catherine passed the trial easily and returned to Siena to minister to those suffering from a new outbreak of the black plague. The Sienese came to adore her.

In the midst of this activity, Catherine continued her contemplative practice, speaking regularly, she reported, with Jesus. These conversations appear in her *Dialogo*, which she dictated to her followers, since she could not write. Her fame grew, and Pope Gregory, in exile in Avignon, employed her as a peacemaking envoy. In 1376, the "bold and fearless" Catherine heard Christ's call to go to Gregory himself and charge him with reforming his see. "Fulfill the vow which you have promised!" she directed him with vigor, alluding to a secret promise that Gregory had made to himself to leave corrupt Avignon and return to Italy. Gregory complied.

Two years later, the Great Schism again split the papacy, with another rival pope at Avignon challenging Gregory's successor. Catherine became a champion of Urban VI, urging obedience in letters to civil authorities and to spiritual leaders, and counseling reform to Urban himself in missives that blend admonition and loving familiarity (she calls him "my sweet babbo"). Urban invited her to Rome, where she tirelessly urged others to support his papacy. She collapsed in 1380 and died at the age of thirty-three.

Catherine was canonized in 1461 and declared a doctor of the church in 1970. Her *Dialogo* and her 400 surviving letters remain spiritual classics. She has been called "the greatest woman in Christendom" for both her mysticism and her untiring activity on behalf of the church.

Moving Forward to Courageous Action

The extent to which Catherine's life blended contemplative and active life is nothing short of amazing. We might think of mystics as remote and intensely private, totally wrapped up in their relationships with God, and, for much of early church history, mystics were considered elite practitioners, sort of otherworldly spiritual athletes. Catherine, however, who never balked at charging into various frays, was also intensely a woman in the world. She tended the sick; she advised her followers. Although she lacked any formal education, she did not hesitate to counsel popes or to serve as a papal ambassador. She was a force to be reckoned with, not some otherworldly figure unwilling to sully herself with human contact.

She had no choice, really, given her account of Christ's instructions. Yes, her three years of cloistered solitude in the "cell of self-knowledge" had been necessary, she wrote in the *Dialogo*, "in order to know better the goodness of God towards her." After her preparation was complete, however, she reports that Christ ordered her to take her practice to the streets. "Love of Me and love of neighbor are one and the same thing," she quotes him as saying. She wrote that Christ gives particular people particular gifts for ministering to others, and anyone who wants to serve him is obliged to listen to his direction about where he wants those gifts employed. Catherine's gifts, besides her direct conversations with Christ, apparently included diplomacy, tireless service to the sometimes ungrateful poor, and motherly firmness with leaders who needed chastening. Catherine employed these gifts without apology.

Few people are as bold as Catherine in putting the fruits of preparation into action. Those of us who teach in higher education all know students who seem to want to go to school forever because they are afraid to test themselves. One of my record-holders is a student now completing her *third* B.A., protesting that she still doesn't know enough to teach. The I'm-not-ready-yet syndrome happens in religious education as well: one of my friends who is a catechist talks about a woman who has been coming to introductory religious education classes for years, but, despite invitations to commit to the church, always demurs. It also occurs in out-of-school adults. I know people who are always planning to do particular useful things–to go to work at the society of St. Vincent de Paul, to volunteer at the hospital—but temporize. It's so much easier to contemplate action, to convince oneself that one needs more time to prepare, than to dig in and begin. Though cells—literal and mental—and ivory towers can be uncomfortable, as Catherine well knew, over time they become safe havens.

Fortunately, though, there are still Catherines among us. One of them is named Tara, and she's my former student. If anyone might be forgiven the wish to remain cloistered, it's Tara. She came to school as a young wife with three children, uncertain of her own ability, coming from a working-class world where her occupations had always been menial. Within a year, she was in the midst of a divorce from her husband, which sorely tested her resources of time, money, and self-confidence. With encouragement from her teachers and some scholarship money, Tara persevered, however, and discovered that school was her element. What a wonderful student she was, someone who made all other students in a room better. How hungry she was for learning, and how quickly she learned! How happy she was with her books and her studies!

Most of us involved with Tara assumed that four years would not be enough for her, that she would go straight on to graduate school. In fact, one afternoon I volunteered to write a recommendation letter for her. But she said that she had found another calling, at least a temporary one: for two years she would volunteer in the AmeriCorps. She was going to work with the local neighborhood housing authority, helping needy families find decent homes. She'd been thinking about this a great deal, reflecting on her own time as a single mother. The position wouldn't pay much, but her children were a little older now, and they could cope. She had a home of her own now, and she wanted to give back to others some of the encouragement and assistance she had received. "Graduate school would be wonderful," she said. She'd probably return to school eventually. But she was sure that this was how she was supposed to use her new self-confidence and communications skills.

I was momentarily disappointed, I'll admit, so I just nodded. If Catherine had been sitting in my chair, however, I imagine that she would have jumped to her feet and embraced Tara to her bony frame with temporarily breath-crushing enthusiasm. Catherine might have declared with her characteristic forthrightness that Tara understood what she understood: that the purpose of cloistered time was to prepare one to do God's will. "You go, girl"—in some fourteenth-century locution, of course—is what she would have said. I like to imagine them smiling at each other—two women who might have found excuses not to act. But neither was/is that kind of woman, and both had confidence, after careful contemplation, that their duty stretched outward, in service to others.

When we encounter students who are loathe to take a logical next step or friends who always mean to get around to acting, we teachers would do well to introduce them to Catherine. Actually, when we find ourselves stalling, telling ourselves that we're not ready to apply our hard-won insight (though we know that we are), we ought to reintroduce *ourselves* to Catherine. "The love of Me is fulfilled and completed in the love of neighbor," Christ told her—words that my Tara would understand, words for all of us to ponder.

For Further Reading

Rudolph M. Bell, *Holy Anorexia* (Chicago: University of Chicago Press, 1985).

Bert Ghezzi, "Miracles that Made Peace–St. Catherine of Siena," in *Mystics & Miracles: True Stories of Lives Touched by God* (Chicago: Loyola Press, 2002), 31–38.

Arrigo Levasti, *My Servant, Catherine*, trans. Dorothy M. White (Westminster, MD: Newman Press, 1954).

Robert McClory, "Catherine of Siena," in *Faithful Dissenters: Stories of Men and Women Who Loved and Changed the Church* (Maryknoll, NY: Orbis Books, 2000), 78–89.

Mary O'Driscoll, ed., "Introduction," in *Catherine of Siena: Passion for the Truth, Compassion for Humanity. Selected Spiritual Writings* (New Rochelle, NY: New City Press, 1993), 7–16.

Butler's, 2:192–98.

Oxford, 96–97.

18

St. Antoninus

1389–1459 ~ Italy ~ Feast: May 10

St. Antoninus was a Dominican reformer and cleric, archbishop of Florence from 1446 until his death in 1459. He was born in 1389, son of a notary, and, inspired by the preaching of Blessed John Dominic, applied to enter the Dominican order at fifteen and was accepted a year later. Antonius was sent to the novitiate at Cortona, along with the artist Fra Angelico. His talent as a leader was soon apparent, and as a young man he served as prior at Fiesole, Cortona, Siena, and San Minerva at Rome, among other places. As prior provincial of the Roman province, Antoninus worked to institute St. Dominic's reforms. In particular, he urged priors to lead by example. "If the inferiors follow the leaders into the same sins, they will follow them also in the same virtues," he told one gathering. "It is therefore very important that you show your friars what should be done and what should be avoided, and show it by your actions more than by your words." Antoninus zealously reformed clerical dress (he is said to have cut one priest's hair himself), and he insisted that all priests have prayer books.

In 1436 Antoninus was called to organize the newly remodeled convent of San Marco in Florence; he was joined by Fra Angelico, who painted for the order. Antoninus preached daily and became a famous confessor, producing a manual for making good confessions. He also continued to consult with popes about canon law and reform. In 1446, much against Antoninus's will, Pope Eugenius IV made him archbishop of Florence.

Antoninus was deeply beloved and especially famous for his care of the poor. Living humbly himself (he owned no plate and no horses, only a mule—which he kept selling to feed the poor, but which patrons kept buying back for him), he followed his own advice about setting an example. Antoninus is said to have torn up the flower beds around his palace to plant wheat for his people; he sold his own furniture and clothes for charity. He patiently saw all visitors and earned a reputation as the "angel of counsel." Although people of great importance frequently came to speak with Antoninus, he was not above dealing with more humble problems: according to one story, when a peasant girl could not be consoled for the loss of a pot that she had broken, he miraculously reconstructed it. He also established a benefit society for people who were ashamed to beg. His personal work during plague, earthquake, and famine were legendary, and he made sure to visit his entire diocese once a year on foot, listening to people's concerns. His extensive, four-volume work, the *Summa Theologica Moralis*, suggests that such beneficence flowed from fundamental belief: a pastor, Antoninus argues, must take Christ the Good Shepherd as his model, and one of his fundamental responsibilities is to feed his flock.

As archbishop, Antoninus did not compromise his reforming zeal; he warred against gambling and black magic, in particular. Although he is celebrated today for his arguments that capitalism can be ethical if conducted in the right spirit, he would not tolerate usury. He also kept a close watch over public morals, once whipping young men out of church when they came only to ogle young women.

Late in his life, Antoninus served as Florentine ambassador and participated in a papal community charged with reforming the Roman court. When he died, Pope Pius II praised him as a man who had "conquered avarice and pride, was outstandingly temperate in every way, was a brilliant theologian and popular preacher." Ironically, given the simplicity of Antoninus's life, he was given an elaborate funeral attended by throngs of Florentines. After Antoninus's death, his writings were widely distributed and influential: his *Summa*, first published in 1477, went through fifteen editions in the next fifty years, and his manual for confession went through one hundred editions during the fifteenth century. He was canonized in 1523. Scenes of his life decorate the church and cloister at San Marco, and his body lies, "visible and incorruptible," under a glass altar there.

Bringing Love into a Classroom

The twentieth-century composer Benjamin Britten's cantata *Saint Nicolas* opens with the chorus invoking the saint after "sixteen hundred years," asking for his inspiration and guidance. Nicholas, in the form of a necessarily vigorous tenor (given the music's demands), appears to them and begins musing about his original congregation. "All who knelt beside me then are gone," he sings reflectively in Eric Crozier's text. "Their name is dust, their tombs are grass and clay." But then he turns to the people actually before him. "Yet still their shining seed of faith survives–/In you!" he sings, his voice gaining volume and pace as he sees them more clearly. "In you!" he repeats, with enthusiasm and affection, now energetically and emotionally committed to telling them his story.

Though Antoninus has become obscure enough outside of Florence that no one (to my knowledge, at least) has written a cantata about him, he too would be an appropriate subject for such a wonderful musical moment. For Antoninus, like Nicholas, loved people. In part, this affection was theologically based (his *Summa* insists that humans have inherent dignity because they are made in God's likeness), and it was congruent with his description of a pastor's role, but his love was too abundant to have been inspired only by duty. Antoninus was a people-junkie, one might say: he turned to everyone who sought him (and some who didn't) with his full, affectionate attention. In turn, his flock loved him back with extraordinary devotion, despite his rigor. While saints' relics are typically treated with affection and pride, Antoninus is unusual in that his whole body is on display for anyone to see in the church of San Marco, lying there preserved (though a little wizened) under glass, provoking children's enthusiastic exclamations of horror in a variety of languages. It appears that the people of Florence and the monks of San Marco are reassured to know that Antoninus is still present in their midst.

Given scandals and abuses, we are often nervous today about speaking of love for those in one's pastoral or temporal care. It's fair to say, though, that true community—in a congregation, a study group, a classroom—can't exist without love, when the term is used in the sense of "agape," nonerotic, mutually supportive affection. When people become emotionally attached to each other, they take greater responsibility for the group's work. They look forward to seeing the others. They throw themselves, heart and soul, more fully into the work. It's a delight to be in a room full of people who love one another in the sense of caring about one another's progress, celebrating one another's joys, encouraging one another through times of aridity and pain.

Antoninus was a genius at building such a Christian community, and his life provides a fine model of how one might be fostered in a classroom, as well as in a diocese. Antoninus shows us that love doesn't mean absolute tolerance; caring for people means correcting their faults as well as ministering charitably to their needs. If love is to be the hallmark of our interactions, though, behind that rigor must be affection and a fundamental optimism about people. A good shepherd reaches out because he believes that people are capable of good. He lights up when he turns to the people in a room, whether they are familiar or new, eager to see what they are thinking, what they can do today. He is energetic in drawing people into community. All needy people were recipients of Antoninus's charity. Everyone had his ear. No one was invisible.

Not every classroom will be full of love, as every teacher knows. But thinking and acting like Antoninus can increase our odds of fostering affectionate concern among our students. The reward is well worth the energy, after all, because classrooms that are full of affection prosper. As I write these words, I've just finished a semester in which my general education freshman class, by the grace of God, became such a community. When I said my good-byes yesterday, a young woman looked back at me with a stricken face. "It's over!" she lamented. Though one or two of her fellow students—who through my fault or their own or a combination never quite felt part of that community—set their faces and looked away, the others laughed sympathetically. "What are you teaching next semester?" someone asked. "All upper-division classes," I replied, but I reassured them that they'd find another "family," possibly in their next English class, and they smiled at me, a little dubiously.

I hope they will, because I do love them. For my part, I'm hoping to overcome my own pangs of loneliness at their departure ("It's over," I've caught myself saying, too), so that I can attempt to resume the role of Antoninus/Nicholas again in a few weeks. "In you!" I hope that I can say as I turn to those new strangers who have become my flock, my eyes sparkling with new attention, new hope.

For Further Reading

Social Theories of Saint Antoninus From His Summa Theologica (Washington, DC: Catholic University of America Press, 1950).

www.op.org/DomCentral/study/ashley/antoninus.htm (Benedict M. Ashley, O.P. "Antoninus of Florence, Christian Community.")

Butler's, 2:263–5.

Oxford, 27–28.

19

Healthy Individualism

St. Josephine Bakhita

1871–1947 ~ Africa, Italy ~
Feast: Beatified May 17 (Feast after Canonization in 2000, February 8)

St. Josephine Bakhita was a former African slave who, after she was freed, chose a life of peaceful service as "Sister Moretta," the "little brown sister" of the Institute of Canossian Daughters of Charity in Italy. Born around 1870 in the Sudan to a village chief, she was taken from her prosperous, peaceful home by armed slave traders when she was nine. The girl never saw her family again; because of the terror of her capture, she even forgot her original name. Like all who were taken as slaves, she was renamed by her master. Her new name, *Bakhita*, means "the lucky one," and her overall life story suggests that it was given with more truth than the master could have known.

The early years of her captivity, however, were full of brutality. Immediately after her capture, she was held for two months in a "hole of a room," then marched for eight days toward a slave market. Bakhita and other young girls in the group (who were only chained at night) escaped, but they were retaken and whipped along in another forced march. At the slave market of El Obeid in Kordofan she was sold to an Arab chief as a maid for his daughter; the family's son beat her so badly that it took her a month to recover. She was then sold to a Turkish general to wait on his mother and wife. She was whipped again in that household and tattooed as a mark of identification, with salt rubbed into her cuts to set the scars. "We had to bear it all in silence," she later reported.

After seven years of suffering, Bakhita returned with her Turkish masters to their native land, and she was sold to the family of the Italian vice-consul to Khartoum, Callisto Legnani, who bought her so that she could escape slavery as a free servant. She was treated kindly in this family and taught European ways, and she insisted on migrating to Italy with them after the fall of Khartoum. In Italy, Legnani found her a position as servant, then nursemaid for a business associate. When the Michaeli family left Italy to supervise a hotel on the Red Sea, Bakhita and her charge, Alice, were sent to board at a Catholic convent and school in Venice run by the Canossian Daughters of Charity. Up until then, Bakhita had received no formal training in religion, although "seeing the moon and the stars, I said to myself—Who could be the master of these beautiful things? And I felt a great desire to see him, know him, and pay him homage," she wrote in her autobiography. Responding to her interest, a trustee of her employer's family told her about God and gave her a silver crucifix; the Canossians instructed her in Catholicism, and she prepared for baptism.

The commitment to faith gave her new resolve. Signora Michaeli returned to Italy to retrieve her daughter and Bakhita and take them to Africa, but Bakhita refused, "quietly but firmly" telling them that "she wished to stay with the Sisters." Her employers entreated her; when she would not budge, they asked the Patriarch of Venice to intervene, but he reminded them that slavery was illegal, and that the young woman was free to do as she wished. The patriarch himself baptized and confirmed Bakhita in January of 1890. Three years later, Bakhita applied for the novitiate of the Canossian order; another Cardinal of Venice, the future Pope St. Pius X, questioned her, "then smiled and welcomed her." She was consecrated in December of 1896. As Sister, then Mother Moretta, Bakhita took up manual work with gladness, serving as a cook, seamstress, porter, and sacristan for twenty-five years in a convent school. "Gentle and tranquil, she led a life of strict poverty and attended to her tasks," a biographer writes. As a doorkeeper, she loved to lay her hands on the children's heads as they entered or left the convent, caressing and blessing them. She was known for "her humility, her simplicity, her constant smile . . . and her inalterable sweet nature . . . and she won the hearts of all."

Josephine Bakhita longed to be a missionary and return to Africa, but that wish was not granted; the closest she came was serving as a doorkeeper for the missionary novitiate in Milan. Her example did become available beyond her own circle, though, when she wrote her life story at the request of her community.

Bakhita died of pneumonia in 1947; though she fretted in fever, imagining that she was chained as a slave, her last words were, "I am so happy. Our Lady . . . Our Lady." She was beatified on May 17, 1992 by Pope John Paul II, and three hundred thousand people came to St. Peter's Square to celebrate. In 1993, John Paul presented her relics to a Canossian sister for return to Africa, pronouncing: "Rejoice, all of Africa! Bakhita has come back to you: the daughter of the Sudan, sold into slavery as a living piece of merchandise, and yet still free: free with the freedom of the saints!" On October 1, 2000, Josephine Bakhita was canonized, the first African to be so honored since the early centuries of Christianity.

ALLOWING THE GROWTH TOWARD INDEPENDENCE

The transformations of Josephine Bakhita's life were amazing. She began as a child in a quiet village, a well-loved girl, with the promise before her of a stable traditional life as a wife and mother. Then, suddenly, she was "a living piece of merchandise," with no defense against any brutality, a girl who might at most hope to live a few years in suffering and to die forgotten. Then she became a kindly treated servant, a retainer who was also a pet project for her employers; in this phase she learned and learned, until she was ready to make her own choice. To make that choice required bravery. But along the way Bakhita had learned to value freedom so much that she could not deny her new convictions. And so she became a nun, devoted to a new kind of service—one that must have seemed a light burden, indeed, given what she had been through as a slave, and a joyful one.

Many aspects of Bakhita's life are possible subjects for meditation: the outrage of slavery, her courage and adaptability, the paradox of her having to be wrenched from everything that she knew to find faith. To me as a teacher, though, the transition between her life as a servant and her life as a nun seems particularly evocative. For, in that change of role, Josephine Bakhita experienced a transformation that students must also experience, if they are to grow to their potential. Josephine Bakhita had to break with her mentors to be true to herself. Her mentors had nurtured her, given her a life exponentially more comfortable than her life of slavery had been—a fulfilling life, in many ways. Still, she had discovered her real vocation, and she had to be firm in breaking free, this time from a good life.

Her determination seems to have shocked everyone. By all accounts, she had been a quiet, faithful servant, devoted to Alice and apparently content. Suddenly she was standing up for herself, respectfully but stubbornly. She must have faced accusations of ingratitude. Her Italian mentors had extended the benefit of the doubt to her, assuming that she could learn and be trustworthy. How could she abandon them? The answer, of course, is that she had found compelling truth and compelling vocation that overrode her obligations. She had found "The Master," as she called God, and she was obliged to turn her allegiance to him, committing to a new life as a Canossian Sister, which meant leaving those mentors behind, angry and baffled.

Time after time, we find our students evolving into people we don't quite know. Educational psychologists have called this process *individuation*, or *self-actualization*. To become fully mature, they say, students must redefine themselves. Sometimes they overtly rebel, as have many saints. They question teachers aggressively, making scenes that are declarations of independence, whether they are loud like young Catherine of Siena or quiet like Bakhita. Sometimes they simply remove themselves from their teachers to pursue interests, careers, and ways of life that teachers would not have chosen for them. This has happened recently with one of my M.A. students, a young scholar of great potential who has decided that she is content with her position in a community college and will not pursue a Ph.D.. I have acted a bit like Bahkita's employers did. My student isn't budging, though, and I've found myself feeling betrayed, as if she's somehow rejected my world. Individuating can hurt when you are the one who's being individuated *from*. The process can be agony for the individuator, too, who, like Bakhita, must be aware that he or she would never have had the chance of reaching this moment, were it not for the mentor.

If the revised vocation comes from deep conviction, however, neither the teacher nor the student has a choice. We must not stand in the way of transformations that help our students evolve into themselves, for there's nothing more joyful than a person who has found a life faithful to his or her true calling. That Josephine Bakhita felt such joy is clear in photographs of her as a Canossian sister. They depict a broad-faced, pleasant woman who looks ordinary—until one notices her small but radiantly peaceful smile. Though one might say that she had simply exchanged one sort of service for another, these images demonstrate beyond a doubt that, as Sister Moretta, she was enjoying the true freedom of doing what mattered most. All of her difficulties—including the moment that she was forced to break with her mentors—had been leading to this marvelous place.

After all her sufferings, Bakhita was given the grace and courage to discover a way of life which allowed her to fulfill herself through serving others, and her life became a blessing. As our own students evolve into themselves—though the process may sometimes be as painful for us as it is for them—let us wish them nothing less.

For Further Reading

Canossian Sisters of Charity Web site, www.fdcc.org/in/canossione/bakhita/menubak.htm.

Maria Luisa Dagnino, Canossian Missionary Nun, *Bakhita Tells Her Story* (Verona, Italy: Canossian Daughters of Charity, 1992).

Kathleen Jones, "Josephine Bakhita," in *Women Saints: Lives of Faith and Courage* (Maryknoll, NY: Orbis Books, 1999), 118–92.

20

Humor at Work

St. Philip Neri

1515–95 – Italy – Feast: May 26

S t. Philip (Filippo) Neri, an important figure in the Counter-Reformation known as "God's clown," was born in Florence in 1515, the son of a mother who died when he was young and a notary father who dabbled in alchemy. Always a good, popular child (he was known as *Pippo buono*, or "good little Phil"), he was sent for his education to the Dominican monks at the Florentine convent of San Marco. Though Neri was later apprenticed to a relative, he migrated to Rome after a mystical experience, determined to devote himself to God. There, he stayed with a fellow Florentine, teaching the household's children during the days and spending his nights in prayer and study.

After three years, Neri began preaching informally in Rome, traveling the streets to evangelize. Although Neri was outside of the church hierarchy at this point, he substantially assisted in the revitalization of the church through his itinerant preaching, which earned him the title "the Second Apostle of Rome." Good-natured, companionable Neri attracted people with friendliness and cheerful conversation; he influenced many to reform their lives, to recommit to participating in the sacraments, and to join him in acts of charity. He still spent nights in fervent prayer, and in 1544, at Pentecost, he had a spiritual experience in which a globe of fire entered his mouth and caused his heart to swell. For the rest of his life, he would feel chest palpitations during periods of extreme spiritual emotion.

In 1548, Neri founded a confraternity of laymen devoted to prayer and to working with poor pilgrims, a mission that would become especially necessary in the Jubilee Year of 1575. Though he was reluctant to become a priest, his confessor convinced him to take orders, and he worked enthusiastically with penitents. To extend his ministry, he began "conferences" for prayer, study, and discussion. These were formalized as the "Congregation of the Oratory," a loosely organized religious society without vows but with communal living arrangements. To help involve potential converts emotionally as well as intellectually in devotional meetings, Neri began commissioning musicians to set the words of the Bible to music; this was the beginning of the musical genre of oratorio, which flourished under composers such as George Frideric Handel. In 1575, the Oratorians received papal approval, and they set about rebuilding the small church of St. Maria to accommodate their rapidly growing congregation.

Philip Neri was famous for his joyful eccentricities. To make people laugh—especially the young, whom he was particularly interested in reaching—he would sometimes wear his clothes inside out or wear outlandish floppy white shoes. Once he shaved off half his beard. He resisted being called a saint and struggled to prevent others from taking him too seriously. He wore a blue cushion on his head; when he heard that others were praising him for his modesty, he paraded the streets in a mink coat. His two favorite books were the Bible and a book of jokes. Though he always prayed intensely, he cautioned others against excessive devotion: he told one young man that if he wanted to wear a hair shirt, he must wear it outside his clothes.

Even with his outlandish ways, Neri was highly respected. He served as St. Ignatius of Loyola's confessor and counted Charles Borromeo and Francis Xavier as his friends. Popes and cardinals consulted him. His faith was so great that his face was said to glow when he said Mass, and he had a reputation for being closely in touch with the supernatural, apt to fall into ecstasy. After he was too old to go about the streets, people came to his rooms, where he celebrated Mass daily. He died in 1595 at the age of eighty and was canonized in 1622.

UNLEASHING LAUGHTER'S POTENTIAL

Teachers and speakers who resort to gratuitous jokes simply to get the audience engaged have never much appealed to me. I once knew a priest who predictably told a joke to begin every homily; only very seldom did these have anything to do with the day's text or the ultimate message of the talk. Though some people in the congregation laughed, I more often winced, embarrassed that he thought we were so uninterested that he had to resort to a Dale Carnegie-style trick to "hook" us. One of my former Girl Scouts now has a high school teacher who does the same thing, and she dislikes it. Even at sixteen, she finds the teacher's attempts to ingratiate himself with the class corny and insulting. "It's an honors class," she says. "We want our teacher to be a scientist, not a comedian."

St. Philip Neri's humor, in contrast, seems never to have been gratuitous, but integral, based on a deep conviction of the interconnectedness of faith and temperament. "Christian joy is a gift of God flowing from good conscience," he once remarked. For Neri, joy was an adjunct to faith: "Cheerfulness strengthens the heart and makes us try harder to have a good life, thus God's servants must always be in good spirits." Neri stood out during this era in which ascetic rigor was encouraged in order to correct the laxity into which the church had fallen. Christians should be happy, he proclaimed, for "a heart filled with joy is more easily made perfect than one that is sad."

One of the qualities that apparently made Neri such a beloved confessor is that he used humor as he corrected faults. He once told a young woman who had confessed to gossiping that for penance she must pluck a chicken while walking through the streets, then go back and gather up all of the feathers. When she complained that the task was impossible, Neri remarked that "it was also as impossible to take back all the damaging effects your gossip has spread throughout the city." Do you think she ever forgot that metaphor? Employing overkill, he assigned a young priest who was proud of his eloquence to preach sermons for six weeks in a row. Always a realist about human nature, he gave this response to a priest who asked what prayer was most appropriate for closing a wedding ceremony: "A prayer for peace."

Neri's own goofy antics in the street were not simply silliness for silliness' sake, but manifestations of his desire to "upset popular expectations about saintliness," as one biographer writes. He clowned to undercut any chance of either the people or himself taking him too seriously. He was human, and he wanted everyone to know it. And yet, he was also as ascetic as anyone in the church, with his racking visions, his nightlong prayers, and his tendency to lose himself in devotion to the extent that he sometimes took long hiatuses within the Mass for contemplation.

Neri's life stands as a marvelous reminder of the complexity and the potential of true humor. Through his example we see that anyone who wants to guide others ought to be realistic about human nature—including one's own tendencies to pride—and should cultivate the ability to smile at human foibles. As leaders, we should admit to our own mistakes; at times we might even make our pratfalls public. Doing so will make us seem to our students like companions on the journey, and thus will make the journey appear more possible.

Neri also demonstrates that "a glad spirit," as he termed it, can coexist with high seriousness. We don't have to choose between a serious classroom and a joyful one; the world does not have to be divided that way. We can let our enjoyment of our subject area show. It's fun to solve problems, after all. Sometimes the subject matter itself is funny. Sometimes our own attempts (or our predecessors') to make sense of the subject matter reveal amusing things about the human mind. We should admit these things to our students, inviting them into our own balanced attitudes. The fact that Neri liked to laugh did not result in his penitents ignoring his advice. So long as it is clear that we take our work seriously, we, too, can let our happiness shine.

After all, why are we teaching if the subject matter is not full of joy for us? If the very process of inquiry is not often a delight? Why are we working with these young people if we do not believe that what we are transmitting will ultimately make them move more happily through the world? "I will have no sadness in my house," Philip Neri once remarked. How marvelous it would be to have no sadness, but only joyful learning, in our classrooms.

For Further Reading

F. W. Faber, *If God Be With Us: The Maxims of St. Philip Neri* (Harrisburg, PA: Morehouse Group, 1995).

Theodore Maynard, *Mystic in Motley: The Life of St. Philip Neri* (Milwaukee: Bruce Publishing Co., 1946).

Paul Turks, *Philip Neri: The Father of Joy* (Staten Island, NY: Alba House, 1995).

Butler's, 2:395–99.

Oxford, 382–84.

21

St. Dympna

Seventh century ~ Ireland (?), Belgium ~ Feast: May 30

St. Dympna, the patron of people with epilepsy, of sleepwalkers, and of people with mental illness, is discussed only in legends. She is said to have been the daughter of a pagan Celtic or British king, perhaps of Ireland, and a Christian princess mother in the seventh century. Dympna was baptized as a Christian. Her mother died when the girl was young; as Dympna matured, she began to look exactly like her. Her father was crazed by Dympna's resemblance to the wife he had adored, and he made incestuous advances to her. Dympna fled with her confessor, St. Gerebernus, to Antwerp, then into the forested country to the southeast. They settled in the town of Gheel in present-day Belgium around the year 650, planning to live as contemplatives.

Dympna's enraged, jealous father pursued them. He sent spies to track Dympna and Gerebernus, locating them when inhabitants recognized that the coins the spies were offering for information were the same as the fugitives'. When the king surprised his daughter and her confessor, he tried to talk Dympna into coming home, but she refused. He then ordered his attendants to kill the two. The retainers quickly murdered the priest but were reluctant to attack the princess. Dympna's father then cut off her head with his own sword.

The two bodies were buried ("by angelic or human hands," Butler says) where they had fallen. Rediscovered in the thirteenth century, they were placed in a shrine, and miraculous cures of people with mental illness and epilepsy were soon reported in the vicinity of the relics. Dympna became the patron of people with mental illness and Gheel a center for the treatment of psychological disturbances. Today it holds a modern sanatorium and has pioneered a residential mainstreaming program in which patients live and work with farmers and other local residents. Patients still are encouraged to walk through a narrow archway under Dympna's shrine when they come to Gheel seeking a cure.

Offering a Compassionate Presence

"Jean-Baptiste de La Salle may be the official patron of teachers," one of my Catholic friends likes to say, "but we all know that it should be Dympna." Along about mid-May, many of us are likely to grin and agree with her, no matter which way we think that cause-and-effect operates: did we go into teaching because we were crazy in the first place, or is teaching driving us crazy? In either case, when the pressure mounts and we begin to doubt our own sanity, it's nice to know that folklore has presented us with a gentle patron saint offering comfort.

Dympna's patronage is complicated, however, for her legend does not quite suggest why she is credited with special powers over mental illness. Most other saints had interactions with their particular realms of influence. Blaise tamed wild animals; Peter Claver worked with black people; Borromeo instituted catechism classes; Lucy lost her eyes. Dympna's connection with mental illness is more tenuous. The most common explanation has been to assume that her father must have been mentally ill to pursue her incestuously. Modern knowledge about incest victims, though, suggests a closer-to-the-bone explanation: that Dympna herself is likely to have suffered psychological scars as a result of her trauma. Flashbacks, guilt, and self-loathing; repression neuroses and psychoses; abuse of others—these can all result from coming into contact with others' sexual madness. A counselor might assume today that Dympna's experience had to unbalance her, even though she attempted to protect herself.

In light of that insight, Dympna's cures at Gheel might be attributed to her empathy for others in the grip of mental torment. "You have to suffer to sing the blues," a musician's cliché goes, and Dympna had suffered plenty. Outsiders could be sympathetic toward people with mental illness, but only someone who knew the true anguish of those so suffering could focus the tremendous compassion necessary for healing.

The question of why innocents suffer—why anyone suffers—is one that troubles practitioners of many religions. Dympna's story, however, can offer one suggestion for a silver lining: our own past suffering can help us reach out to others. Teachers, who often have their students' trust to begin with, are in a particularly strong position to help others in this way. That doesn't mean that we're qualified to act as psychiatrists. Several of the most empathetic young teachers I've known have self-destructed professionally as they attempted to counsel deeply troubled students, students who became emotionally dependent, then angry when their problems did not go away. That's why counselors study their trade for so many years—to gain specialized professional skills. Those of us teachers who have lived through disturbance and trauma ourselves, however, will have something just as useful as counseling to offer our students: the ability to recognize the signs of what we have been through and to compassionately direct students to people who are qualified to help.

Recognizing trauma and guiding people to others may seem like very minor steps in the process of dealing with psychological disturbance, but they're essential ones. "I *can't* see a counselor," a student of mine once said, after she'd spent an hour weeping in my office. She was a young married woman whose husband had just walked out—for the fourth time—and she was struggling not only with the pressures of going to school and raising a toddler alone, but with his parting words:

"Why don't you just quit school? You're too dumb to go to college." He had called her "selfish," too, for wanting to pursue her dreams. She wasn't sleeping. She cried all the time. She hadn't submitted her latest paper for my course because she couldn't concentrate, and she was sure that she couldn't do the assignment, anyway. She had come to ask me whether she might be able to retrieve any tuition money when she dropped out of school this late in the semester.

I had recommended that she see a counselor; our campus health center provides free appointments. But she protested. Everybody in her family was happy, and she would be ashamed to admit that she couldn't handle things herself. She would let everybody down. She had to deal with this herself. And so I found myself telling her about my own period of depression twenty years before, when my youthful first marriage was breaking up and I was sure that I was a bad person. I was in serious trouble then, despite my high functioning at the surface. My counselor had saved my life with her gentle listening and tough advice, and with the medication she prescribed. Depression is chemical as well as circumstantial; I made sure to tell this to my student, just as my counselor had reassured me, for this insight had helped me feel not quite so guilty (I, too, had come from a background where no one had ever admitted that he or she couldn't handle things alone). I told her about my own long struggle with myself, before I ventured to a mental-health clinic, and about how wise the decision had been.

"*You* were depressed?" she asked with wide eyes. Yes, I told her, and, moreover, I had just emerged from another bout that began when my sweetheart—the wonderful teacher, the mountaineer, the poet—died of cancer sixteen years into our marriage. I'd recognized the symptoms this time; I'd gone to a counselor immediately, and we'd worked together until I reached more solid ground. "How did you know that you were depressed?" she asked cautiously. I told her, and a marvelous thing happened: before long, we were laughing ruefully together about some of the things both of us had done and thought. We talked for a long time as the afternoon shadows deepened in the office, not teacher and student now, but two human beings together. I explained that I'd come to think of depression as something like a tendency to bronchitis or back spasms. I wasn't particularly ashamed, and she shouldn't be, either. She began asking questions about therapy sessions. Before she left, she let me call the campus health center so that she could set up an appointment, and she kept it two days later.

Who knows why we suffer—depression, anorexia, abuse, even serious garden-variety loneliness or doubt in ourselves? It's certain, at least, that our work as teachers enables us to make something from our suffering—as I was blessed enough, that day, to touch my student. "You're not alone," we can literally or figuratively say to young people when they feel isolated. "Your life is not over—you can feel better." Or, at the very least, "I know how you feel"—something that no one else may have ever said to them, because they have been afraid to admit their suffering, afraid that they would be stigmatized.

Dympna is truly our patron at such moments. For our simple compassionate presence, like hers, can be the archway through which our troubled students might pass to hope.

For Further Reading

Butler's, 2:320–21.

Oxford, 155.

22

St. Gottschalk

Died 1066 ~ Denmark, England, Germany ~ Feast: June 7

St. Gottschalk is the patron saint of lost vocations. Though very little is known about him, his story appears in several martyrologies, and he has been the object of "a sporadic cultus," according to Butler. He is reported to have been a Germanic priest trained at the Abbey of St. Michael in Lüneburg during the eleventh century. After his father was killed by Saxon Christians, however, Gottschalk bitterly repudiated Christianity, left the abbey, and spent twenty years battling the Saxons. He served the Danish King Canute (whose daughter he married) in Europe and in England.

Eventually, however, for reasons not reported in his story, Gottschalk regained his faith and returned to the priesthood. He converted thousands, founded monasteries, and "henceforth fostered [Christianity] with great zeal." His recommitment cost him his life, for his brother-in-law led an anti-Christian revolt, and Gottschalk was one of the first killed at Lenzen on the Elbe in 1066.

Recommitting to Vocation

We know less about St. Gottschalk than about almost any other saint in this book (Butler admits that "no solid reason appears for regarding him as either a saint or a martyr"), but I've included him because I believe that his life will resonate particularly with teachers. Gottschalk is famous because he *quit*. And I believe that all of us who teach, if we are honest, will admit that we've wanted to quit sometimes.

Actually, what I believe goes further than that: I believe that all of us who are honest with ourselves will admit that we *have* quit sometimes. I certainly have. Over the course of my career I've encountered several groups of students with whom I simply could not work well. To put it bluntly, I came to hate them during the semester, and I know that they were not fond of me. Nothing that I tried would engage them with the material. They complained about the class's difficulty (though I had taught the same material to other students with no problem in earlier semesters); they disliked the readings and the assignments; they sat sullen. The last was calculated particularly to rile me, for I am proud of being able to foster lively discussion, and I proclaim to teaching assistants that discussion should be a classroom norm (pride going before a fall, as usual). Each of those classes held a few enthusiastic students preternaturally eager to make the class work—they sat in the front, tried to answer every question, conspicuously told me how much they enjoyed the material at every opportunity—but I came to dislike even them, telling myself that their brownnosing was simply inspiring greater resentment in the others.

After unsuccessfully attempting to retrieve these classes with a palette of tricks familiar to all experienced teachers—building in cunning teaching strategies designed to warm up students and include their voices, asking them directly what was wrong—I quit, I'll admit it. I lectured more; I let the eager beavers talk; I put students in groups so that they'd at least be doing *something* during the class hour, and I wouldn't have to look at all those drooping eyelids. If I'd had access to movies of all the novels on the syllabus, I would have showed them. With each of my impossible classes, I lapsed into resigned passivity, waiting for the glorious hour when we would finally all be free of one another. I actually hummed a rude popular song about saying good-bye out loud as I left the building after one final exam. Quitting is quitting, and I did it with those classes, as surely as if I'd abandoned teaching during the middle of the school year, as I once fantasized when I was a first-year high-school teacher.

Though the language of contemporary popular culture aligns giving up with pathetic weakness and flawed character ("Just do it!" we are admonished, as if we could perform any miracle if we had enough determination), I suggest that rather than losing hope when we temporarily quit, we ought to remember Gottschalk. How easily he could have turned his back on the priesthood permanently, because he was disillusioned for a justifiable reason, bitter at a religion that had been commandeered by hypocritical practitioners. Christians had killed his father. Moreover, his culture, which embraced a feudal code of honor and revenge, mitigated against forgiveness. To identify himself once again as a Christian would have exposed him to derision, as well as to an internal sense that he was betraying his family. He must have been ashamed of his earlier repudiation, and he might well have doubted his calling. And yet somehow—we don't know how—at long last he came back to Christianity "with great zeal," and he died for it.

The sketchiness of Gottschalk's story actually makes him a more useful mentor saint, in my opinion. I like the fact that we don't see a big dramatic scene in which Gottschalk heroically regains his faith, a scene depicting angel choirs and bolts of lightening. To so dramatize the moment would be to distance us from Gottschalk . . . or at least to distance me, for I've found that my own recommitments to my vocation are more dogged than dramatic. After classes that did not go well, I've most often felt as if I've simply dusted myself off and stubbornly put my hand to the plough again, rather than experienced a life-changing epiphany. Occasionally I learn things when I analyze the horrible classes, but more often I find that I can't tell exactly what went wrong. I just begin again, and usually the next time is much better.

Gottschalk teaches us that what matters ultimately is not making perfect sense of our failures in some self-justifying conclusion, and not waiting for some conclusive sign that we are still called to our life as teachers. What counts is the action of taking up the work again. Even after we have temporarily betrayed our most central calling, we can choose to continue. Indeed, we must. Of course we'll examine our failures after the fact, attempting to learn from them. Of course we'll feel ashamed of ourselves and doubt ourselves. Ultimately, though, we can't allow temporary losses of vocation to paralyze us. With Gottschalk as our mentor, we must turn from the unresolved past and recommit ourselves. The good that we may do tomorrow demands it.

For Further Reading

Benedictine Monks of St. Augustine's Abbey, Ramsgate, *The Book of Saints: A Dictionary of Servants of God Canonized by the Catholic Church: Extracted from the Roman & Other Martyrologies*, 4th ed. (New York: Macmillan Co., 1947), 272.

Michael Freze, *Patron Saints* (Huntington, IN: Our Sunday Visitor, 1992), 151–52.

Butler's, 2:496.

23

THE GIFT OF
ECCENTRICITY

St. Lutegarde

1182–1246 ~ Belgium ~ Feast: June 16

St. Lutegarde was a mystic nun, born in 1182 in the Netherlands. Her parents were ambitious for their children's success and arranged a marriage for Lutegarde, but her dowry was lost when a ship in which her father had invested sank. Pretty, intelligent, lively Lutegarde was sent to a Benedictine convent at age twelve. She first lived as a boarder, free to come and go and fond of receiving visitors, but one day Christ appeared, "blazing before her astonished eyes," as Thomas Merton writes, and revealed his spear wound. "Seek no more the pleasures of unbecoming affection; behold, here, forever, what you should love, and how you should love," he commanded her.

Lutegarde responded to this vision with a transforming passion. When a young man later came to visit her, she said, "Get away from me, thou bait of death. I belong to another Lord," an outburst that must have flabbergasted him. She also dismissed a soldier who was courting her, literally running away from him. From that moment Lutegarde took Christ as her bridegroom, devoting herself to mystical prayer. She encountered some jealousy from other nuns who declared that her fervor would not last, but she persisted, and St. Catherine appeared to her to reassure her that she would never fall into mortal sin.

Lutegarde had many mystical experiences: she is said to have floated, glowed, and received Christ's wounds in the form of blood

drops on her forehead and hair. She also received the power of healing and became so busy with petitions that she complained to Jesus,
"Why did you go and give me such a grace, Lord? Now I hardly have
any time to be alone with You. Take it away, please . . . only give me
another grace, give me something better." On Christ's asking her what
she would prefer, she requested an understanding of Latin, but she discovered that this gift left her heart "empty and dry." After a dialogue
in which her heart was merged with Christ's, and a vision of Christ on
the cross during which she pressed her lips to his bloody wounds, her
"spiritual betrothal" was perfected, and she redevoted herself to blissful
contemplation and love. Lutegarde maintained an intimate conversa-
tional familiarity with Christ: once when she was interrupted at prayer,
she said, "Wait here, Lord Jesus, and I will come back directly after I
have finished this task."

Lutegarde professed as a Benedictine, but after she was chosen
prioress ("Lutegarde regarded it as a disaster," Merton writes), she
transferred her allegiance to the Cistercians, an order that emphasized contemplation. She proclaimed that Christ ordered her to go to
a French-speaking convent in Aywieres ("if you do not, I will have
nothing more to do with you," she reported that he told her), and she
complied. Since Lutegarde did not speak French, she was thus safe
from administrative responsibilities and could devote herself to prayer.
She once burst a blood vessel in the fervor of her prayer, and that event
was taken as an indication that, although she was not granted the favor
of dying for God, she had received the stigmata in her heart, an equiva-
lent of martyrdom. She became known for the efficacy of her prayers,
for her prophesies, for the seven-year fasts she undertook for various
causes, and for the spiritual consolation she offered others. For the last
eleven years of her life, she was blind, accepting the affliction "with joy,
as a God-sent means of detaching her from the visible world," Butler

writes. Christ instructed her to spend her last years praising God, praying for the conversion of sinners, and relying on God alone.

Lutegarde died on June 16, 1246, as she said that Christ had told her. Celebrated as "one of the great precursors of the devotion to the Sacred Heart of Jesus," she is remembered as a wonderfully quirky saint. "Amongst the notable women mystics of the twelfth and thirteenth centuries there is no more sympathetic or loveable figure than that of St. Lutegarde," writes Butler.

Dealing with Those Nonconformists

We'd call St. Lutegarde a *character* today if she showed up in one of our schools—to say the least! As with Catherine of Siena, whom she predated, Lutegarde was paradoxical, at once a mystic capable of tremendous austerities and a woman connected to practical earthly concerns. She once took pity on a deaf nun and healed her so that she could hear the convent singing, and she energetically prayed against the Mongol invasion and for the conversion of the apostate Emperor Frederick II. "Very matter-of-fact and very Flemish," Thomas Merton judges this woman who is said to have received otherworldly visions "almost daily."

Lutegarde was also eccentric because of her confidence in what one might term her "alternate reality." Though she was humble and at times insecure about her own worthiness, she was absolutely convinced of the truth of her mystical experiences. Her daily relationship with Christ was a fact to her, though no one else saw him. Her reported conversations are actually quite amusing, for, while revering Christ to the point of asking for wounds, she addressed him as one might an earthly husband, even chiding him.

Despite the time-and-place particulars of her eccentricity, however, Lutegarde will be a recognizable type for teachers. For, among the many hundreds or thousands of students we meet over the course of our careers, we're likely to encounter at least a few individuals who, like her, forge confidently on, unapologetic about their nonconformist convictions. Many of us, actually, might count ourselves among them, for we, too, believe in the truth of realities that could only be called "alternate" from the perspective of mainstream culture. The catechists among us consider matters of faith so important that they talk about them "as if they were true!" as a new catechumen once exclaimed to a friend of mine. Those of us who teach secular subjects are dedicated to transmitting knowledge that many consider hopelessly esoteric— foreign languages, music history, literature centuries old, philosophy, theoretical mathematics or economics, inorganic chemistry. There's no arguing with us that these things are interesting and that knowing them makes life richer.

It's easy to see why Thomas Merton was so drawn to Lutegarde that he wrote a book about her, for he also marched to the beat of a different drummer, to use a term coined by Henry David Thoreau. Merton was a Cistercian who embraced Buddhist mysticism, a monk who sought enclosure at his home monastery but became famous for his writing and public speaking. Lutegarde and Merton would have been very comfortable reading Thoreau, actually, and reading other American Romantic thinkers such as Ralph Waldo Emerson. "To believe your own thought, to believe that what is true for you in your private heart, is true for all men,—that is genius," wrote Emerson in "Self Reliance," an essay in praise of "original and not conventional" behavior that also includes the famous line, "a foolish consistency is the hobgoblin of little minds." Emerson waged a lifelong battle with lowest-common-denominator conformity, surrounding himself with inspired eccentrics, writing and giving speeches that urged his listeners to live according to their own visions of the truth.

Emerson, Thoreau, Merton, and Lutegarde, whatever their dif- ferences might have been—and they would have been explosive and entertaining in conversation, no doubt—would certainly sigh together in sorrow over the spectacle of teaching systems that assume that everyone should think and act alike. They'd be appalled by my home district, for example, where a conservative majority insists that it is near-heresy to question "the American way" or certain other party lines. Still, Lutegarde et al. would see cause for hope in the high-school career of the son of my closest friends, recently graduated. Independent-thinking Ted baffled his speech coach by presenting an impeccably researched talk arguing the perils of capitalism (he lost to a speech composed of platitudes); he shocked a gymnasium full of people by presenting a graduation speech that challenged his classmates to address America's social injustices (even emphasizing that there *were* any was shocking) and questioned the war in Iraq. At times, Ted's blunt honesty seemed almost suicidal, as when he confronted a policeman giving a DARE presentation and insisted that taking one drink did not automatically lead to a spiral of alcoholism. Many other students in the room undoubtedly had more firsthand ability to challenge this alarmist "fact" than the abstemious Ted, but they sat back and let him fight the hopeless battle. Long hair, seriousness, talent at soccer and skiing, National Merit Scholarship finalist status and all, Ted has gone on to one of the best liberal arts colleges in the country and is studying physics, though he's taking a semester in Japan as I write these words. The drummer that he's hearing is every bit as unconventional as Lutegarde's, but he marches confidently, and all of us who love him are intrigued to see where he'll end up.

Granted, students like Ted can be difficult, even infuriating. I can't imagine being Lutegarde's abbess, or Merton's abbot. Still, the world needs eccentrics precisely because they make us uncomfortable and force us to reexamine our own worldviews in light of theirs. Christ's presence in the convent at Aywieres must have seemed infinitely more real to the nuns because of Lutegarde; Ted's insistence on the world's complexity certainly modeled intellectual courage for other students at Century High School; Merton's influence reinvigorated the Christian contemplative prayer movement. Emerson's words still inspire young people, and teachers' brave insistence on their own versions of reality can do the same.

Independent idealism is leaven for the world, challenging all in its vicinity to take their own measures. As teachers, we attempt to suppress it—in ourselves or in our students—at our peril. Here, Lutegarde laughs her boisterous Flemish laugh and says, "As if we could—."

For Further Reading

Bert Ghezzi, "The 'Accidental' Mystic: St. Lutegarde of Awyieres (1182–1246)," in *Mystics & Miracles: True Stories of Lives Touched by God* (Chicago: Loyola Press, 2002), 39–43.

Thomas Merton, *What Are These Wounds? The Life of a Cistercian Mystic, Saint Lutegarde of Aywières* (Milwaukee: Bruce, 1950).

Butler's, 2:557–58.

Oxford, 330–31.

24

St. Thomas More

1478–1535 ~ England ~ Feast: June 22

Thomas More is a well-known saint in America, thanks to a 1966 Oscar-winning film about his life, based on a play by Robert Bolt. More is celebrated for having defied the English King Henry VIII, refusing to acknowledge the king's supremacy over the English church. A defender of papal authority, More debated the validity of the king's marriage to Anne Boleyn, arguing that Henry had been married to his first wife, Catherine of Aragon, by papal dispensation. More was martyred for his convictions in 1535.

More was born in 1478 and studied at Oxford and in London. After considering a clerical career, he became a lawyer, and he married. Throughout his life, however, he adopted clerical practices, wearing a hair shirt, saying the Little Office daily, and inflicting penance on himself. His intelligence and talent quickly became apparent, and he attracted a circle of learned men, including the scholar Erasmus (who called More "magnificent"); they avidly discussed classical texts, humanist subjects, and theology. More was a Renaissance man in the sense of having a varied personality, as well as in his learning. For all of his high seriousness, he loved the life of the street; he was gentle but could be intolerant, even cruel.

More's first wife, Jane, died six years after they were married, leaving him with four small children; he remarried a widow, Alice. Around 1524, the family moved to Chelsea, where they were painted by Hans

Holbein as a model of cultured, virtuous domesticity. More believed in the education of women, and he taught his daughters to read; his favorite, Margaret, became a scholar in her own right. Besides practicing law, More wrote extensively. His best-known book today is *Utopia*, a description of an ideal kingdom (which tacitly satirizes England by contrast) where there is no private property and education is free to men and women. More also produced books about law and about history, tracts against heresy, and theological texts.

More's ethical competence attracted the attention of Henry VIII, who promoted him quickly in public office and became his personal friend (though More understood that Henry was not to be trusted, once remarking, "If my head would win him a castle in France, it should not fail to go"). As a judge, More was known for his refusal to accept bribes and his energetic defense of Catholicism. He became Lord Chancellor in 1529. When Henry insisted on defying the pope's authority so that he could marry Anne Boleyn, however, More stood firm in his refusal to condone the action. He did not attend Anne's coronation. Sure in his own conscience, he resigned the chancellorship. With the loss of his salary, More's family was reduced to poverty. Henry continued to pressure More for support, but the latter stood firm, enraging the king. In 1534, Henry caused Parliament to issue an Act of Succession, which required subjects to recognize his and Anne's children as lawful successors to the throne and to acknowledge that Henry's marriage to Catherine had been "no true marriage." More agreed to the first but kept silence on the latter, for it entailed a repudiation of papal supremacy. He was committed to the Tower of London for treason. There, he wrote spiritual works, including *A Dialogue of Comfort Against Tribulation*. Though his family took the oath, he continued to refuse.

Weak and ill, More was finally brought to trial in Westminster Hall. He defended himself ably, but he was unjustly charged with having presented perjured testimony, and convicted. After More's sentencing, he finally made his position clear in bold, impassioned speeches, arguing that "no temporal prince can presume by any law to take upon himself a spiritual pre-eminence given by Christ to St. Peter and his successors in the See of Rome." After a last meeting with Margaret, More was beheaded on July 6, 1535, forgiving his executioner and proclaiming himself to be "the king's good servant, but God's first."

More's death shocked observers both in England and on the Continent. After his head was exhibited for a time on Tower Bridge, it was reclaimed by Margaret. Margaret's husband, William Roper, soon published a laudatory biography. Long considered a hero of conscience, More was canonized in 1935. He remains an object of fascination: a journal, *Moreana*, has been devoted to him; biographies have proliferated; *Utopia* remains in print and is widely anthologized; and Bolt's *A Man for All Seasons* has been performed both on stage and in several film versions.

MERGING YOUTHFUL IDEALISM WITH REALITY

Young people can be so idealistic! A twenty-year-old I know, the daughter of friends, has decided that she wants to work to help alleviate poverty after she graduates from college. Camille is so smart that she could do anything, yet her good heart (and her parents' example—this is a family that has served in soup kitchens every Thanksgiving for many years) has led her to altruism rather than to a career that would make her wealthy. Another young woman I know longs to visit India so that she can study comparative religion. A slightly older young person, our new parish priest, has claimed the Kyrie from us lectors; he's singing it himself with great solemnity. My purist heart has responded so warmly to this gesture that I'm almost able to forgive him for using the phrase "like totally" in a recent homily.

I remember vividly when, as a young idealist myself among many others in a high school honors English class, I first encountered Sir Thomas More. We were assigned Bolt's play, and we devoured it. "What heroism," we said. "Standing up to that pressure, when everyone around him was willing to compromise to save their own necks!" We all understood that the subtext on our teacher's mind—which accounted for the resurgence of interest in More in the 1960s—was the Vietnam War. Our teacher explicitly raised themes of civil disobedience, conscience, and obedience to authority in class discussion, and we avidly discussed the implication of More's actions for our own time. Those were among the most exciting high-school classes I ever experienced.

"Lives of great men all remind us / We can make our lives sublime, / And, departing, leave behind us / Footprints on the sands of time," reads an inspirational poem, "A Psalm of Life," by Henry Wadsworth Longfellow. Though I wince a little now at the determined rhymes, plodding meter, and clichéd didacticism of that verse, I loved that poem as a teenager, and I applied it to More. More was such a great man, I thought when I encountered him, and reading about his life made me dream of making my own life "sublime," somehow.

It turns out that More was more complicated than we believed during our discussions half a century ago. All recent biographers emphasize, for example, that More persecuted Protestants vigorously. More declared of one "inoffensive bookseller" whom he condemned to burn at the stake that "there never was a wretch, I wean, more worthy." He caused a friend's house to be searched for Protestant texts, and, finding them, threw him in jail, where the friend died. More was also a complicated man psychologically: energetic, melancholy, intellectual, precise, cynical, obstinate, devout. He wrote bawdy epigrams and made fun of his wife when she did not recognize the stones in a necklace he'd bought her as fake. "A cruelly divided man, torn between the necessity of making his way in the secular world and the devout longing to simplify life and to prepare his soul for the eternal world to come," one biographer calls him, arguing that More found peace only in prison, as he proved to himself that he had the courage of a martyr.

Though all of this information certainly tarnishes More's halo—at least the idea of him wearing one throughout his life—I like to think that my idealistic classmates and I would still have admired him, had we known such things. I'm almost certain, in fact, that we would have. Though we were idealistic, we knew that the world was morally complicated, and we liked fictive worlds that weren't bifurcated between absolute right and absolute wrong. We knew that Vietnam protesters and conscientious objectors were not complete angels. *We* weren't angels. And so we battened onto the unbending obstinacy that Bolt's play dramatizes in More—and avidly debated the intersection of conscience and what was then called "situation ethics." We recognized that, in his stubbornness, More was a person with whom we could identify, and yet he was so extreme! Like any classic tragic hero (oh, that Aristotelian pride!), he made us reflect on what it means to be human yet to live an extraordinary life.

Those of us who work with young people—or idealistic catechumens, no matter what their ages—should never underestimate the potential influence of historically-documentable saints like More. Our students long for inspiration, long to dream of doing great things, and some of them, at least, are likely to take those models to heart. I can't say that ardently looking up to More as a teenager has caused me to make my own life exactly sublime, but remembering him all these years *has* inspired me to take deep breaths and think twice at some key points. We might say that this is what saints are for—to inspire new generations to make difficult choices honorably. Yet we teachers also have a responsibility not to pretend that the models are somehow superhuman. Historical saints, saints whose lives can be researched and psychoanalyzed, provide us with a unique opportunity to inspire our students with human examples. A flawed person can make a tough, transcendent ethical choice. A flawed person can grow.

Thank heavens that the young are so idealistic, because the best of them, not yet bored and cynical about ethical choices, can be society's conscience. We, in turn, can feed their consciences by introducing them to people whose lives have the potential to spark the liveliest discussions about what it means to live honorably yet as fallible human beings. And few people embody the paradoxes of the human condition as well as More. The introduction to the standard edition of More's works terms him an "exasperating, annoying, boring, hateful, obtuse, brilliant, witty, demanding—and somehow very much an indispensable ideal we cherish for ourselves." Our students need such ideals, in all of their human—yet still, as Erasmus said, "magnificent"—complexity.

For Further Reading

Peter Ackroyd, *The Life of Thomas More* (New York: Nan A. Talese, 1998).

Alistair Fox, *Thomas More, History and Providence* (New Haven: Yale University Press, 1982).

Richard Marius, *Thomas More: A Biography* (New York: Knopf, 1984).

A. L. Rowse, ed., *A Man of Singular Virtue: Being a Life of Sir Thomas More by his Son-in-Law William Roper, and a Selection of More's Letters* (London: Folio Society, 1980).

Butler's, 3:49–55.

Oxford, 374–77.

25

St. Peter and St. Paul

First century ~ Rome, Middle East ~ Feast: June 29

The joint feast of Saints Peter and Paul has been celebrated since 258, and Christian tradition pairs them in many other ways, too: they are said to have both been martyred under Nero on the same day; they are invoked together in the Litany of the Saints; 283 English churches, according to the *Oxford Dictionary of Saints*, were dedicated to them jointly. Historically, though, Peter and Paul were very different men, separated, one writer has said, by "a deep and permanent gulf," men who engaged in direct confrontations with each other. What was at stake between them, they believed, was the very nature of the church itself.

Peter was the more conservative of the two, the one who sought to maintain continuity between Christianity and Jewish law—developing Christianity as a sort of reformed Judaism, one might say. Peter had been the most prominent of Jesus' disciples. He was the first chosen, the one in whose house Jesus stayed, the one who acclaimed Jesus. Jesus gave him central teachings and renamed him Cephas, and remarked "on this rock I will build my church" (Matthew 16:18, NRSV). Despite these honors, during Jesus' life, Peter revealed himself as a flawed man, sinking beneath the waves for lack of faith, betraying Christ in the garden. Such actions, as Alfred McBride has argued, make his "credibility as a leader . . . all the more appealing" because they provide "the backdrop of his noticeably human personality: impulsive, inadequate, faltering, yet able to respond." Peter, McBride writes, "was a real leader who might at once be brave and fearful, sometimes insightful and occasionally blind, capable of passionate loyalty and yet prone to slip, able to sin and yet willing to repent."

After the crucifixion, tradition suggests that Peter was the first apostle to see Christ; he became the Apostles' spokesman. He performed the first miracle in Christ's name. Tradition makes him the Bishop of Antioch. At first, Peter assumed that some Jewish customs— circumcision, particular food practices—would apply in the new religion, and only gradually did he see that the new religion must be inclusive toward gentiles. He presided at a council in Jerusalem that set rules for Christian customs which some felt were not distinctive enough. Despite Peter's prominence, he was severely rebuked by Paul at Antioch for compromising with Jews who disapproved of Christians' contact with gentiles:

> And when Kephas came to Antioch, I opposed him to his face because he clearly was wrong. For, until some people came from James, he used to eat with the Gentiles; but when they came, he began to draw back and separated himself, because he was afraid of the circumcised. And the rest of the Jews [also] acted hypocritically along with him. . . . But when I saw that they were not on the right road in line with the truth of the gospel, I said to Kephas in front of all, "If you, though a Jew, are living like a Gentile and not like a Jew, how can you compel the Gentiles to live like Jews? (Galatians 2:11–14)

Like most of the apostles, Peter was persecuted; one famous episode credits an angel with helping him escape from prison, though he was chained between two soldiers. He was crucified head-downward by his own request, church lore says, to deliberately intensify his suffering. Legend makes him the first bishop of Rome, and his relics are supposed (with much debate) to be beneath St. Peter's Basilica.

St. Paul was a striking contrast to St. Peter. He was born a Jew and became a Pharisee; he was an intellectual, while Peter was a man of the people. Paul had been Saul, an energetic persecutor of Christians; in one of the most famous episodes of early Christianity, recounted in the ninth chapter of the Acts of the Apostles, he was converted on the road to Damascus by a vision of Christ, who asked, "Saul, Saul, why are you persecuting me?" Literally blinded by the light that flashed around Christ, foregoing food and drink for three days, Saul sought baptism from the skeptical Ananias then, renamed Paul, retreated to Arabia for prayer and solitude. Three years later, Paul began preaching in Damascus, where Jewish opponents of Christianity were so hostile that he had to escape by being lowered from the city walls in a basket. When he arrived in Jerusalem, the apostles greeted him with understandable suspicion, but Paul earned their trust with his preaching. He went on three (possibly four) mission journeys to the gentiles in territories including Greece, Macedonia, Cyprus, and Asia Minor. His adventures during this work, along with those of his followers Timothy and Silas, are heroic: he was imprisoned and escaped; he healed the sick and cast out demons; he effected myriad conversions despite persecution. Even when he was imprisoned for two years, he continued to write to Christian colonies that looked to him for leadership, as the Acts of the Apostles and his New Testament letters demonstrate.

Paul was particularly concerned with converting gentiles to the new faith, and his insistence on a new covenant based on spirit rather than traditional law brought him into conflict not just with Jews but with more traditional apostles. One modern biographer has suggested that some of Paul's fervor for more definably new religious practice and theology may have been fueled by his sense of being an outsider among the apostles. His ideas, however, became central to Christian theology.

Like Peter, Paul was martyred in Nero's persecution around AD 65 (although as a Roman citizen he was beheaded rather than crucified).

His epistle to Timothy predicted his own death. Besides his canonical letters, apocryphal books including the *Acts of Paul* tell of his adventures. Along with Peter, he has been a favorite subject of Christian artists.

Understanding Deep Concern and Discord

"Wait a minute," said the friend to whom I was talking last summer about my research. "You're saying that Peter and Paul didn't get along? They're the two big guys; didn't they found the Catholic Church together? How could they manage that, if they were fighting?"

My friend isn't an especially devout or theologically informed man, but he does attend church and reads the Bible. Yet, learning of the feud between Peter and Paul, he was flabbergasted, as I suspect that the vast majority of practicing Christians would be. Peter and Paul, not get along? Peter and Paul, overtly mean to each other? Squabbling and one-upping the other to his face, behind his back? How can that have been?

Though the church doesn't often draw our attention to the fact of Peter and Paul's feud, it seems to have indisputably existed. The passage in Galatians is unambiguous, with its strutting, superior tone. Another document, the *Kerygmata Petrou* ("Preachings of Peter"), produced a century later, suggests that Peter did not take Paul's abuse lying down. In that account of the early days of Christianity, he calls Paul a false prophet. Both biblical and legendary evidence confirms that the two seem to have spent as little time as possible near each other, except for the convergence of their martyrdom.

No wonder they were arguing. What was at stake in their debates was the nature of the new religion—its fundamental systems of belief and practice. Both were championing positions to which they were deeply committed, positions that could not coexist. Even given that, however, the extent of their rancor might take us aback. "In front of all," Paul is careful to point out. This is not polite debate. This is intimidation.

Teachers might be especially disillusioned by the historical record of Peter and Paul, because their conflict may remind us of the debates over policy we frequently encounter in our own constantly evolving organizations. What should we teach, exactly? What requirements should we ask students to fulfill? Should colleague X, who some people think is doing a weak job, be given notice? Should we hire this candidate, or that one? We understand that the more fundamentally such questions touch on who we are as an organization, the more blood is going to be spilled. Such confrontations can end in real hurt: humiliation for those who lose, discomfort for others in the room. "I sure hope that King Kong and Godzilla will take it easy this afternoon," one of my colleagues muttered to me as we entered a department meeting several years ago.

When we are playing King Kong or Godzilla, however, the noise of our quarrels can seem like necessary damage, given the larger question at hand. Of course we care deeply, we say to ourselves; of course we must fight for what we believe.

I'm not sure whether thinking about the historical Peter and Paul should be encouraging or discouraging when we participate in or listen to such discussion. Their conflict gives us a precedent for vigor in argument, yes. It reassures us that even legendary figures of the faith thought themselves justified in taking off the gloves when fundamental issues were involved. But the rancor of Peter and Paul's feud can also discourage us about human nature. *Even the best of us have always been nasty to each other*, we might think. *Infighting will never end. I'll have to listen to this until I retire.* And yet their story suggests another message, one about institutional memory. Worthy institutions can absorb even the bitterest quarrels and still persevere. Peter and Paul, those archrivals, have become Peter-and-Paul, treated since the third century as Siamese-twin apostles. We celebrate their joint feast today. We see them side by side in religious art, not glaring at each other. We run their names together in the liturgy. Most of us remember them simply as great men who helped shape the church.

And so, when the Peters and Pauls among us rear up at each other, we can take some comfort, I think, in remembering their precursors. Uncomfortable as we may feel during debates, good may come of them, for we must examine alternatives in order to reach the strongest position. Even the heat of our debates may be considered encouraging, for never getting angry means that no one cares. If Peter and Paul had not argued, the church might have fractured into gentile and Jew, with no compromise ever reached.

Beyond such reassurances, though, the long-term fate of Peter and Paul can also help us gain some distance on ourselves when we engage in such quarrels, recognizing that it is the policy that our arguments effect, rather than the blow-by-blow circumstances of our arguments themselves, that people are likely remember. We might even smile when we remember these two old antagonists, going down the centuries hand in hand, imagining whose hand might be placed in ours, someday.

For Further Reading

Michael Grant, *Saint Paul* (New York: Scribner, 1976).

Alfred McBride, "Peter," in *Saints Are People: Church History Through the Saints* (Dubuque, IA: W. C. Brown Co., 1981), 3–8.

Richard P. McBrien, "Peter and Paul, Apostles," in *Lives of the Saints: from Mary and St. Francis of Assisi to John XXIII and Mother Teresa* (San Francisco: HarperSanFrancisco, 2001), 261–65.

Pheme Perkins, *Peter: Apostle for the Whole Church* (Columbia, SC: University of South Carolina Press, 1994).

Butler's, 2:664–72.

Oxford, 414–15; 422–24.

26

The Endless Task
of Making Peace

St. Elizabeth of Portugal

1271–1336 ~ Portugal ~ Feast: July 4

St. Elizabeth of Portugal ("Isabel" in her own country) is known as the "Patroness of Peace" for her efforts at averting war, largely among her own relatives. She was a princess of Aragon, born in 1271, named after her great-aunt St. Elizabeth of Hungary, and her very birth fostered peace, for it reconciled her capricious grandfather to her father. Elizabeth was married at twelve to the king of Portugal, Don Diniz (Denis). Diniz was a celebrated and beloved king, an agricultural reformer and promoter of economic progress, a poet and patron of the arts, and a builder of city walls that protected the country. He was also famous for engaging in extramarital affairs, which produced numerous illegitimate children. Elizabeth, though, so charitably insured that all of these children were well cared for that Diniz made her their guardian! A deeply religious woman, she founded a convent of Poor Clares and an institution in Coimbra that taught orphan girls the skills necessary to be farmers' wives. She then gave them farms as dowries.

Elizabeth's peacemaking efforts began early in her marriage, when she called a council of arbitration that averted civil war between Diniz and his brother. Her long-term work, though, was inspired by disagreements involving her children. Her daughter Constance married Ferdinand of Castile, who soon was at war with Elizabeth's own brother, Jayme II of Aragon. After she healed this quarrel, a short "golden time" ensued, but it was interrupted by rivalry between her son Affonso, and Diniz's illegitimate son Alfonso. Alfonso lived at the palace with his father while Elizabeth's son lived on his own estate, and Affonso became so jealous that he plotted to kill his half brother. When Diniz discovered the plot, he accused Elizabeth of collusion and banished her from Lisbon to Almequer, where she built a church and worked with lepers. During her exile, she also made peace between her brother Frederic and Robert of Sicily. She was so beloved that the common people and the courtiers offered to rise in her defense, but Elizabeth refused. "Let us commit our ways to Providence," she said, forbidding them to go to war. The rift between Elizabeth and her husband was finally healed when she convinced her son (who had been actively fighting in revolt against his father) to beg Diniz's pardon on the condition that all insurgents be spared.

The illegitimate son was still his father's favorite, though, and soon Elizabeth's son was again at war against Diniz. The former's army was notoriously undisciplined, sacking convents and royal tombs and killing a bishop. After "a bloody but undecided battle" at Elizabeth's beloved Coimbra, she again orchestrated peace, which lasted for a year and a half before fighting resumed. In the most famous scene of Elizabeth's career, she prevented parricide by riding between the armies of her husband and her son on a mule, "with no other weapon than her weakness, her hands joined in supplication." "The effect produced was irresistible," an historian says. "Everyone stood still and ceased to fight. Meanwhile the king and his son, touched to tears by such great heroism and love, made a reconciliation once more on the field of blood."

This peace lasted until Diniz's death from illness a year later, after he had repented of his sins and had been pardoned by the pope. Elizabeth took the habit of a Poor Clare for the last twelve years of her life, retiring as a Franciscan tertiary to a monastery she had founded at Coimbra. She still retained her property for charitable use, however. She was soon occupied making peace again between her son Affonso and his son-in-law, the king of Castile. Even as Elizabeth was dying, she met with the two to urge that war be averted, arguing that in war "no care is taken of the people; and this alone is your sovereign charge." Sadly, after her death in 1336 (during which she told her daughter-in-law to "bring a chair" for the Virgin Mary, whom she saw), the warfare that she had so hated continued for many years. One of the most serious disruptions involved Affonso's son Pedro ("The Cruel"), who fell in love with his wife's Castilian maid of honor, Inés de Castro. After Inés was murdered in a political coup, civil war broke out, and Pedro, whom historians judge had always been "half crazy and loose in morals," defied the pope, proclaiming that no papal letters be published without his approval. Portugal was disrupted well into the next century.

Still, Elizabeth's peacemaking efforts were so celebrated that she was hailed as a saint in her lifetime and after. She was formally canonized in 1625.

Working for Peace in the Classroom

It's easy to proclaim, "Blessed are the peacemakers." It's harder actually to make peace, and it's hardest of all to *persist* in attempting to make peace when the world seems bent on strife.

Reading Elizabeth's story, one wonders how she found the strength to persist in working for peace. Her extended family members brought repeated bloodshed to Portugal, Spain, even Sicily during her lifetime. Whenever she might have imagined that she had talked sense into them, they were off again at each others' throats, mowing down who knows how many innocent people as collateral damage of their quarrels. One imagines her sighing to learn that her husband and son were rampaging *again* across the area where she had established young farm women and their husbands, knowing that those to whom she had given such hope were likely to be dead, their crops and houses burned. Having recognized Diniz's nature early in their marriage, she must have been devastated to see her son, despite her love and example, turning out to be even more irresponsible and volatile than Diniz. How could Elizabeth not become disillusioned, terminally cynical about human nature?

Teachers have many temptations to such disillusionment. We work for peace daily in our own ways, and we can see how hopeless achieving peace often seems. Some of us must come between physical combatants, as Elizabeth did, for playgrounds in all neighborhoods see children squaring off, fists raised and battery threatened. In our post-Columbine times, we know that greater violence is also possible. All of us, too, no matter what kind of teaching we do and no matter what the age of our students, must keep more subtle peace in our classrooms. Someone is always feeling resentful of someone else, it seems—believing that the other student gets more attention, more respect, favoritism in grades, or more opportunities to hold the floor. Or students are playing power games among themselves, for it is a rare class that does not have cliques and outsiders. Personalities clash.

No matter how we try to smooth feathers, those resentments seem to return. "She put me in a group with *him*!" I overheard one of my adult students telling another in the hall, to my chagrin. I thought I'd been clever and that cooperation might lead to tolerance between antagonists. "Thank God, though, we've just about got our report done. Only one more week to work with that jerk; then I never have to speak to him again."

The efforts we make to interest our students in peace in a broader context can also seem hopeless. Some of us work overtly for social justice, arranging internships and spring-break trips for student volunteers, opening our students' eyes with statistics and anecdotes about injustice. We attempt to foster curiosity about other cultures and tolerance for differences. If we teach catechism or religious education, we inevitably talk about peace and forgiveness over and over again.

And yet the world seems bent on war. As I write this essay, I'm in the midst of planning for a new semester, and yesterday I was reviewing exercises that I've used in the past for freshman composition. One of them asks students to work with very general theses, revising them into workable claims with an outline of specific potential support. One of those generic sentences is "The United States should/should not have sent troops to _____ because _____." To my sadness, I see that in former versions of the exercise, many countries have filled in the first blank: Vietnam (from my teaching assistant days), Haiti, El Salvador, Nicaragua, Bosnia, Iraq, and so on. It's discouraging to look at that proliferation of examples.

How could Elizabeth keep herself from despair? Her deathbed message to combatants (that bellicose son, again!) includes a hint: she considered the cost of not intervening. When war comes, she wrote, chaos engulfs bystanders as well as combatants, for "justice will not be distributed," and good people will be "harrowed by fear and every sort of ill." Someone had to speak for peace; to be silent and give up would sanction human suffering. Even a short interval of peace helped people live out their dignity as God's creations. A person of good will had no choice but to work for peace.

I like to think, too, that Elizabeth's difficult family offered a lesson in reality, providing tough but helpful insights that enabled her to persevere. She learned early from her grandfather (who had not only gone to war but had torn out a bishop's tongue when he protested that grandfather's remarriage) that people were naturally violent, and she kept learning from her husband, her brother, her son, her son-in-law, her grandson . . . She might hate that violence and oppose it, but she could not make it go away. Thus, instead of worrying about the cause of the violence, Elizabeth matter-of-factly addressed the results.

That may well be the best course for us, too, as teachers. We cannot allow ourselves to despair when we consider prospects for peace in our own classrooms or in the world. We cannot take an all-or-nothing view; we cannot afford the disillusionment that leads to apathy. Given human nature, Elizabeth knew that one never *made* peace but was always *making* it. That the same is true in our time should not weaken our resolve.

For Further Reading

John Dos Passos, *The Portugal Story: Three Centuries of Exploration and Discovery* (Garden City, NY: Doubleday, 1969).

A. H. De Oliveira Marques, *History of Portugal* Vol. 1 (New York: Columbia University Press, 1972).

Fr. Vincent McNabb, O.P., *St. Elizabeth of Portugal* (New York: Sheed & Ward, 1937).

Oxford, 169–70.

27

The Importance
of Order

St. Benedict

c. 480–547 ~ Italy ~ Feast: July 11

S t. Benedict is considered the father of Western monasticism because of his Rule, a remarkably clear set of instructions for monastic life. While the Rule holds monastics to the highest standards of faith and behavior, it was revolutionary in its day for its flexibility and its assumption that practical, manual labor would be part of monastics' lives. That thousands of men and women, both monastics and oblates, still live the Rule 1,500 years later is a testament to St. Benedict's wisdom.

Benedict was born around 480 in Nursia, Italy, to a well-off family; the little that we know of his life comes from St. Gregory's *Dialogues*. He studied in Rome but found the disorderly atmosphere there oppressive. Rome had been sacked by barbarians who subscribed to Arianism; pillage and licentiousness were endemic. There was "almost no effective political order in Italy," one scholar reports; ecclesiastical order had also broken down. Benedict retreated to Subiaco, outside of Rome, where he encountered the monk Romanus and became a hermit, living alone in a cave for three years. After shepherds discovered Benedict, his fame spread, and a community of monks requested that he serve as their leader. "It soon became evident that his strict notions of monastic discipline did not suit them," Butler remarks dryly, for they tried to serve him poisoned wine. Benedict miraculously discovered the attempt in time and left without rancor.

Men of more congenial temperaments and many backgrounds, including noble Romans and Goths, began gathering around Benedict as his disciples, and he established them in twelve monasteries under his direction, each with its own prior. At this point he had written no Rule, but led by example. After a jealous priest attempted to slander him and to literally poison him again (this time with tainted bread), Benedict migrated to southern Italy. The people there had fallen into paganism and sacrificed to Apollo on the summit of Monte Cassino. Benedict fasted, prayed, and preached to them, and he converted them. The pagan temple was pulled down and a Christian chapel was erected; around 530 the foundations of what would be a great monastery were laid on the mountain.

Benedict composed his Rule at the monastery, drawing on both eastern and western monastic traditions, including the work of St. Basil the Great. Some evidence suggests that Pope St. Hormisdas commissioned the text in an attempt to standardize western monastic practice. During a period in which monks commonly practiced self-torture in the name of heroic self-discipline, the Rule was distinguished for its moderation; rather than counseling flagellation, it emphasizes orderly prayer and reading of the psalms, healthy physical labor, and quietly structured days. Full of common-sense understanding of human nature, the Rule warns leaders against vanity and favoritism, and it emphasizes the dignity of all members of the community, from the youngest to the oldest. It forbids private property and recommends humility. Among its most influential provisions is the instruction that visitors are to be "welcomed as Christ."

Benedict became a famous man, consulted by religious and secular leaders, including Totila the Goth, who is said to have reformed after their meeting. Benedict was also beloved for his stewardship of the people who lived around Monte Casino. Gregory gives Benedict a reputation for miracles, including the ability to raise the dead, to interpret men's thoughts, and to foretell the future, including his own death. Benedict died in 547 and was buried with his sister Scholastica, who had supervised a convent of nuns under his rule.

Paying Attention as a Daily Habit

As a provider of discipline and order, Benedict is among the most obviously relevant mentor saints for teachers. He inherited a world of monastic anarchy in which each monastery determined its own code of conduct. Individual monks wandered from foundation to foundation whenever they were bored or irritated or simply had wanderlust; devotion to God was sometimes subordinated to intrigue and the quest for personal status. Benedict understood that if religious life were to properly glorify God, such behavior had to stop. And so he wrote his "little rule for beginners," posed in simple, straightforward language, setting guidelines for everything: the order in which psalms would be sung; the hours that monks would sleep, pray, and work; the clothing they would wear at various times of year; the duties of the abbot and cellarer; the protocols for greeting visitors and treating monks who had misbehaved. As many commentators have remarked, Benedict's Rule is moderate and humane as well as practical, stipulating, for example, that monks be given ample food and drink (with special provisions for the sick), that schedules for sleep change with the length of days, that the order of the psalms might be changed "if people find this distribution . . . unsatisfactory," even that malefactors be given multiple chances to reform before they are dismissed.

Benedict's attention to detail stabilized monastery life. Suddenly, monastics knew what to expect from each other, what was normative. Equally important, they also knew what was a transgression and when they had a right to correct behavior that was damaging the community. Under the Rule's guidelines, people were free to pursue their work—rather than constantly having to react to others' whims—and they understood clearly what their work was. Everyone had responsibilities to the whole, especially the abbot or prioress, who was reminded that he or she would be called to God's judgment for the conduct of the community and was obligated to model "all that is good and holy."

All of this is obviously relevant to the work that we do as teachers, for one of our core roles is arguably "bringer of order" on many levels. We bring order whenever we construct and maintain disciplined classrooms. Our students can no more learn in chaos than Benedict's monks could pray in that condition. Like Benedict, however, we also work to establish internal discipline in our students, to train them in inherent responsibility to others and themselves. As we teach subject matter systematically, too, we give our students paradigms of inquiry and organization. People learn best when they are secure. People learn best when they are organized and disciplined and have committed to the task. And yet, like Benedict, we pride ourselves in building flexibility into the structure we enforce, understanding that we must allow humane exceptions to the rules sometimes, and that, since learning isn't easy, we must grant our students many chances to succeed.

Benedict's Rule also carries a lesson that is applicable to teachers' broader lives: its insistence that everything a monk does should reflect his disciplined service to God. Benedict did not just discuss prayer and penance; he also provided structure for eating, drinking, sleeping, and working. He suggested that these aspects of life were included in the core of monastic responsibility. Perhaps most revolutionary of all—given that the ascetic tradition in monasticism had actually honored dirt (that is, ascetics were known to refrain from bathing or cutting their hair)—he even noted that housework was important, for it reflected community members' respect for the property that God had given them. "Whoever fails to keep the things belonging to the monastery clean or treats them carelessly should be reproved," he insisted.

As many modern commentators on Benedictine life including Joan Chittister, Wil Derkse, and Kathleen Norris have suggested, such directives blur the line between the secular and the sacred. "Tasks and activities may indeed differ in weight," Derkse writes, "but the one is not worthy of more attention (is 'more sacred') than the other." "If indeed we walk in the womb of God," argues Chittister, herself a Benedictine, "then reflection on the meaning of every action and the end of every road is the constant to which we are called. There is no such thing as the idle decision, the thoughtless act." Benedictinism, these commentators note, shares Zen's insistence on the importance of every moment: in a Benedictine monastery, Derkse writes, applying a phrase by Iris Murdoch to this context, one can observe a constant attention "to attend and get things right."

While teachers don't live in monasteries (though our salaries may suggest that we do), the Rule's blurring of the secular and the sacred can encourage us, too, to live more consciously. Everything we do, Benedict suggests, even the most apparently mundane action, offers us an opportunity to glorify God. Everything reflects our attitude and has bearing on the community of which we are a part. Our lives are of a piece: "the integration of prayer and work, body and soul [are] essential parts of the journey to wholeness," Chittister writes.

So, if Benedict had written a Rule for teachers consistent with his Rule for monastics, it would probably have mentioned such things as planning class, answering the telephone, speaking to supervisors, straightening our desks, eating lunch, going out for drinks after school on Friday with colleagues . . . even what to wear to work. It would have insisted that such things are crucial, for they impact the teaching community and reflect the practitioner's commitment. That's a daunting thought, but it makes sense. If we preach order and discipline to our students in the classroom but lead chaotic, irresponsible lives outside, we're bound to betray ourselves sooner or later in class sessions without focus, careless commentary on student work, or some lapse of attention or too-hurried moment. If we get into the habit of performing slapdash work when we're dealing with things "that don't really matter," that habit is likely to infect our work on the bigger matters. If we let ourselves speak sharply to our colleagues, or ignore them, we'll carry that behavior into our interaction with students. If, on the other hand, we learn to act as if everything we do is "holy," as Derkse puts it—and to pay attention even when no one is watching us—we will find ourselves modeling discipline and care. The Zen emphasis on the importance of "practice" in shaping a fully lived life has relevance for us teachers, too.

Benedict's Rule ultimately reminds us that everything we do influences everything else. Every moment takes our measure. It is not just our students who need to learn to be responsible; we do, too.

For Further Reading

Joan D. Chittister, *The Rule of Benedict: Insights for the Ages* (New York: Crossroad, 1992).

Wil Derkse, *The Rule of Benedict for Beginners: Sprituality for Daily Life*, trans. Martin Kessler (Collegeville, MN: Liturgical Press, 2003).

Timothy Fry, "The Rule of Benedict," in *RB1980: The Rule of St. Benedict in Latin and English with Notes* (Collegeville, MN: Liturgical Press, 1981), 65–112.

Butler's, 1:650–55.

Oxford, 49–50.

28

TEACHERS AS

TALENT-SPOTTERS

The Magi

First century - Bethlehem - Feast: July 23

The Magi are such a familiar fixture of the Christmas story that it might come as a surprise to realize that they appear only once in the Bible, in Matthew's account of the Nativity. According to that story, they come from the east, telling Herod that they have seen the star of the newborn king of the Jews at its rising and have traveled to pay him homage. Herod is disturbed by this information; he asks his chief priests and scribes where that king is to be born. On learning that Bethlehem is the place, he sends the Magi there, requesting with hidden menace that they return after they have seen the child. When they tell him the king's exact location, Herod says, he will go and pay homage, too. The Magi follow the star until it stops over the Christ child's birthplace. "Overjoyed," they enter and find him with Mary, prostrate themselves, and offer gifts of gold, frankincense, and myrrh. "Warned in a dream not to return to Herod," they leave for their country "by another way."

That is all the detail that Matthew's account contains, and, thus, many of the images and attributes that we associate with the Magi are later additions. Matthew doesn't say there were three of them, just three gifts, and other traditions give other numbers. Early Christian art shows two, four, eight, or twelve magi as well as three. The names by which they are commonly called today—Gaspar, Melchior, Balthasar—are apparently the result of medieval lore, originating around the eighth century. In other traditions, they have other names. The Syrians call them Larvandad, Hormisdad, and Gushnasaph; the Armenians Kagba and Badadilma. Some writers make all three from the same country; others suggest that they formed an alliance representing the continents of Europe, Asia, and Africa, or the tribes of Shem, Ham, and Japheth.

They were also probably not kings, for the word *magi* suggests "magician" or "astrologer". The Greek historian Herodotus suggests that magi were a priestly caste in Persia, perhaps Zoroastrians specializing in the interpretation of dreams. Other texts, including the Bible, suggest that magi were present at Roman courts, and they were also associated with Arabia, Mesopotamia, and beyond. They were praised for their learning about the natural world, their knowledge of the stars, their embodiment of "the world's oldest learning."

Thus, "almost every detail of the Magi story and tradition is the object of doubt and uncertainty," as the *New Catholic Encyclopedia* notes. Still, the Magi have always been considered important saints. They were venerated by the early church, and the cathedral at Cologne claims to house their relics, brought from Milan in the twelfth century. Their story appears in the *Golden Legend*, in Butler, and in many other collections of saints' lives. They have been the subject of much commentary and interpretation. Most commonly, the Magi are said to represent Christ's call to, and eventual acknowledgment by, all peoples of the earth. The Magi are also held up as evidence of prophesy fulfilled, as commentators point to passages in the Old Testament that presage their coming (Isaiah 60:6; Psalms 72: 10–11). Their story, writers note, underlines that a new Israel is being born; it suggests that Jesus is a new Moses. Their homage symbolizes the acknowledgment of the true wisdom of Christ by older wisdom traditions.

GUIDING OTHERS INTO THEIR DESTINIES

"Whatever conclusion one might adopt in regard to the historicity of the Magi episode," the *New Catholic Encyclopedia* notes, "It is most important to recognize that the story has great theological value." The same might certainly be said of its value as a subject of meditation for teachers. For, though most of us would never claim to be magicians, soothsayers, or even people of great wisdom, we can see ourselves as having a great deal in common with these travelers, when we consider our interaction with our students.

They come out of nowhere, these Magi. No one is expecting them, and even the later scholars who try to account for them disagree about their origin. Persia? Arabia? A multicontinent alliance of like-minded seers? Who can tell? What observers *can* see is that they carry such confident insight that everyone must take notice. They bring knowledge unglimpsed by Herod's court; they help confirm the truth that Mary held in her heart. They shake things up.

We must seem like that to our students, like odd forces of nature suddenly blown into their previously predictable lives. "I've got Jones," you can hear them saying in the halls, as if, like the plague of frogs, we'd been visited on them by God. Sometimes, perhaps, we have.

Our experience is so different from theirs, and our knowledge so much broader. We attempt to bring them new information every day, helping them glimpse a world beyond theirs, as the Magi did. Beyond knowledge, though, we also show them what it can mean to use one's brain. We know how euphoric discovering something new can be. A Buddhist might say that we know how to be mindful at those times when time disappears and we are consumed by the task and the wonder of the work. Absentminded professor stereotypes come from such engagement, as do students' head shaking and comments: "She's

obsessed with Shakespeare/butterflies/the American Civil War/quarks/
three-dimensional geometry . . ."

Who cares if they think we're crazy? Through such engagement, we
can show our students what it means to be a student—a wise person.
So many of them have never seen such concentration, have never imagined that striving to explore something, to understand something,
could be so exciting. We're foreign in the best sense in those moments,
helping them imagine a richer world. We represent learning.

Beyond such modeling, we also have the potential to be witnesses
to our students' nascent possibilities, as the Magi were. "Scouts," my
baseball-loving late husband said once about working with student creative writers. "That's what we are. Talent spotters." So many of our students, whether six years old or forty, haven't any idea of their capacities.
Some truly believe that they are earthbound and ordinary, when they
have extraordinary potential. Others, though they feel sparks in themselves, have been told by their culture or their families that they ought to
disregard those inklings of power. They fear pursuing their talents, for
they believe that the pursuit would make them eccentric, abnormal, and
unhappy. So, when they come to us, they're in the process of settling for
safe careers, pedestrian lives, and work far below their capacities.

We've all seen students who have gifts that they do not yet imagine. Some of us have been those students. When I was a college freshman, in my first honors English literature survey, a professor legendary
in the department scouted me. She had been the first woman PhD
on that department's staff, and she was moving then, in 1969, toward
retirement. Still, she was tough and smart and intimidating, with her
neat, formal skirt suits, her tiny frame, and her decisiveness. The study
of literature was a discipline, she insisted, not a process of emoting
pretty little insights (as our high school training had largely suggested).
Midway through the semester, her comments on a paper changed
my life. "You're just the sort of student who should go on to graduate

school," she wrote. "But you *must* do something about your spelling." I'd never heard of graduate school, but I sensed that it was a big deal, and I was daunted and amazed, guessing that she didn't suggest it to everyone. Though I was embarrassed about the spelling comment, I followed her advice on both counts, and I found my calling.

Like such teachers, the Magi were confident that they knew talent when they saw it—or, in the case of that baby, transcendence so marvelous that they fell down and worshiped. They didn't hedge, fearing to shake up that family's life by acknowledging a wild, risky future. They didn't second-guess the truth that had drawn them, magnetically, to that cradle. They trusted their insight, even though that scene in the stable must have seemed less than promising.

We're not doing anybody any favors, of course, if we make our announcements about talent lightly. After a few years of experience, however, I think we can recognize real vocation in our students when we see it. It can be intimidating. Sometimes students can amaze us with their insight, their quickness, their ability to manipulate words or paint or fingers or intellect. *He's smarter than I am*, we think, with a flash of jealousy. *I could never have done that.* But, if we are to be good scouts, like the Magi, we must swallow those feelings. Then, we can begin—gently, firmly—to invite the inexperienced one to imagine the path for which he or she has been born.

We must also recognize in such moments, however, that the gifts we bring are likely not to be harbingers of unalloyed joy, any more than the Magi's were. "You're never going to be rich," I tell my undergraduates who turn from safe professional paths into the cave of graduate school in the liberal arts. Whatever those exceptional students' fields are—even the ones in which they will be rich, eventually—our talent-spotting will inevitably lead students to unbelievably hard work, and to risk. That's the myrrh. We know that life will never be the same again, if they accept the burden of their talent. They will be transformed.

Still, we have no choice, if we are really teachers. Like the Magi, we must be brave, for we've been born, ourselves, to bear witness at so many beginnings, at so many cradles.

For Further Reading

Matthew 2:1–12.

George Arthur Buttrick, ed., *The Interpreter's Dictionary of the Bible: An Illustrated Encyclopedia* (New York: Abingdon Press, 1962), K–Q:221–23

New Catholic Encyclopedia. Prepared by an Editorial Staff at the Catholic University of America (New York: McGraw-Hill, 1967) 9:61–65.

Jacobus de Voragine, *The Golden Legend: Readings on the Saints*, trans. William Granger Ryan (Princeton, NJ: Princeton University Press, 1993), 78–84.

Butler's, 3:168–69.

Oxford, 338–39.

29

THE NECESSITY
OF REFLECTION

St. Ignatius of Loyola

1491–1556 ~ Spain, Italy ~ Feast: July 31

Ignatius, founder of the Society of Jesus (the Jesuits), was a saint whose work changed the shape of the modern world. He was born in 1491 to an old and noble military Basque family not long before the Moors and the Jews were banished from Spain. Sent to court as a young man to serve as a page, Ignatius loved chivalric romances and lived a life that emphasized gallantry, romance, and proud personal honor. In 1517, he became a knight and distinguished himself. A few years later, though, he was badly wounded during the French siege of Pamplona. His broken leg was poorly set and had to be rebroken; when it healed, one leg was shorter than the other and disfigured by a protuberance, so the determined, vain Ignatius demanded another operation.

Unable to walk during the long convalescence from this second operation, he returned home, confined to bed. He asked for chivalric romances to pass the time, but none were available, so his sister-in-law gave him a four-volume life of Christ and *The Golden Legend*. Inspired by these books, Ignatius changed his allegiance and dreamed of being a knight of Christ, vowing to offer penance in Jerusalem when he recovered. He set out in 1523, first performing a vigil at Montserrat (where he surrendered his armor and sword), then purifying himself for nearly a year during a sojourn near the town of Manresa, where he was staying with Dominicans. During this period, Ignatius worked in a hospital, he begged, and he worshiped with the Dominicans. But, most crucially, he began to do penance and to pray in a cave. In his zeal, he imposed severe penance on himself, eating and sleeping very little and letting his hair and nails grow wild to mortify his pride in his appearance. This was a period of spiritual searching, when he alternately embraced his new vocation and doubted it, when he experienced altered states of consciousness and lived through nearly suicidal depression. Finally, he began to feel consolation and he moderated his penances. The journals he kept during this period would become the core of his *Spiritual Exercises*, a practical plan for the discernment of God's will in a person's life. "One of the most influential works in Western civilization," according to a biographer, the *Spiritual Exercises* use militaristic and chivalric metaphors to help participants become aware of their own sinfulness, commit to serving Christ, and understand both the costs (poverty, self-denial) and the rewards of salvation.

Ignatius then proceeded to Jerusalem but found his visit hampered by restrictions imposed by Turkish officials, who controlled the city, although he bribed guards to let him see the Mount of Olives. He soon returned to Spain and, at age thirty-three, began study that would allow him to help souls to salvation. After a course in Latin grammar, he attended the University of Alcalá, where his preaching and instruction in the Spiritual Exercises drew a group of enthusiastic followers. The Inquisition, however, looked suspiciously on his work, and Ignatius was jailed for a time in 1527 and ordered to stop instructing others until he progressed in his studies. Impatient at this hindrance, Ignatius traveled to the University of Salamanca but was forbidden to teach there without credentials and was again briefly imprisoned. He left Spain to study in Paris.

Ignatius found a more congenial intellectual and spiritual climate in France. He greatly admired the rational educational system he discovered there—one that featured small classes, a curriculum that built in incrementally difficult lessons, and recreation—and it would become the basis for later Jesuit schools. Once again, he drew followers, "friends in Christ," including Francis Xavier and Peter Favre. The young men formed an informal brotherhood, took vows of poverty and charity, and decided that helping souls to knowledge of God and to salvation would be their mission. The group vowed to walk to Jerusalem to assist the pope, currently troubled by the rise of Lutheranism and a corrupt church hierarchy.

They met in Venice to begin their journey, but, because of hostilities with the Turks, were unable to find a ship to the Holy Land. Instead, they traveled to Rome, where, recognizing their merit, Pope Paul III soon began employing them. Their assignments were scattered, however, and so, to prevent the dissolution of their company, they decided to establish a formal order, which was approved in 1540. Ignatius remained in Rome for the rest of his life, drawing up the Jesuit's rule of life and doing good works, which included establishing homes for converted Jews and for penitent fallen women. The order grew rapidly, from ten to a thousand before Ignatius died in 1556. The Jesuits focused on teaching, especially teaching of the catechism to young people and to those who had not heard of the church. To that end, they became missionaries to the far ends of the world, with Francis Xavier traveling to India and Japan. Wearing no distinctive dress, but simple priests' clothing, they established a reputation as learned and practical men who understood how to get business accomplished in the world. These traits inspired suspicion and paranoia, however, and even persecution from within the church, as the order was suppressed in the late eighteenth century.

By the nineteenth century, however, the Jesuits were reconstituted to lead more missions and found more schools. In the late twentieth century, they again inspired controversy as they took up the cause of social justice around the world. Today, Ignatius's legacy lives on in the incalculable number of Catholics whose ancestors were originally converted by Jesuits, in the hundreds of schools and colleges founded by the order, and in the *Spiritual Exercises*. Ignatius was canonized in 1622, and dozens of his fellow Jesuits have followed him in that path.

Taking Time Off, Taking Stock

Although Ignatius's work continues to be a major influence on Catholic education today, his way of thinking can seem very foreign in the early twenty-first century. Despite the Jesuits' respect for the foreign cultures in which they labored (Matteo Ricci, working in China, is particularly well-known in this regard), Ignatius's own attitude unabashedly lacked cultural relativism. Soon after leaving Montserrat, on the initial stage of his journey to Jerusalem, Ignatius seriously considered beheading a Moor whom he met on the road simply for making remarks about the Virgin Mary. Ignatius also suffered from scruples that can now seem extreme. Before embarking for Jerusalem, he had a crisis of conscience that made him sick, obsessing over whether he should take sea biscuit for his voyage. Would so providing for himself indicate a lack of faith in God? His militarism is also likely to make us uneasy, now that we pray in church regularly for peace, though he came by it naturally, having internalized the feudal model as a young aristocratic. His Christ is a valiant knight jousting with the devil. Though his Jesuits, like Peter Claver, attempted to mitigate suffering in the wake of the armies of imperialism, they arrived with those armies as self-defined soldiers of Christ. Though I admire Ignatius's intelligence, stubbornness, and dedication to teaching, I do sometimes catch myself thinking when I read about him, "Not my culture; not my church, anymore . . . thank heavens."

Virtually everyone will agree, though, that another aspect of Ignatius's thinking still glows with relevance: his insistence that a teacher's life must be both active and contemplative. Jesuits, Ignatius insisted, would not only instruct others and serve as missionaries and counselors; they would also regularly take time away from their work to foster their own discernment of God's direction in their lives. The Exercises were intended to provide a guide for those "sabbatical" sessions. In consultation with a spiritual director, the retreatant worked through a structured series of meditations on the knightly Christ, the suffering Christ, and the resurrected Christ, seeking guidance, consolation, and a renewed sense of vocation. Ignatius insisted that every Jesuit do this every year.

Ignatius's disciplined plan for reflection has come to form the spiritual core of the modern retreat movement. Working to discover their "own way of discipleship in a particular set of circumstances," as David Lonsdale has written, modern retreatants go to a place without distractions to pray and reflect, opening themselves to listen for God's voice. Through discernment, they take their spiritual pulses, looking back over the past and noting whether promptings from God or from their own consciences bring "desolation or consolation" in conjunction with each memory. By the retreat's end, participants should feel "more in tune with the presence and leading of God in all aspects of . . . daily life," aware of necessary changes or correct choices in decision making. Ideally, they will be renewed and recommitted, as Ignatius intended his sixteenth-century Jesuits to be, though the exact particulars of that commitment will vary from one individual to the next.

Whether for spiritual renewal or for practical refreshment, modern teachers need to take time for disciplined reflection, too. Caught up in the whirl of our daily responsibilities, it's so easy to let one thing lead to another, until we're acting, thinking, and believing in ways we hadn't planned, operating on autopilot. It's so easy to become disillusioned and sterile unless we take time to reflect on what we're doing. Some of us are lucky enough to have regular sabbaticals; most of us have summer breaks. Ignatius would say that we are losing a key opportunity if we spend those times only in play, or only in work. Anyone with a vocation, he'd tell us, should take time to focus inward, to reflect on his or her immediate past experiences, to spend focused time in discernment.

If we do decide to discern, most of us will not want to adopt Ignatius' exact plan or language, which even the most sympathetic modern commentators admit are hard going. Few of us will relish flag-ellating ourselves with our teaching sins, imagining as blows to Christ's body the times when we were impatient with students, underprepared, or unfair. It will do us good, though—whatever terms we use—to bring Ignatian honesty to our reflections, remembering without flinch-ing what we've done that gives us pain, as well as the moments of which we're proud. Self-reflection can help us make decisions about the direc-tion our careers or our next terms will take, can help us re-form our practice and rededicate ourselves. We can even undertake this reflec-tion whenever we're uncomfortable in our work, during a weekend. We can take ourselves off, alone, to a quiet place we love, to walk a beach, a mountain, or a woodland trail, to sit before a fire, perhaps with our journals beside us, opening ourselves to what God wants to tell us.

When I was a young teacher, one of my mentors, who was a bit of a Thomas Merton-Buddhist-Catholic, was awarded a sabbatical at the end of what had been a particularly difficult year for her. "I'll bet that you're glad to be getting this time away!" I said to her, in my blithe innocence.

"Oh, I'm not going away," she smiled quietly. "You see, I'm going *in*."

For Further Reading

Thomas Green, *A Vacation with the Lord: A Personal, Directed Retreat Based on the Spiritual Exercises of Saint Ignatius Loyola*, rev. ed. (San Francisco: Ignatius Press, 2000).

Douglas Letson and Michael Higgins. *The Jesuit Mystique* (Chicago: Jesuit Way, 1995).

David Lonsdale, *Eyes to See, Ears to Hear: An Introduction to Ignatian Spirituality* (Maryknoll, NY: Orbis Books, 2000).

W. W. Meissner, *Ignatius of Loyola: The Psychology of a Saint* (New Haven, CT: Yale University Press, 1992).

30

St. John Vianney

1786–1859 ~ France ~ Feast: August 4

John Vianney, the "Curé of Ars" and patron saint of parish priests, is one of the most widely beloved of Catholic saints—although, as Butler writes when comparing him to St. Thérèse of Lisieux, "the halo of sentimentality . . . is far less easily fitted to *his* head." Vianney was born in 1786 in the French village of Dardilly to a devout peasant family. When he was three years old, the French Revolution disrupted religious and secular life. Vianney passed his childhood working in the fields; he received no formal education and only occasionally heard Mass from fugitive priests sheltered by his family (at the time, the revolutionary government in France banned all religious observance). When worship was permitted again, he longed to go to seminary, but his father forbade it. Only when Vianney was twenty could he begin his education, entering a preparatory class taught by Abbe Balley in a nearby town. Vianney was "the oldest and most stupid boy in the class," John P. Kleinz writes. "He had a pathologically weak memory, little proficiency in French, to say nothing of Latin." He was a nervous young man who compulsively twisted his scarf when he was upset. He was unkempt, ill-favored, and given to rashes when he tried to control his temper, but Balley recognized his potential, for Vianney was hard-working and of high moral character.

Vianney became discouraged, particularly with Latin, which he could not master no matter how hard he tried. Asking God's help, he made a pilgrimage to the shrine at La Louvesc; when he returned, he took up his studies with new conviction, though he was not much better at them. Then his preparation for the priesthood was interrupted by conscription into Napoleon's army. Vianney never had to fight; he inadvertently deserted through a characteristically awkward comedy of errors (he was late and his company left without him; while trying to catch up, he became lost in the mountains and was sheltered by a family who counseled him to stay lost, since he was already technically a deserter). Still, he lost two years of study. Finally, after a pardon of all deserters in 1810, when Vianney was twenty-five, he was finally free to pursue his study for the priesthood.

Thanks to Abbe Balley, who continued to believe in him, Vianney was admitted to "a minor seminary, where he ranked last in a class of two hundred students." With Balley's intercession once again, he was subsequently allowed to study theology in Lyons. Vianney continued to struggle with Latin; he failed his first try at examinations because his nervousness prevented him from continuing. Balley argued for the goodness of this "most unlearned but most devout seminarian in Lyons," and through special dispensation of the archbishop, Vianney was ordained in 1815. He went to work as a curate to Balley, and the two ministered together until Balley died of a gangrenous ulcer in 1817.

That the diocese continued to distrust Vianney's powers is clear in the next assignment he was given: to the village of Ars, "a remote and neglected place of 230 souls." Ars had a reputation as a wild town where religious observances had not been properly restored after the Revolution; it was known for its taverns, dances, immorality, and the absence of Sabbath rest on Sunday. "Good heavens, how small it is!" Vianney said when he first saw the place in 1818. Setting out to restore Ars to Christian order, Vianney began with hellfire-and-damnation preaching and stern pastoral supervision (he refused confession to those who had been to a dance). His significant breakthrough came, though, in 1824, when he helped establish an orphanage for homeless and deserted children: La Providence. Two holy women supervised the work, but Vianney treated the group (which included up to sixty children) as his family. Miracles connected with his provision of food for the group spread his fame as a holy man. "Our curé is a saint, and we must obey him," people said. During this period, Vianney began to suffer what everyone considered persecution by the devil: loud noises, personal battering, on one occasion the burning of his bed. These manifestations continued for thirty years. Vianney was also subject to complaints from jealous neighboring priests, some of whom forbade their parishioners to see him for confession. He was mad, they said. To these accusations the bishop replied, "Gentleman, I wish that all my clergy had a small grain of the same madness."

Crowds began to flock to Ars as Vianney attained a reputation as a marvelous confessor and miraculous healer; between 1830 and 1845, he saw more than three hundred people a day, and a special booking office in Lyon was set up to handle railway reservations for those who wanted to travel to consult him. Vianney began hearing confessions at midnight to prepare penitents for 6:00 a.m. Mass; he ministered for up to sixteen hours a day. Not surprisingly, he became exhausted and attempted to run away and become a monk, but he was caught and brought back three times. He was also known for his ability to read souls; once, for instance, he refused to bless a medal a child brought to him because he intuited that it had been stolen, and he walked up to a girl in his church whom he had never seen before to tell her, accurately, that her application to a convent would be granted soon. In the confessional, he sometimes reminded penitents of particular sins they had "forgotten" to confess. He became widely beloved, for, as Butler says, "with advancing years came greater experience of the needs and capabilities of souls, and deeper insight into moral theology, and pity, kindness and tenderness modified his severity."

During the last year of his life, more than one hundred thousand pilgrims came to see Vianney. Exhausted, he died a peaceful death in August 1859. He was canonized in 1925 by Pope Pius XI.

KEEPING AN OPEN MIND, STAYING PATIENT

Though John Vianney already has an official assignment in hagiographic ranks as patron of parish priests, we teachers might also want to claim an unofficial share of his beneficence. For every time we meet a struggling adult learner, a nontraditional student who, though earnest and dedicated, appears nevertheless to be a square peg attempting to fit into a round hole, John Vianney can give us good counsel.

Like such students, Vianney was distinguished by his apparent lack of promise. This was clear even to Abbe Balley—who loved him and saw his goodness, "to whose clear-sightedness and perseverance is due . . . the fact that St. John Mary Vianney ever attained to the priesthood," as Butler writes. Vianney was totally unprepared and slow on the uptake; he had a terrible memory. He studied hard and yet made little progress. Teachers who work with adults will recognize this type instantly. These students struggle with the subject matter because they have either never learned foundational concepts or have forgotten them. They are always in our offices for extra help that appears to do little good. They panic and fail exams; they can't address the simplest test questions, though we know that they've prepared. During class discussions, they're painfully awkward, either attempting to answer every question from their seats in the front row or sitting dumb with terror in the back. Other students laugh at them behind their backs, as classmates reportedly laughed at Vianney. They appear hopeless.

In another sense, though, they are our best students: the most serious about the enterprise in which they are engaged, glowing with earnestness. They *work*. Unlike younger classmates who take education for granted, they know what a privilege it is to study. Unfortunately, this awareness can actually contribute to their misadventures, for they can become overwhelmed with a sense of their own unworthiness and prone to breaking down in a self-fulfilling prophesy.

Such students challenge us to patience. It's tempting to write them off, for they defy conventional expectations about the characteristics necessary for success in study. We must work with them harder than with anyone else, yet we are likely to see only glacial progress, as my late husband used to put it. Sometimes we might wonder if it would be a mercy to have a frank talk with them, a talk that respectfully encourages them to try another path in life. Even if our efforts succeed and these unconventional students begin to catch on and move to higher levels, they can be a trial. If they claim us as mentors (and they will, if we've been kind), their ineptitude can embarrass us when they perform badly for other teachers. We may find ourselves having to make extenuating arguments for them when they fail exit exams. Why should we pour our energy into hopeless cases, we might wonder every time we encounter a new student of this kind, when so many more promising students also need us?

Abbe Balley must also have asked himself such questions—he was human, after all—but he stood by Vianney because he sensed the potential in this awkward man. He accepted and retained Vianney as a student; he recommended him to the seminary at Lyon and advocated for a special dispensation to allow him to become a priest. He took Vianney under his wing as a curate. Somehow Balley was able to perceive that Vianney had gifts that promised an unconventional but transcendent career. The vicar-general of Lyon recognized the same: when he ordained Vianney, he commented, "The Church wants not only learned priests but even more, holy ones." Vianney turned out to be holy beyond anyone's dreams, agent of a one-man revival in his lifetime, and an inspiration still to millions. His life defied all the predictions that might have been made based on his schoolroom performance (imagine how Vianney would have scored if there had been such things as aptitude tests!). Asked about Vianney's miracles of healing, the schoolmaster at Ars is said to have replied, borrowing words said about St. Bernard, "The most difficult, extraordinary and amazing work that the Curé did was his own life." That work could not have taken place, though, without a teacher with foresight who was willing to persevere.

Vianney was one-of-a-kind, of course, and it would be foolish to assume that all of our underprepared yet driven nontraditional students will achieve miracles. Still, one never knows. We must remember, as Balley did, that it is not our job to predetermine our students' fates based on a one-size-fits-all model of success. Our job is to teach all comers, encouraging them and honoring their various gifts, unconventional as they may be. Our job is to be patient, and to be open . . . so that if a latter-day Vianney ever does chance to come into our care we will not turn him away.

For Further Reading

John P. Kleinz, *The Who's Who of Heaven: Saints for All Seasons* (Westminster, MD: Christian Classics, 1987).

Daniel Pezeril, *Blessed and Poor: The Spiritual Odessey of the Curé of Ars* trans. Pansy Pakenham (New York: Pantheon Books, 1961).

Francis Trochu, *The Insight of the Curé d'Ars: Selected Stories* (Westminster, MD: Newman Press, 1957).

Margaret Trouncer, *Saint Jean-Marie Vianney: Curé of Ars* (New York: Sheed and Ward, 1959).

Butler's, 3:280–86.

Oxford, 521–22.

31

St. Edith Stein

1891–1941 - Poland, Germany, The Netherlands - Feast: August 9

St. Edith Stein was born into a devout Jewish family in present-day Poland in 1891. She was the youngest of seven children, and her widowed mother ran a timber business. Stein was an intense, intelligent, quick child with tendencies toward hypersensitivity. When she was a teenager, she became an atheist. She began to study philosophy at the university in her hometown of Breslau, but transferred to the University of Göttingen to study with the philosopher Edmund Husserl, whom she greatly admired, pursuing her work with much ardor ("like a person in love," someone observed). She completed her dissertation on empathy in 1916 and was awarded highest honors.

Stein followed Husserl to the University of Freiburg. Despite her militant feminism, she served as his assistant rather than pursuing her own independent writing and research, organizing his papers and tutoring his students in what she called condescendingly "philosophical kindergarten." She longed to do her own work. During this time she became interested in Christianity after she visited the widow of one of Husserl's associates who was killed in World War I; Stein was impressed by the woman's peaceful acceptance of death—the "divine strength of the cross," as she later called it. In 1921, Stein accompanied new Christian friends to their country house for a vacation. When they temporarily left her to her own devices, she found Teresa of Ávila's autobiography in a bookcase. She read all night and recognized a kindred spirit. Buying herself a missal and catechism, she studied Christianity and was baptized on New Year's Day, 1922, making her profession of faith in Latin. When Stein returned to Breslau and informed her mother of her conversion, Mrs. Stein wept. To comfort her, Edith accompanied her to the synagogue and said prayers.

Stein determined to take up a contemplative life, like Teresa, but her priest counseled her to teach and continue writing instead. She became a teacher in a girls' school at Speyer. Though one commentator has claimed that her pupils loved her, most biographers suggest that Stein was not a particularly effective teacher. "She knows much, but she cannot teach," her supervisor is on record as saying. Stein's teaching was characterized by "a Prussian exactitude," one biographer writes. "She taught standing motionless, without gestures, speaking in a low monotone, and she made scathing remarks about their work." Brilliant herself, Stein could not understand why others could not quickly grasp concepts that seemed easy to her, and she came across as intolerant, "a narrow and rigid personality." In 1931, she left her position and worked on translating the works of Cardinal Newman and Thomas Aquinas. She also produced original treatises on the role of women in contemporary life and on philosophical subjects.

Though Stein repeatedly sought a lectureship at a major university, she was not hired (biographers suggest because of her gender and her religion), although she worked for one year at the Institute for Pedagogy at Munster. When Hitler came to power, all university teaching was legally closed to her. Appalled by Hitler's persecution of the Jews, she attempted to gain a papal audience to urge for an encyclical protesting the Holocaust, but her request was refused. After praying for guidance, Stein determined that she could best serve God as a nun in Teresa's order, the Carmelites, and she entered as a postulate at the age of forty-two, bringing only her books as a dowry and taking the name of Teresa Benedicta of the Cross. There she found a new world of expectations. "I hope that she can sew," an elderly nun remarked when she heard of this new postulate. As someone who had always worked with her mind, Stein had never performed domestic labor, but now it was expected of her. She found herself inept at housework and dish washing, constantly subject to correction—a potentially humiliating situation for someone who had always excelled at everything she valued doing. Through this trial, Stein remained cheerful, enthusiastic, and dedicated, determined to devote herself to contemplation and humble work, cultivating obedience, and learning to laugh. Her superior wisely insisted that she supplement her domestic labors and prayer with writing, and while she was a Carmelite, Stein produced work on church prayer, on Christmas, on finite and eternal being, and on knowledge of the cross.

After Stein made her final vows in 1937, she was sent to a Carmelite convent in the Netherlands for her own protection. Hitler invaded the Netherlands in 1941, however. Though Jews baptized as Christians were initially exempt from persecution, after Dutch bishops protested Hitler's anti-Semitism all non-Aryan Christians were arrested. Stein could have escaped, but she submitted to save her convent from reprisals. She was deported, and witnesses reported that she was seen in a holding camp "walking among the women comforting, helping, soothing like an angel," rocking children in her arms, sad but calm. She died in the gas chamber at Auschwitz in August, 1942.

Edith Stein was beatified in 1987 and canonized in 1998.

Discovering Unsuspected Talents

No one who knew Edith Stein as an intense young scholar or girls' school teacher would have imagined that the last human glimpse of her would have shown her calmly comforting women and children. Edith

Stein comforting ordinary women, whom she'd scorned in her youth as given to "vanity, curiosity, gossip, indiscretion, and frittering away energy"? Edith Stein cradling babies? Edith Stein, once an atheist, in a nun's habit? Edith Stein, she of the volatile temperament, always ready to dispute a philosophical point, "calm," even?

Vocation can bring out curious, unexpected things in people. It taught Edith Stein compassion, for instance, and it demonstrated that she had a talent for obedience and patience. As a young scholar, she had written abstractly about empathy. Now she recognized that empathy was one of her gifts—and it might be fair to guess that no one was more surprised by this than she was. Like her mentor saint, Teresa of Ávila, Stein had been self-willed and high-strung, used to getting her own way. But once she decided to follow Christ as a Carmelite, she focused her considerable energies on obedience and love—and, like the first Teresa, she experienced conversion and transformation.

Similar transformations can happen in other vocations, too, for when people commit themselves to callings they cannot resist, they may need to tap previously undeveloped parts of their personalities in order to succeed. That's certainly true for teachers, as I can testify from my own experience. Anyone who knew me as a teenager or young adult would be shocked, I'm sure, to see me in a classroom now, hamming it up if the students need to be encouraged, energetic and outgoing, apparently the ultimate extrovert. I used to be very shy. Though I possessed a good singing voice and my choir directors encouraged me to try out for solos, I could not make a sound when my turn came to audition. In my undergraduate oral interpretation of literature class, I used to get dizzy and nauseated before I was due to present. When I began student teaching, I prepared my lessons with obsessive thoroughness to counteract my fear that I would find myself speechless before my students, writing out an exact sequence of questions (including follow-up questions for all possible answers that I could imagine), phrasing the answers in the margins so that I would not forget them. Even so, I was nervous enough in those first few years that I sometimes forgot which question I had asked before the students answered it.

If one is going to teach, though, such fear obviously can't continue, and, over time I've literally found my voice ("I'll say," I imagine my current students remarking). A talent for extroversion? Me? Apparently so. Over the years, too, I've seen others, my colleagues and my students, discover their own unexpected talents when their commitment to teaching demanded it. One of my friends has learned to be organized; another has learned, like Stein, to be compassionate toward those not as mentally quick as she is. An undergraduate who appeared to be somewhat ditzy has turned out to be mentally disciplined as an instructor. Another has learned to laugh at himself.

One of the finest things about vocation, indeed, is how it can round us out as human beings. If we really want to do whatever it is we believe we're called to do, and we lack attributes or skills that are essential, we will find them. Edith Stein is one of the best illustrations imaginable of that principle. Cutting, intolerant, and impatient, she became a gentle, obedient woman. She was still herself in good ways— the incisive abstract thinker, the brilliant writer—but that self could be kinder and more at peace than she'd imagined. Her transformation was clearly a delight to her, for all accounts paint her happier in the convent than she had ever been, radiant among her household trials. It was also a gift to others, leading her to the apotheosis of vocation as she forgot herself in ministering to those who were suffering.

We, too, have the chance to grow into new versions of ourselves in our vocation as teachers, and we must be open to such growth, letting God work. For, as Edith Stein's experience—and mine—suggest, we will be given what we need, almost in spite of ourselves. "I really admire the way that you're so relaxed in front of the classroom," one of my teaching assistants said to me earlier this year. "I wish I could be like that, but I know I'll never be."

"Oh, I don't know," I said, grinning. "I'd wait and see."

For Further Reading

Waltraud Herbstrith, *Edith Stein, A Biography*, trans. Bernard Bonowitz (San Francisco: Harper & Row, 1985).

Kathleen Jones, "Edith Stein (Theresa Benedicta of the Cross 1891–1942)," in *Women Saints: Lives of Faith and Courage* (Maryknoll, NY: Orbis Books, 1999), 31–37.

Edith Stein, *Knowledge and Faith*, trans. Walter Redmond (Washington, DC: ICS Publications, 2000).

Joyce Sugg, "Edith Stein 1891–1942," in *The Journeying Ladies: Agnes McLaren, Elisabeth Leseur, Margaret Laurentia McLachlen, Edith Stein* (London: Burns & Oates, 1967), 173–223.

Oxford, 484–85.

32

A HOLY INSISTENCE
ON HIGH QUALITY

St. Pius X

1835–1914 ~ Italy ~ Feast: August 21

Pope Pius X, a vigorous reformer and man of the people, was born Giuseppe Melchiorre Sarto in 1835 in the Veneto region of what is now northern Italy. He was one of eight children of a seamstress and a janitor for the local government offices. Dedicated to the priesthood as a boy, he walked fourteen kilometers round-trip to junior seminary with his shoes over his shoulders to save leather. He studied for the priesthood at Padua, beginning a lifelong admiration for Gregorian chant and the writings of Thomas Aquinas. The future saint was ordained in 1858, and feeling "a special calling to help the poor," according to one biographer, worked as a priest in farming villages. He was known for his "open-hearted" and down-to-earth nature; he ate only what the poor ate, even giving up his food and pawning his clothing for the hungry. He became the chancellor of his diocese, then the bishop of Mantua ("the most lovable of all bishops"), then cardinal and patriarch of Venice in 1893.

In Mantua, Pius began to speak of modernism as an enemy of the church—a position inspired by leftist, anticlerical control of Italian government at the time. "The capital crime of our day," he pronounced, "is the substitution of man for God." He forbade the faithful to see a controversial painting, and he harshly criticized the separation of church and state, the ascendance of science, and "exaggerated realism" in the arts.

In 1903 Pope Leo XIII died, and Pius gathered with the other cardinals in the Vatican. He was so sure that he would not be called to succeed Leo that he bought a return ticket to Venice, but he was elected pope. Pius retained his common touch in office, for he disliked pomp and he identified with ordinary working-class people. He also used his position to advance his convictions. His first encyclical decried the "illness" of modernism, and he ordered priests to combat rationalism, ignorance, and socialism. Later encyclicals decried French and Italian anticlericalism and communism and termed modernism "poison in the bowels of modern society." Religion was not adaptable and individualistic, he argued; values were not relative. Pius was also known for his advocacy for social justice; he spoke against slavery and for workers' dignity. He opposed the formation of a nondenominational political party in Italy.

Pius also actively labored to reform practices within the church. During the period immediately proceeding his papacy, Jansenists had popularized the idea that communion should not be taken frequently. Promoting the Eucharist as central to the Church's beliefs and practice, in 1905 Pius urged daily communion, and he decreed that the age of first communion be lowered to seven. He reformed seminaries, decreeing that priests should serve the poor as poor men themselves. One cause particularly close to his heart was the reform of church music. At this time, "tawdry operatic" and popular dance music had crept into use in the Mass; Gregorian chant had been debased into rote syllable-based droning that obscured the sense of the chant's words and blunted its emotional force. Drawing on the nineteenth-century research done by the Benedictines of Solesmes using ancient manuscripts, Pius supervised publication of an edition of chants restored to their original beauty. "His love of music became inseparably linked to his love of God," a biographer wrote, and one of Pius's greatest legacies is the re-adaptation of the "primitive purity" of liturgical chant.

Late in his life Pius attempted to prevent World War I, but his efforts failed. He died in 1914 "with a reputation for miracles, simplicity, and poverty, having written in his will 'I was born poor, I have lived poor, and I wish to die poor.'" A popular demand for his canonization began immediately, and he was made a saint in 1954.

TREATING PEOPLE AS CAPABLE

On the surface, Pius X is an unlikely saint for me to have chosen for this book. Ever since I was an undergraduate, I've enjoyed modernist literature, music, and painting, and I wrote my dissertation on a postmodern novel—Thomas Pynchon's *Gravity's Rainbow*—of which Pius would certainly have disapproved. My tastes in theology lean toward the liberal, whereas Pius's were extremely conservative. Even the *Oxford Dictionary of the Saints* admits that his encyclicals provided "the occasion for reactionary zealots to impugn the orthodoxy of a number of eminent Catholic scholars," setting off a "crisis" from which "it took years to recover." I'm generally on the left in my politics, and I'm happy that church and state are separated in America.

When one considers Pius in the context of his era, however, his attitudes become more understandable. Pius's church was beleaguered: persecuted by the civil government in France, and a subject of disdain in Italy (a "spent sun," according to one contemporary writer). Pius feared the human costs of modern anarchy. His age was marked by the rise of totalitarianism, massacre of the Jews in Poland, a general strike and economic disarray in Italy, and the aggressive militarism that would lead to World War I. He had witnessed hunger and poverty, and he spoke for the rights of immigrants and slaves. One must admire him for swimming against the intellectual tide in the service of human rights, even if some of his positions can seem reactionary today.

Whatever a person concludes about Pius's taste in art or theological positions, one can still admire his insistence on quality. This insistence issued from a democratic viewpoint: ordinary human beings, he maintained, should not be treated as if they were incapable of appreciating the best of human culture and the full practice of faith. When he was a new priest, shoddy music dominated church liturgy, and even monastic chant was corrupted by such features as ploddingly slow time in the supposed service of seriousness. Churches were often gaudily decorated (with "red rags," he once lamented). Priests were often poorly prepared and Mass ill-attended. One could say that the church's critics had some basis for their assertion that Catholicism seemed to be a corrupted, fading tradition.

As a man of the people Pius combated this tendency, arguing that "good enough" was *not* good enough. He implied that a great deal should be expected of ordinary Catholics; they should be full participants in a liturgy that reflected the highest standards. "I want my people to pray in beauty," he insisted, and so he helped remake churches into physically inspirational places (not "an annex to the theater," as he put it), and to develop music into an experience that challenged listeners to rise to the height of devotion. He urged Catholics to make themselves worthy of the Eucharist, and he insisted that priests be trained to help them. To do less was to patronize, to dehumanize.

As teachers, we too have a responsibility to bring high-quality experiences to those in our care. One good way to do that—a way that Pius favored—is to refuse to settle for content that has become diluted, instead insisting that our students encounter the best of what people before them have done and thought. In the early twenty-first century, *culture* will mean "popular culture" to most of our students, no matter what their ages. I've met college students who have never heard of Beethoven or Botticelli, and cradle Catholics who have no idea who Aquinas or Augustine were, much less what they said. I know avid readers, people in book clubs, who would never have encountered fine contemporary writers if Oprah hadn't introduced them. Please understand that I'm not arguing that movies and videos, popular music and books and pop theology are worthless in the classroom. Of course we can teach effectively using them. But, if that's all we employ, I'd argue that we're letting our students down.

It can be difficult to ask students to deal with the highest-quality materials, particularly from periods that will be unfamiliar to them. Such experiences require the hard work of understanding new aesthetics, conventions, concepts—just as Pius's reforms challenged Catholics of his day to readjust their sights. Whether we are presenting meditative prayer, medieval poetry, actual texts by Kant or Einstein, Byzantine art to adults or age-appropriate classical music, like Saint-Saëns *The Carnival of Animals* to children, our students are likely to resist. "This is hard," they'll say. And it surely is. No wonder they long for comfortable "red rags" and "tawdry music."

I certainly understand such longing from a student's perspective, as well as a teacher's. When I was an undergraduate, my choral director conducted the university concert choir along lines that could not have been further from my high school experience as a singer. In the latter context, we had sung engaging melodies—show tunes, popular songs—in dramatically emotional ways, impressing the dickens out of our parents and ourselves. In college, though, we faced complicated compositions, the best of many centuries of music. Our college choir director emphasized technical precision and faithfulness to what the composers had written. Confronted with very unfamiliar musical conventions, we sometimes had to work for fifteen minutes on a short phrase, going over it again and again, when we yearned just to sing a pretty melody. Ironically, given that I'm remembering this experience in an essay about Pius, some of that college music was distinctly modernist. If Pius could have allowed that such compositions had merit, though, he would have loved my voice teacher, for both of them refused to allow their charges to simply make do. They would have agreed that learning, like practicing faith, should take us out of our comfort zone.

And so we wrestled with those difficult pieces, and we learned, to our surprise, that we were capable of singing them, and well. Moreover, we were given other things incomparable in those hours: awareness of and a vocabulary for understanding past human achievements. When I entered college choir, I knew music through the AM radio. When I left, I took with me a much wider world.

It's funny to think of elitism and populism together, but Pius melded them seamlessly, as did my voice teacher. Both knew that true respect for the people in one's care demands that they be treated as capable, and that means not watering down the world (or the faith) for them. Though the people might sometimes protest that "good enough" is good enough, comfortable and easy, real leaders know that it's not.

For Further Reading

René Aigrain, *Religious Music* (London: Sands & Co., 1931).

Pierre Combe, *The Restoration of Gregorian Chant: Solesmes and the Vatican Edition*, trans. Theodore N. Marier and William Skinner (Washington, DC: Catholic University of American Press, 2003).

Benedict A. G. Ehmann, "Church Music," in *A Symposium on the Life and Work of Pope Pius X,* Episcopal Committee of the Confraternity of Christian Doctrine, eds. (Washington, DC: Confraternity of Christian Doctrine, 1946), 196–215.

Igino Giordani, *Pius X: A Country Priest,* trans. Thomas J. Tobin (Milwaukee: Bruce Publishing Co., 1954).

Raphael M. Huber. "Biographical Sketch of Pope Pius X," in *A Symposium on the Life and Work of Pope Pius X* (Washington, DC: Confraternity of Christian Doctrine, 1946), 1–49.

Butler's, 3:474.

Oxford, 436–37.

33

CONVERSION AS
JUST THE BEGINNING

St. Augustine of Hippo

354–430 ~ North Africa, Italy ~ Feast: August 28

St. Augustine was a native of Tagaste, in North Africa. Born in 354 to a Christian mother, St. Monica, and her violent idolater husband, Patricius, Augustine was instructed in the Christian religion but not baptized. At seventeen, he began studying rhetoric in Carthage. He was a talented, exemplary student, but he was driven by ambition and pride and lived a profligate life. During this period he took a mistress who remained loyal to him; they had a son together in 372.

Besides classical authors, Augustine also read Christian writing. He embraced Manicheanism, with its dualistic teaching about good and evil. The saint ran his own school of grammar and rhetoric, chafing at the boys' lack of discipline ("they break in improvidently and like a pack of madmen play havoc with the order which the master has established," he noted, in words with which any teacher whose lesson plan has been exploded by student disruption must empathize). In frustration, he went to Rome to teach but was also dissatisfied with those students and continued to Milan. There, Augustine met St. Ambrose, and he admired the latter's combination of eloquence and learning. St. Monica had followed Augustine, and she continued to pray for his conversion. Augustine struggled with doubt for some time. Finally, with the help of St. Paul's epistles and an African teacher named Pontitian, Augustine underwent a sudden, violent conversion. Monica was delighted, and Ambrose baptized him. Augustine's mistress was dismissed, though the son stayed with his father.

After attending a short retreat with friends for study and penance, during which time Monica died, Augustine returned to Africa, eager to live a monastic life in Tagaste. One day in 391, however, he went to church in Hippo, and the bishop, against Augustine's will, called him to be an assistant. Though Augustine distrusted pastoral life (he feared temptation to pride, flattery, and dissipation from prayer and study), he acceded and became celebrated as a preacher. Working from emotion and example rather than logic, he used biblical quotes to instruct listeners who could not read; he also incorporated many powerful statements and anecdotes taken from ordinary life. The people's response was "electric," according to one biographer, and hundreds came to hear him whenever he preached.

In 395, Augustine became Bishop of Hippo. He regulated clerical and monastic life and emphasized learning and discipline. He was also known for caring for the poor. Despite the fact that he was widely beloved, he sometimes expressed frustration with his "intractable people . . . on whom all my zeal and insistence is spent in vain" when they seemed not to have heard his words. To counter his own tendency to impatience and arrogance, he continued to evoke "the bonds of human feeling" in his sermons, identifying with his congregation and inviting them to identify with him.

Besides his public work, Augustine was also a prolific writer. His most famous work is his *Confessions*, a narrative of his own life that details his early sin and conversion. He also wrote many instructive letters to laypeople and to clergy, including letters sent to address and heal quarrels, including one over points of doctrine between St. Jerome and Rufinus. In his writing, Augustine was untiring in his attempts to defend the church from heresy, especially the Manicheanism he had once embraced, and Donatism, a heresy which held that the effectiveness of a sacrament depended on the moral character of its administrator. He continued to be an active scholar throughout his career as bishop, publishing many books, including his great *City of God.*

Augustine's last years were marked by destructive Vandal invasions of North Africa. He died of fever in 430, asking for penitential psalms to be displayed near his bed where he could read them and weep for his own sins, and speaking of the love of Christ.

PERSEVERING IN LONG-TERM VOCATION

So much of the commentary on Augustine emphasizes his conversion, and for understandable reasons. It was a remarkable story indeed, chronicling a wild young man who suddenly turned from prodigality to faith, a Manichean who had exploited his great intellect to lead others astray who turned his gifts to good purpose, becoming one of the great doctors of the church. We have so much evocative information about that conversion in *Confessions:* so many titillating details of the wild time; so much soul-searching and regret; such a brave vision of starting over.

For teachers, though, I think that the rest of Augustine's long life, postconversion, constitutes perhaps the more important story. Though most of us probably haven't led such wild lives or been heretics, we can probably cite "conversions," or at least epiphanies, in our pasts. A catechist might remember a moment of insight when he or she was a catechumen and vowed to help others to such moments. A person who spent an early career practicing a remunerative, practical profession and then turned to teaching might often recall the day that he or she finally recognized his or her true vocation, took a deep breath, and rethought life. Even those of us who were always relatively sure that we knew what we wanted to do can remember moments in our early careers when a class session or a conference was pure joy, and we knew that we would be happy doing nothing else.

Those are the moments we dramatize when we tell our stories. The trouble is that those are only *beginnings*. Like Augustine, after those exhilarating conversions we must face the challenge of deciding how we will put our new resolutions into practice. The stronger the call, the more intimidating this can be. My late husband used to talk about "now-what moments," times when we have peak experiences, but after the momentary exhilaration passes, we wake to find ourselves washed back onto the shores of ordinary time, wondering how we will live out our commitments and afraid that our efforts are doomed.

Augustine can be a wonderful mentor at such moments, because his long life gives us a model of how to live postconversion. One of the most comforting things about him, to me, is his awareness that a person will never have all of the answers in hand as a perfect practitioner. A few years before he died, Augustine wrote a book that reexamined his earlier writings, and he called it *Reconsiderations*, a title that says everything about the need to rethink one's positions. Even on his deathbed, he recognized the need for penance. Augustine's life affirms that vocation is an ongoing process. We don't automatically choose the best course, even after we have made our commitments. A misstep isn't cause for despair or for doubting our calling. It's human nature to make mistakes. What matters is that we recommit to our vocation each day, growing as we do. Augustine recognized that faith is a process; we ought to recognize, similarly, that learning to teach is a process.

Augustine also reminds us that our nature does not necessarily change completely after a conversion experience. Rather than deliberately discarding everything we've been, we should focus on turning our extant talents to new purpose. He turned his eloquence, his ability to command a room into effective preaching. He also accepted that ingrained faults as well as strengths were likely to persist. In Augustine's case, that meant that his old enemy vanity would always be something against which he had to guard. Even as he railed against his "warped, misshapen" people, he recognized vanity, entwined in a complicated way with righteous, justified anger inside him. And so he confessed, and this humility about his own sins helped make him an effective pastor, and a saint.

"Show yourself an example for the believers," Augustine liked to quote from Timothy 1, and his writing accomplished that. Augustine's postconversion life, from this perspective, becomes perhaps his greatest challenge to the black-and-white worldview of Manicheanism. God's universe—our universe—is more complicated than a good/bad system. Rather than telling ourselves that we must be angels or else everything that we do is a lie, we must accept our humanness.

"It's going to be a long career," a young teacher once said to me, when she realized that her idealism would not translate automatically into student learning. *Yes*, I thought as I smiled to her then, in recognition, *I feel that too, sometimes.* Armed with St. Augustine's example, though, I might now offer a stronger reassurance: that persevering despite the frustration of my own continuing weaknesses is the true proof of vocation. Conversion is just the beginning.

For Further Reading

Saint Augustine, Bishop of Hippo, *Confessions of St. Augustine* (New York: Sheed & Ward, 1942).

Joseph R. Bernardine, "St. Augustine as Pastor," in *A Companion to the Study of St. Augustine*, ed. Roy W. Battenhouse (New York: Oxford University Press, 1955).

David Bentley-Taylor, *Augustine, Wayward Genius* (London: Hodder and Stoughton , 1980).

Peter Brown, *Augustine of Hippo: A Biography* (Berkeley: University of California Press, 1967).

Luc Verheijen, *St. Augustine: Monk, Priest, Bishop* (Villanova, PA: Augustine Historical Institute, 1978).

34

Blessed Jeanne Jugan

1792–1879 ~ France ~ Feast: August 29

J eanne Jugan, beatified October 3, 1982, devoted her life to serving the aged poor. She was born in 1792, the sixth of eight children of a French fisherman and his wife; her father died when she was a toddler. Her mother, one of the "sturdy, confident" women of Brittany who "had little time for self pity or tears," kept the family together in a one-room cottage and made sure that her children attended secret Catholic services, though public worship was forbidden after the French Revolution.

When Jugan was sixteen, she went to work as a kitchen maid for a rich woman with a kind heart, the Viscountess de la Choue. France was experiencing civil war, and Brittany suffered from famine, poverty, and pillage. The Viscountess (who was perhaps one of the "Trotting Sisters," an underground order of Catholic women) took Jugan with her when she went to give food and clothing to the needy. From her, Jugan learned a lesson that she would remember all her life: let the poor keep their dignity when you help them. "Treat the poor only as you yourself would wish to be treated," the Viscountess told her. "The good we do must be offered with the deepest respect and love."

Jugan herself joined the Trotting Sisters when she was twenty-five and became a hospital worker in a town where four thousand out of the ten thousand residents were classified as beggars. Exhausted after six years, she again took employment as a lady's maid. Finally, in 1837 at age forty-seven, she discovered her life's work. She and two other women began taking in homeless old women, giving them their own beds. Soon, "the little hospice" attracted two more helpers, and Jugan devised a simple rule for their lives. Committed to serving the needy, they moved to a place where they could nurse a dozen old women. Jugan walked daily through the streets with a basket, soliciting donations to support their home. Once it became known how happy the old women were and how well cared for, donations flowed in. Before long, the community was able to buy and renovate a former convent, and by the early 1840s Jugan and her companions were caring for forty-four "good women," as they called them, "in dignity and cheer." Jugan's community earned the local bishop's blessing and began calling itself the "Little Sisters of the Poor"; Jugan won a French Academy prize for this work in 1845. In 1846, Jugan established a second home in a nearby city; by 1851, the group had attracted two hundred sisters caring for 1,500 people in a dozen homes and had received a papal blessing.

But in 1852, a trial began that would haunt the rest of Jugan's life. The community's Father Superior, Father La Pailleur, suddenly ordered Jugan to stop collecting money, to stop having any contact with benefactors, and to retire to the motherhouse to supervise the manual work of postulants. His motives are unclear, though he was apparently mentally unbalanced and jealous. Despite the injustice of this command, Jugan obeyed cheerfully and became beloved by the young women she supervised. A few years later, La Pailleur ordered her to suspend that work and assigned her no particular duties. Once again, Jugan obeyed with "absolute discretion about the wrong that had been done her," living as a cheerful, ordinary sister among the young nuns, whom she gently counseled about their work with the aged, telling the girls to take walks when they were worried and to remain good-humored, since "our little old people do not like long faces." Many had no suspicion that she was the founder of the flourishing Little Sisters of the Poor order, which by then enrolled more than two thousand sisters. Meanwhile Father La Pailleur had taken on himself the day-to-day management of the order, even personally screening candidates. When Jugan died in 1879, he directed that she be buried as an ordinary member of the order in the cemetery, her tombstone noting erroneously that she was the third sister to enter.

Jugan was not doomed to obscurity, however, for Father La Pailleur's conduct, increasingly more domineering and strange, attracted notice from Rome, and an inquiry was held. He was eventually removed. On her deathbed, the order's Mother Superior (who had been one of Jugan's earliest recruits) revealed that Jugan had indeed been the order's founder. In a dignified and joyful procession of sisters in March, 1936, Jugan's body was moved to a place of honor inside the mother church.

Working beyond Praise and Ego

How could Jeanne Jugan do it, I wonder when I read her story. How could she meekly endure a series of demotions, then a deliberate attempt to change institutional memory to exclude her? All of those days on the street with her basket, those nights on the floor in the first years of her work! She had a right to be proud, for she had inspired others to join her in an enterprise that brought "dignity and cheer" to thousands of lives. How could she bear being anonymous? Why didn't she stand up for herself?

Self-abnegation is a difficult model in our time, when self-promotion is among the most popular topics of self-help seminars and books. The way to get ahead is to take all of the credit that's coming to you, we're told. It's healthy to stand up for yourself, to be "proactive" in making sure that others are suitably impressed with you.

Many of us teachers have taken such advice to heart. A friend of mine who teaches high school once told of how she set her colleagues straight in a faculty meeting when a male teacher assumed credit for a program she had planned. Still trembling with remembered emotion, she told me how she stood up (literally) and proclaimed that he was misrepresenting the facts. "It was *my* idea," she said. "Not Bob's, and I wanted everybody to know that. I felt so powerful for finally telling him off."

Another woman I knew years ago, who had run her parish religious education program for a long time, suddenly found herself replaced by a new parish member who had advanced training in theology. Rather than work in a diminished position under the new leader, she quit. "What would people think of me if I just went quietly?" she said. "If I just rolled over and took it? What a doormat I'd seem like! They'll find out before too long how much they miss me!"

How could Jeanne Jugan do it, I wonder when I hear my young colleagues insist that they must teach in their areas of specialty, and when I catch myself irritated at being given an assignment anyone could do. *Don't they know who I am?* we think in such situations. We're all so eager to maintain our prerogatives, so afraid that we're going to be devalued, overlooked. So insecure.

Jeanne Jugan, in contrast, was the epitome of security, for she knew that the work she had begun was prospering, and *that* was what mattered. She was able to see a larger picture: that the overall goals of the organization, not her own reputation, should be sustained at all cost. She knew that contesting the Father Superior's order might well have distracted attention from caring for the aged, with people taking sides and precious energy expended in argument. She also knew that to disagree with the Father Superior would have been modeling disrespect for religious authority.

And so, trusting that God had a reason, she took up her new assignment contentedly. Soon she discovered a marvelous truth: that bearing her own cross with patience taught her how to help others bear theirs. She had a new role now, a superficially more humble role, but a role no less crucial to the order's survival. The order had grown so large that the novices had little daily contact with the oldest, most experienced sisters. To keep the charism vital, she needed to inspire them, as she had inspired the original recruits. To accomplish that, she told the younger women what had apparently always worked for her: keeping the central mission of the Sisters always in their minds, giving up their egos and their temporary irritation with the old people who depended on them for sustenance and cheer. I imagine Jugan every bit as happy to see a restless young nun with whom she'd spoken smiling at an elderly man as she would have been in the central office—perhaps more, for by that time the order was established enough that someone else could run it. These young women, on the other hand, needed her. It would soon have become apparent to her that these young nuns loved her—an apparently obscure old woman—for herself. It was her day-to-day gentleness and wisdom, not her résumé, that constituted her worth. What a marvelous gift such recognition must have been!

When we feel slighted, we teachers can learn a great deal from Jeanne Jugan's later life. We may fantasize about being vindicated, borne back to recognition by a triumphant procession of supporters (preferably over the dead bodies of our enemies). We may attempt to do the bearing back ourselves by promoting ourselves loudly in public. Still, what shows our mettle, really, is what we do when we find ourselves set to work in a capacity we believe to be below our dignity. Jeanne Jugan's life reminds us that, though it might not seem fair, what we've done for God and our students today should be our focus. Rather than spending our energies on resentment, we'd do better to turn our attention to what we can accomplish in our new, "demoted" status. For only when we allow ourselves to lose our lives—our past lives, with all their bragging rights—can we begin to enjoy the new work God has waiting, radiant with possibility, for our hands.

For Further Reading

Ferdinand Holböck, "Jeanne Jugan," in *New Saints and Blesseds of the Catholic Church: Blesseds and Saints Canonized by Pope John Paul II during the Years 1979–1983*, trans. Michael J. Miller (San Francisco: Ignatius Press, 2000).

Paul Milicent, *Jeanne Jugan: Humble So As To Love More*, trans. Alan Neame (London: Darton, Longman, and Todd, 1980).

35

THE TENSION BETWEEN
WORK AND AVOCATION

St. Gregory the Great

c. 540–604 ~ Rome ~ Feast: September 3

Gregory the Great has been called "one of the most remarkable figures of the medieval world." Though he became pope at a particularly troubled time in Roman history, his thirteen-year pontificate was full of gains for the church. He championed and reformed monasticism, sent missionaries to England, produced books that greatly influenced church practice, introduced Gregorian chant, battled heresy, and reformed the administration of church and state. "His achievements," one biographer says, "were prodigious."

Gregory was born about 540, the son of a Roman senator, and he inherited a sense of civic responsibility that would help shape his career. The Rome of his youth was a "run-down, depopulated and decaying city, fever-ridden and famine-prone." Its inhabitants had faced repeated outbreaks of the plague and natural disasters; the city had been besieged and invaded by Goths and Lombards. Gregory received a good classical education just before the schools closed, and he seemed destined for a life of secular public service. In 573, however, he sold his considerable property, gave his profits to the poor, and founded seven monasteries, joining the one in Rome himself the next year.

Although Gregory loved contemplative life, he was called from his monastery to be one of the seven deacons of Rome, then to serve as an ambassador to Byzantium. "I have to bear with secular business,"

Gregory lamented, noting that he felt "fouled with worldly dust." Legend has it that Gregory saw several Anglo-Saxon slave boys in Rome during this period and, calling them "angels, not Angles" because of their fair complexions and hair, asked to be sent as a missionary to England, a request that was denied because he was needed in Rome. After Pope Pelagius II died of the plague, Gregory's hopes of returning to monastic life were permanently foiled, for Gregory was chosen as his successor. "I have lost the deep joy of my quiet," Gregory wrote, "and while I seem outwardly to have risen, I am inwardly falling down."

Soon, however, despite almost crippling anxiety and its physical effects (gastritis, colitis), Gregory made his peace with the inevitable and began his illustrious service to a faith and a city he loved. He negotiated with the Lombards, and he systematized church and civic administration. He reformed the liturgy, supervising the codification of plainsong into what became known as Gregorian chant. Gregory was also a noted author, "the last of the great Latin patristic writers." He wrote commentaries that made the Bible and the work of such church fathers as Augustine and Ambrose accessible to the barbarians. Among Gregory's many works are the *Dialogues*, a book that chronicles the lives of holy men (including Benedict), the highly influential *On Pastoral Care*, and many pastoral letters. In addition to his duties in Rome, Gregory vicariously took up the work of conversion of the English, sending a missionary delegation of forty monks in 596. Reportedly, ten thousand people were baptized within a year. Gregory continued to supply monks, relics, and church supplies to England, and he continued to direct that mission himself.

Despite his active public life, Gregory's heart was always with monasticism, and he promoted it tirelessly, reforming monastic rule and encouraging the foundation of monasteries. He has been called the "first monk-Pope," one who "translated his deep personal commitment to monasticism into a very practical policy of protecting, advancing, and defending the rights of Italian monasteries" against secular and clerical authority. His writing makes it clear that, though he recognized the importance of active service to the church, he held contemplative life in a place of honor. "Conversion, culminating in a life of contemplation, is the object of understanding the scriptures," he wrote. Under Gregory's influence, monasticism—which had been somewhat distrusted and not much written about—flourished.

Gregory died in 604, as the Lombards prepared to invade again. Though a mob is said to have tried to make him a scapegoat for the invasion, his fame as a champion of the church spread, and he became one the four Doctors of the Latin Church. He is frequently depicted in art, and his books have had great influence in the Middle Ages and after. He is especially beloved in England, where legend claims that he "will present the English people to the Lord on the Day of Judgment as their teacher and apostle."

BEING TRUE TO ONESELF DESPITE DISTRACTION

Stories of the saints so often recount their reluctance to accept high office that the gesture is "a commonplace of the literature," according to one scholar of hagiography. In Gregory's case, though, his reluctance to assume the papacy seems to have been ardently felt and Gregory sincere when he remarked that "I have been stricken with such sorrow that I can hardly speak." For Gregory had avocations—interests and commitments that meant everything to him—plans that would be seemingly impossible to pursue, now that he was pope.

Many teachers will find it appropriate, in that light, that Gregory's modern feast day comes just as most of us are beginning a new school year. No matter how much we love our jobs, it's always a wrench to realize that we will now have much less time for our avocations: less time to read, to pursue hobbies, to meditate or pray, to celebrate the beautiful natural world, to volunteer. Knowing that we, too, will be "divided among many cares," we might even feel a little of the anguish that Gregory did as we gather ourselves and struggle psychologically to make our own peace with the inevitable.

Gregory believed that he would have to say good-bye to two particular heart's desires as he took office. One was his wish to lead a mission to the Anglo-Saxons. Though recent scholarship about him has called the exact details of this inspiration into question—some scholars argue that Gregory may never actually have encountered the captives who reminded him of angels—his personal concern for the English is well documented. Gregory's other focus was his long-term attraction to monastic life. Though he had emerged from contemplation to serve the church, he always called his time as a monk the happiest period of his life, and his writings demonstrate that he believed contemplation to be the highest calling. When he was chosen as pope, he was torn forever from that life, and he became so melancholy that he made himself sick.

The irony, of course, is that Gregory *was* able to be faithful to these interests, to serve them more effectively, actually, than he might have been able to do had he not become pope. Under his direction, missionaries converted England, and, though Gregory never visited the island himself, he has been hailed ever after as the beloved father of the English church. He has also been recognized as one of the fathers of western monasticism, the man who did more to define, reform, and establish the centrality of contemplative life than anyone else. Thus, Gregory *was* able to live a life that served his convictions, though not quite in the way he had initially expected.

As we begin the new school year, Gregory's life can present a useful reminder that it is possible to be true to our avocations even in the press of daily business. Many teachers find creative ways to bring their heartfelt interests directly into their work. A religious education teacher passionate about social justice incorporates discussions of that subject into her classes; another who loves religious music introduces topics to her catechumens through hymns. One high-school teacher in my town who works during the summers with disadvantaged young children has mobilized her honors students to teach reading year-round to elementary school students in the city's less-affluent neighborhoods; another, who is a conservationist, takes his general biology classes outdoors often, arguing that once students learn to pay attention to the natural world they are less apt to abuse it. Such actions multiply the effectiveness of those teachers' commitments, as Gregory's stature as pope was able to multiply his.

If we are assigned administrative jobs, Gregory becomes a particularly appropriate mentor, for he reassures us that becoming a manager does not necessarily mean that we have to abandon the causes that have defined us. That can happen, of course. It's easy to become so ground down in the press of small daily business ("fouled with worldly dust"— what a psychologically useful expression!) that we come to believe we have only enough time to manage those responsibilities. It takes energy to propose new directions for an organization, and it entails risk. But Gregory understood conviction, and he understood delegation. He stayed true to his heartfelt interests and made them organizational priorities. Many of us have the chance to do the same.

Gregory's story suggests that the encroachment of "secular business" can actually serve as a helpful wake-up call, forcing a person either to be serious about what he or she would like to accomplish or to give it up. I like to think that, as Gregory looked back many years later at his early days as pope, he would have recognized just how well he had met this challenge. The melancholy was only a passing, misleading fancy. Despite what he had once considered overwhelming distractions, he had remained true to himself . . . and God had been true to him.

For Further Reading

F. Homes Dudden, *Gregory the Great: His Place in History and Thought*, 2 vols. (New York: Longmans, Green, and Co., 1905).

R. A. Markus, *Gregory the Great and His World* (Cambridge: Cambridge University Press, 1997).

Jeffrey Richards, *Consul of God: The Life and Times of Gregory the Great* (London: Routledge & Kegan Paul, 1980).

Butler's, 1:566–71.

Oxford, 229–31.

36

THE TEMPTATION
TO DESPAIR

St. Peter Claver

1580–1654 ~ Spain, Columbia ~ Feast: September 9

St. Peter Claver, who called himself a "slave of the slaves," was born in Spain in 1580 or 1581. Pious and intelligent, he studied with the Jesuits in Barcelona and decided early on a religious career. Around 1600, he entered the novitiate and was sent to the Jesuit college in Palma, where he came under the spiritual direction of St. Alphonsus Rodriguez.

These were heady, heroic years for the Jesuits. Matteo Ricci was working in China; other Jesuits were busy in India, Africa, and North and South America. In 1599, news came that Fathers Bogado and Verez had converted fifteen thousand blacks in Africa. Ignatius of Loyola himself was beatified in 1609. The idealistic Claver flourished in Jesuit seminary, known for his blend of humble obedience and fiery dedication. Claver's initial bent, though, was for contemplation, until Rodriguez, an advocate of missionary work, convinced him that service in the Americas was his duty. "Are not these souls worth the prize of God's life?" Rodriquez asked. "Ah, Pedro, my beloved son, why do you not go, you also, to gather the blood of Christ?" In 1610, Claver accepted the call and sailed for South America, bearing handwritten notebooks "of spiritual principles" from Rodriguez, which he kept all his life.

After completing his studies at the College of Santa Fe de Bogata and becoming ordained, Peter Claver was assigned to the port of

Cartagena (in present-day Columbia) in 1616. Cartagena was a center of the slave trade; ten thousand slaves passed through each year, bound for work in the region's gold and silver mines and on plantations. Arriving after long sea voyages in inhuman conditions (during which it is estimated that a third died), slaves were penned—hungry, thirsty, filthy, diseased—in the harbor town until they were sold. Conditions were so bad that the noble Father Alfonso de Sandoval, to whom Peter Claver became an assistant, was said to have broken out in a cold sweat every time he heard that another ship had arrived. After the slaves were sold, their lives hardly improved: as property, they could be beaten, starved, and worked to death by their masters. Those masters were actively hostile to the ministrations of clergy.

Peter Claver immediately threw himself into service of these slaves. Every time he heard that a slave ship had landed, he hurried to the slave pens, bearing food and water. His empathy is suggested by the fact that he attempted always to bring food that would be familiar to them: sweet potatoes, bananas, oranges, lemons. By begging from the rich, he was able also to provide decent clothing. He ministered to the sick; he separated men and women for decency's sake. He also attended to the slaves' spiritual needs: he baptized children and all babies born on the voyage; he taught the adults about Christianity (with the help of pictures and interpreters who could speak African languages). Some were so thirsty that they tried to drink the water he used to baptize them. "Tell me, my child," he would say, "do you not remember the great pleasure your body felt when it received that joy of water so nice and cool? Just as your body was happy because of that water, there will be much more and greater happiness in your soul when sin is gone and you are God's child." Such ministry, as Butler points out, helped give slaves "some degree of self-respect . . . some idea that as redeemed human beings they had dignity and worth." Late in his life, Claver estimated that he had baptized three hundred thousand captives.

Once a year Claver visited all of the region's plantations and mines, staying in slave quarters rather than with the masters. His visits were not welcome by most owners, who complained that he was wasting the slaves' time with worship and who feared that his attentions would make slaves insubordinate. Ironically, some later commentary on Claver's life has criticized him for not actively encouraging slave rebellion, offering instead faith that, as he once remarked, made captivity as pleasant as possible.

In Cartagena, Claver kept careful watch on the morals of converted slaves (he is said to have chided a woman who spoke to a male relative in the marketplace, so zealous was he to preserve sexual decorum). He also reached out to those who were not slaves, attempting to convert dissolute sailors and criminals; to heal and comfort the sick, especially lepers; even to serve the spiritual needs of the rich, including Dona Isabella de Urbina, who became his patron. Claver's personal life was a model of austerity; he ate and drank little, imposed penances on himself, and worked and prayed tirelessly.

After thirty-five years, Claver became ill and crippled. During his last four years of life, he was rarely able to go among the poor, and he was neglected by the young man assigned to care for him. He died on September 8, 1654, having lived (amazingly, given the harms' way in which he regularly put himself) more than seventy years. On his death, even those who had criticized him celebrated his memory; colonial authorities and blacks held large (but separate) services in his honor. He was canonized in 1888 (at the same time as his mentor Alphonsus Rodriguez) and is the patron of all missionary efforts among blacks.

Addressing Big Problems, One Small Gesture at a Time

Of all the heroic Jesuit missionary saints who traveled to remote lands and served destitute or initially hostile peoples in places where disease was prevalent, Peter Claver arguably faced the most overwhelming challenge. Hundreds of thousands of slaves labored in unspeakable conditions around Cartagena, and ten thousand more arrived every year, diseased, starving, and broken in spirit. It's one thing to be an idealist, but, as that river of unending human misery continued to flow into Claver's life, year after year after year, the sheer scale of the problem might well have broken his spirit. He couldn't hope to end slavery, or even prevent the suffering he saw every time a ship arrived. He couldn't convince most of the masters to be more humane. All he could do was comfort suffering slaves a few at a time, bringing food and faith, knowing that the next day, the next week, and the next month would bring the work to do over again, in exactly the same way.

When I was a child in the Presbyterian Church, we were taught a cheerful little hymn entitled *Brighten the Corner Where You Are*. It assured us that doing little helpful things in the context of ordinary life was morally important—that we should work contentedly wherever we were planted. "Someone far from harbor you may guide across the bar," a line in that song says, invoking the image of a lighthouse keeper who must trust that his beacon will make a difference. Though I liked that song as a child, when I became a cynical teenager and young adult it came to symbolize for me many things that I was fleeing. *No smug little corners for me,* I thought, *but grand gestures.* I was going to change things. Big things. Corners were fine for those without ambition. But what person with any spirit could be content to stop there?

As I have thought about Peter Claver, though, that childhood song has come rushing back into my head, and it sounds very different when juxtaposed with his life. For, despite the grandeur of Claver's effort taken as a whole, his daily work seems to me to have been exactly that: brightening in very tiny ways the very dark corner where he found himself. A banana, a drink of water, a coat. A dose of medicine. One baptism. Another. Comfort for one dying man. Small things, all.

It would have been so easy for Claver to become overwhelmed by the big picture. But he kept on, doing one small thing at a time, relighting that tiny light. He continued to trust that each gesture was important and that every one of these stricken people mattered. He was right, of course, and his life made an incredible difference. We teachers would do well to remember his example. For, in our own way, we are daily confronted with challenges that might drive us to despair, if we thought of the whole problem as an indivisible unit. Every time we begin with a new group of students, we begin from the same old baseline. Every time we work with a new student whose attitude is bad or whose skills are minimal, we confront the same overwhelming odds. "There's so much to do. Where do I begin?" young teachers often say, and even we old ones think it. We all know people who have let those big pictures overwhelm them. One of my companions in student teaching, who began with dreams of working with inner-city youth, spent two agonizing weeks in the classroom trying to gain her students' trust, expecting that her caring would somehow magically make them love learning, as she'd seen in the movies. At the start of the third week, I heard that she had quit and run away to Boston to be a jazz singer. I suspect that most teachers have been tempted to do something similar at one time or another.

Yet sometimes small things are all we have. When my husband and I moved to the country and joined the volunteer fire department, I once confided to our chief's wife, herself a fine firefighter and my mentor in that group, that I felt useless. I couldn't yet drive the engines or run the ancient pump panels. I didn't have the courage to charge a fire front. With my claustrophobia, I couldn't even wear a self-contained breathing apparatus. Frances, a very wise woman, smiled gently and asked me what I had done on the last fire. "I sprayed burning sagebrush," I said, shrugging off this meager contribution. I'd helped turn soil to ensure that the fire wasn't still burning underground. I'd briefly directed traffic around the scene. Then she smiled more broadly. "Useless?" she said. "Not at all. If you do one thing on a fire, you've helped. And you've done a lot of things."

If Peter Claver had heard those words, he would have nodded in agreement. He couldn't stop the slave trade, he knew, or even prevent a large part of the suffering in his own city. But that didn't free him from the responsibility of doing what he could. He understood that the Lord's work got done one person, one small gesture at a time. It's the same for us teachers, and we must learn to let one tiny step in understanding, one student's small accomplishment, be enough. We are not failures if all of our students don't have life-changing experiences under our tutelage. We aren't failures if individual students make only modest progress. "Someone far from harbor," the song says. Not "everyone."

For Further Reading

Mabel Farnum, *Street of the Half-Moon: An Account of the Spanish Noble, Pedro Claver* (Milwaukee: The Bruce Publishing Company, 1940).

Sir Arnold Henry Moore Lunn, *A Saint in the Slave Trade, Peter Claver (1581–1654)* (London: Sheed and Ward, 1935).

Angel Valtierra, *Peter Claver, Saint of the Slaves* (Westminster, MD: Newman Press, 1960).

Butler's, 3:519–24.

Oxford, 109–10.

37

The Right Discomfort

Martyrs of Korea

Nineteenth century ~ Korea ~ Feast: September 20

The 103 Martyred Saints of Korea were canonized in 1984 by Pope John Paul II as representatives of the thousands of Catholics who died for their faith in that country. Catholicism came to Korea—called "the Hermit Kingdom" because of its insularity—in the late eighteenth century, when Korean intellectuals, curious about the outside world, encountered Christian books sent from China. One of them, Ni Seung-houn, traveled to China in 1784; he studied Catholicism, was baptized, and returned to teach others.

Interest in Catholicism spread rapidly in Korea (a Chinese priest who came just ten years after Ni Seung-houn's return reported that he found four thousand Catholics). Persecution developed just as rapidly. Korea had adopted Buddhism as the state religion; by the eighteenth century, Confucianism was widely practiced. Christianity contradicted both, for it posed an animate God and human soul, and it challenged class structure and the practice of sacrificing to one's ancestors. Perceived as an instrument of westernization and foreign aggression, the new religion was thought to be a threat to "the beautiful customs and rituals" that defined Korean life. The first martyrs, labeled "foreign traitors," died in 1785. A few years later, in 1801, Catholics were explicitly declared heretics, and many laypeople, along with the first Chinese priest sent to Korea, perished in a massacre.

Korean Catholics were without a priest for thirty years. With worship forbidden, and the ownership of Christian books and objects outlawed, "it seemed impossible to reconstruct the devastated Korean Catholic community," wrote one commentator. Still, Catholicism flourished underground. When one convert, Yu Chin-gil, went to China on a diplomatic mission, he was examined by the Bishop of Beijing after requesting baptism. The bishop was amazed at his knowledge of the catechism in a country that had no clergy. "This is indeed a miracle of God," the bishop said.

Korean Catholicism found a champion who would bring it into the open in Paul Chong Ha-sang, son of one of the 1801 martyrs. Ha-sang was a government official who traveled to China to study the faith, crossing the border many times and traveling two thousand miles. In 1831, Ha-sang composed a letter to the pope detailing the fervor and desperation of Korean Catholics; in response, the first Korean diocese was formed. In 1837, Bishop Laurence Imbert and two other priests were sent to minister to the estimated nine thousand Catholics in Korea. Since the government had forbidden all foreign influence, the priests worked at night, underground. When their presence became known in 1839, the priests "allowed themselves to be taken, to avert massacre and apostasy," the *Oxford Dictionary of the Saints* reports, and were beheaded, along with some of their followers.

Catholicism did not die in Korea, however, and several young Korean men traveled to Macau to study for the priesthood. One of these, Father Kim Tae-gon, a member of a noble family and the first native priest to be ordained, returned to Korea in 1845 only to be martyred the next year. Korean Catholics fled to the mountains, establishing new parishes in exile. During another persecution in 1864, bishops, French missionaries, Korean priests, and many laypeople died. Not until Korea negotiated a treaty with the French in 1886 did persecutions officially end, although Korean Catholics were also martyred in 1901 and later expelled from North Korea.

The 103 Korean martyrs represented all social classes, from aristocrats to peasants, but they were united in their faith. Most were laypeople; many of them were women (who added saints' names to their own, including Lucy, Agatha, Barbara, and Theresa). The youngest was thirteen years old. Fiercely dedicated, they leave a proud legacy in Korea, which, its Christians claim, is the only country where Catholicism was not initially preached by foreign missionaries, "but sponsored by the native people themselves."

HELPING STUDENTS SURVIVE SHIFTING PARADIGMS

Paradigm shifts are always threatening. Vatican II is probably the transformation that most Catholics would consider the prime example, but more localized revolutions can be equally disturbing. They challenge participants to discard comfortable worldviews and undertake the unsettling process of redefining values, behavior—even self-concept—in light of a new way of seeing the world. No one knows better than teachers how people resist paradigm shifts, for we are in the business of initiating them all the time. A child who has been the center of a family world comes to kindergarten and must learn to share the spotlight. A seeker who has been drawn to the beauty and humanity of Catholic worship comes to a religious education class and realizes that faith is challenging as well as comforting. A bright teenager who has always performed well with little effort encounters a course in which she doesn't immediately succeed; her old patterns of thinking, her former standards of "good work" are suddenly inadequate. One of my friends who teaches fourth grade reports that resistance to paradigm shifts occasionally happens even in the context of basic mathematical skills.

"I know how to multiply," students say plaintively. "Why do I have to learn to divide?" One common response to a paradigm shift is, sadly, to transform anxiety about the shift into hostility toward the person who poses it. The lives of the Korean martyrs present an extreme case of such transfer. Championing a faith that challenged their culture's class system and the ancestor worship believed to insure stability and prosperity, they were persecuted as enemies of the state, the advance guard of westernization. Their real motives were much different: to worship in a way they believed best glorified God and to spread what they considered the important truths of human existence. They believed that the new religion would enlighten their culture, not destroy it. But Korea's rulers, police, and the common people who made up the mobs could not see this, and so the believers became martyrs.

Compared to beheadings and torture, what teachers suffer when they introduce paradigm shifts is minor: the resistance, the barbed questions, the guilt trips, and outward rebellion. These things can hurt a great deal, though, and, at the risk of sounding presumptuous, I'd insist that teachers can be inspired by the Martyrs of Korea when they encounter such behavior. For we, too, are making people uncomfortable for their own good when we ask them to reexamine their habitual ways of making sense of the world. Our students must discard limiting presuppositions if they are to encounter an academic subject, or their faith—or themselves—in full complexity. Of course they will kick and scream, for every human being enjoys the sense of security that comes with understanding the grammar of existence. If we don't know the rules, we're vulnerable. The more precisely we have defined ourselves in terms of the previous paradigm, the stiffer our resistance to the new one is likely to be. Of course we blame the person who has dislocated us; of course we're furious.

Defining the process of teaching as the process of making people uncomfortable may seem off-putting, but I'd argue that this is essentially what we do whenever we attempt to move our students to a new level of understanding. Such work can seem thankless if we allow ourselves to dwell on the grumbling, the digging-in-of-heels, or even the going-away, if our students have that choice. Like the Martyrs, though, if we truly believe in the worth of what we're teaching, we must stand up and take the heat. For our students must face these changes if they are to grow, and our backing down constitutes not just a betrayal of our profession but a betrayal of our students. We can only hope that, with time, they will see that we were not traitors at all but bearers of a message that, while temporarily uncomfortable, would move them to places they never could have imagined on their own.

For Further Reading

Matthew Brunson, et al. "Martyrs of Korea," in *John Paul II's Book of Saints* (Huntington, IN: Our Sunday Visitor, 1999), 52–54.

Kim Chang-seok Thaddeus and Ch'oe Sok-u Andrew, *Lives of 103 Martyred Saints of Korea* (Seoul: Committee for Bicentennial Commemorative Projects of the Catholic Church in Korea, 1984).

www.catholicculture.org/docs.doc_view.cfm?

Oxford, 303–04; 306.

38

The Courage
to Be a Shepherd

St. Lioba

Died c. 780 ~ England, Germany ~ Feast: September 28

St. Lioba was an English missionary nun and abbess called to Germany by St. Boniface in the eighth century. Much of what we know of her life comes from a biography that Rudolf, a monk, compiled sixty years after her death, drawing on the testimonies of four of her nuns. She was born in Wessex to aged, previously barren parents who consecrated her to God. They sent Lioba to a convent at an early age, where she was instructed by the abbess St. Tetta. Lioba was distinguished by her love of prayer and reading and by her pleasant disposition.

St. Boniface, who was preaching in Germany by the decree of St. Gregory II, was related to Lioba's mother, and the girl sent him encouraging letters as her "brother." In 748, Boniface requested that Lioba lead thirty nuns to Germany to help him establish foundations for women. Though, according to Rudolf, "the Abbess Tetta was exceedingly displeased at [Lioba's] departure," she agreed. As a young woman Lioba became abbess over the new monastery of Bischofsheim, banishing homesickness in her zeal to do God's work. She attracted so many women to religious life that other houses were soon established under her direction. "There was hardly a convent of nuns in that part that had not one of her disciples as abbess," Rudolf writes.

Lioba was known for her energy, her fairness, and her quick intelligence. She tolerated no excessive penances, especially sleep deprivation, because she wanted her nuns to be alert and fresh. "When sleep is taken away, sense is taken away, especially for reading," she remarked. She herself was a hard worker, and her love of learning blossomed in Germany. "So great was her zeal for reading that she discontinued it only for prayer or for the refreshment of her body with food and sleep."

Her studies were sometimes interrupted, however, because both the nuns and the people relied on her powers to avert trouble. Once when she was reading to her nuns, the village caught fire. As flames spread from thatched roof to thatched roof, a crowd of people came to the monastery doors and begged her to help. "Unruffled and with great self-control," Lioba requested a bucket of water from a stream that flowed near the monastery and added salt blessed by Boniface. She told the people to throw the bucket of water in the river and use water taken from below that point to fight the fire. In no time at all, the fire was extinguished "just as if a flood had fallen from the skies." At Lioba's urging, everyone thanked God.

On another occasion, a fierce thunderstorm turned day to night, tearing off roofs and shaking the ground, and the people, "shrieking with fear," sought Lioba in the church, where she was praying. Again, Lioba was calm, inviting them all to join her in prayer. She fell at the foot of the altar herself, but soon they roused her, begging her to take action. Lioba rose "as if she had been challenged in a contest," flung off her cloak, and opened the church doors. Making the sign of the cross to the storm, she asked three times for Mary to intercede with Christ, and the storm ended abruptly. "The people's faith was stimulated by such tokens of holiness," Rudolf writes.

In 754, Boniface left his convent at Fulda, near Lioba's monastery, for a mission in Friesland. He was martyred there. According to his wishes, his relics were returned to Fulda, and Lioba visited them often. In her later years, she served as a friend and advisor to Charlemagne's queen, Blessed Hildegard. After many years of service as an abbess, Lioba died around 780 and was buried by the altar in the abbey church of Fulda, but not in Boniface's tomb, as he had wished, for the monks did not want to disturb his relics.

Releasing our Rightful, Confident Power

If you asked a group of people who have never stood in front of a classroom to list words they associate with teaching, *bravery* would almost certainly not be among them. They might say "altruistic" or "caring" or "intelligent" or "patient." But "brave"? Not likely.

As all teachers know, however, our profession requires a great deal of bravery. Ask any student teacher, hyperventilating in front of his or her first class, lesson plan forgotten in sheer nervousness. To teach is to assume authority, after all, and to assume authority is to assume responsibility. *Authority* isn't a popular word in some pedagogies right now, especially the theory that identifies teachers as facilitators, posing as simply another learner among many in the classroom. While that theory rightly questions pompous authoritarianism in the classroom, the extreme of "student-centered learning" (as if there were any other kind) can be equally disastrous. Last semester I observed a teaching assistant who had swallowed the decentralized classroom theory, hook, line, and sinker. She told her freshmen outright at the start of the semester that her opinions were no more valid than theirs. She sat them in a circle and tried to plan the semester's content by a committee of the whole. Initially her students played along, but the first time she returned papers with suggestions and grades, she faced overt rebellion, and by midterm the class was out of control, not listening to her when she spoke, not reading assignments, and questioning everything she said with the glee of adolescents who knew they'd been given permission to act out. Nobody except the teaching assistant learned much in that class.

The fact is that sheep need a shepherd, and by accepting the responsibility of teaching we assume that role. It's frightening to be in charge, but we must be brave, for, as Lioba discovered, sheep ultimately *want* a shepherd. She had loved the quiet English monastery and would have been content to stay with Tetta, reading, studying, and praying. But she was ordered to Germany in God's service, a country of strange language and strange ways, never to return home, and she accepted her new responsibilities.

These turned out to be more extensive than she had imagined, because she found herself not only leading her nuns but also serving as a mother to the frightened, leaderless laity. It must have been so difficult for the scholarly, meditative Lioba to pull her attention from reading and prayer to solve this problem and then that one. I imagine her sighing as she closed her book or opened her eyes to tend to the mob's panic; I imagine her after repeated interruptions, tempted to retort with some medieval version of "Deal with it!" Lioba did not yield to temptation but gathered her forces with great bravery, as befits her name, which is reminiscent of the Latin word for *lion*, as well as meaning "beloved." She accepted authority, and she triumphed.

In a less dramatic way, the situation is the same for us. By standing in front of students, we take on the responsibility for changing their lives for the better, and, if we do not, we appear culpable. Fortunately we can learn some key lessons from Lioba about how to be leaders. First, Lioba knew that a leader must lead *unambiguously*—the flashing eyes, the clear regulations for the nuns—that to dither when action was needed was to put people in danger. Of course, she did not act impulsively as a leader—she prepared and prayed and thought about the people's best interests—but after preparation she was decisive. She recognized, too, that becoming a leader meant changing her style of behavior when the occasion demanded it, from gentle scholar to warrior. Rather than worrying about consistency or protesting that the latter role was "not my style," she recognized that various roles demanded various personae, and she found the courage to be fierce when she had to be. What apparently helped her do so—perhaps the greatest inspiration she offers us—is that she knew she was not acting simply from the springs of her personal power. The strength she was able to employ as a leader came from her role as a conduit for something beyond herself. She was God's delegate, and in times of great challenge she reached out to him before she did anything. Lioba's prayer, her meditation, and her reading all connected her to power beyond her own mere will. How could she not be confident?

It's the same for us. Whether we're drawing on God's help directly, as catechists might do through prayer, on our confidence in the knowledge that has been transmitted to us by our own teachers, or on our careful preparation, we need to believe in something beyond our personal power when we teach. Even given such grounding, it's unlikely that we'll always be brave; and a constant face of bravery could mean that we've simply become cavalier. "Anyone who isn't nervous on the first day of class shouldn't be in the classroom," a mentor of mine used to say. The challenge for all of us is to face down those fears and accept responsibility—and its risks—every time we stand before a class. As Lioba did for her flock, we must address our students' needs with bravery born of careful preparation. We can't do things halfway. We must be leaders.

For Further Reading

Marie Anne Mayeski, *Women at the Table: Three Medieval Theologians* (Collegeville, MN: Liturgical Press, 2004), 55–104.

Rudolf, "St. Leoba," trans. C. H. Talbot, in Thomas F. X. Noble and Thomas Head, eds. *Solidiers of Christ: Saints and Saints Lives from Late Antiquity and the Early Middle Ages* (University Park, PA: The Pennsylvania State University Press, 1995), 255–77.

Butler's, 3:668–71.

Oxford, 323–24.

39

UNLIKELY DISCIPLES

St. Jerome

c. 347–420 ~ Italy, Antioch, Constantinople, Bethlehem
Feast: September 30

St. Jerome, one of the four Latin Doctors of the Church, is known for his translation of the Bible, his learned commentaries on scripture, and for his irascible, contentious temper. He was born in Dalmatia around 347 to a rich gentleman farmer, who sent him to school in Rome. There, Jerome studied with the illustrious pagan grammarian Donatus and fell in love with books and rhetoric. Jerome possessed strong physical passions, and in later life he bemoaned his "vanity" and sexual experimentation during this period. Nevertheless, he enjoyed visiting the catacombs and he was baptized while in Rome. He then went to Aquileia to serve under its bishop, St. Valerian.

A few years later, after Jerome made enemies in the group of priests and scholars surrounding Valerian, he traveled to Antioch, where he had a dream in which Christ chided him for being a Ciceronian at heart (that is, a disciple of secular rhetoric) rather than a true Christian, and ordered him to be flogged. Deeply shaken, Jerome joined a monastic order in the desert southeast of Antioch, abandoning his beloved classics and learning Hebrew "as a penance." He was assailed by terrible temptations, including visions of dancing girls. "I came to dread my cell," he wrote. During this period, the famous episode in which Jerome pulled a thorn from a lion's paw is said to have taken place.

After five years, Jerome left for Constantinople, where he studied the Bible with St. Gregory Nazianzen. In 382 he became secretary to Pope Damasus and revised the extant, flawed Latin texts of the Gospels and psalms to accord better with original Greek texts. Jerome—an uncompromising champion of virginity and ascetic life—also produced biting satires of clergy and of Christians who lived worldly lives; he attained a reputation as a man "so violent, so easily provoked into harsh words and caustic phrases" that many feared him.

Jerome found a softening influence, however, in a group of noble, wealthy Roman women (some of whom became saints themselves) who had devoted themselves to study and prayer in what Eugene Rice has termed "virtually domestic nunneries in their palaces." Jerome first met Marcella, a widow who approached him with questions about the Scriptures, and through her the widow Paula, who was destined to become Jerome's closest friend. The thirty-five-year-old Paula was distinguished for her intelligence, learning, and strict conduct (she would not eat with a man). Jerome became spiritual director for these women; recognizing their seriousness of faith and intellectual potential, he began to teach them Hebrew. They were "overjoyed," one of Jerome's biographers writes, "at having the secrets of profoundest scholarship laid out before them." Jerome also kept a strict watch over their character, writing cautionary letters and holding conversations that emphasized the importance of chastity and asceticism. He convinced Paula's older widowed daughter Blesilla to turn from worldly pursuits before her early death, and he directed his favorite, Paula's obedient youngest daughter Eustochium, to a life of study and prayer.

After Damasus's death (and the removal of his protection of Jerome) in 384, however, indignation at Jerome's "reforming zeal," controversial revisions of the Bible, and closeness to the women forced him to leave Rome for Antioch. Paula and Eustochium joined him, and they settled in Bethlehem, where Paula used her fortune to establish a convent of women (which she oversaw) and a convent of men for Jerome. In this monastery, Jerome wrote his extensive biblical commentaries and translated most of the books of the Old Testament from Hebrew. Combative as ever, he also "spent almost as much time in doctrinal and personal dispute as in translating and commenting on the Bible." Among Jerome's most famous works of disputation was a treatise against Helvidius (who had questioned Mary's perpetual virginity); he also furiously attacked a longtime friend, Rufinus, in a debate over Origenism. Throughout his quarrels, Jerome resolutely refused to compromise. "I never spared heretics and have always done my utmost that the enemies of the Church should be my enemies," he wrote late in his life.

The last two decades of Jerome's life were troubled. Paula died in 404, and Jerome grieved deeply; a few years later, Alaric sacked Rome, and refugees came to the east. In 418, Pelagian heretics violently attacked the monasteries in Bethlehem, setting fire to them and killing a deacon. Jerome's beloved Eustochium died, and he followed her in 420, leaving a commentary on Jeremiah uncompleted. Jerome was initially buried close to Eustochium and Paula in Bethlehem, but his body was later taken to Rome. In art, he is frequently depicted studying and often accompanied by a lion. As Butler remarks, "a lion is a far from inapt emblem for this fearless and fierce defender of the faith."

MOVING BEYOND PREJUDICE

In my youth, I was assigned in a women's studies class to read a book about Judeo-Christian attitudes toward women. One chapter in particular shocked me: a compilation of passages by church fathers criticizing women. Jerome stood out as a misogynist even in that collection, I remember, bitterly condemning women for their vanity, their nagging, their lechery and hypocrisy. Returning to commentary on Jerome's work in the course of preparing this book, I've found much to corroborate my decades-old impression. One of Jerome's letters—to the teenaged

222 Susan H. Swetnam

Eustochium, no less—has been called "the greatest slander against women since Juvenal's sixth satire." Scholars have even attributed the tradition of misogyny in medieval literature to Jerome's influence.

Yet, as feminist Elizabeth Clark has written, Jerome's life presents a striking paradox, for this man "who could scarcely have been more vicious toward women in his writings" was "extremely supportive of them—at least the ones who accepted his tutelage—in real life." Jerome's closest ties, in fact, were with women. A misogynist in print, he treated actual women as intellectually and spiritually capable human beings, able to learn Hebrew, to read and discuss difficult texts, and to live a life of ascetic discipline that matched his own. "Self-willed and sharp-tongued, irascible to the point of morbidity, inordinately proud," Jerome nevertheless exhibited "spontaneous and almost childlike affection" for his female friends. Had I read widely enough during my undergraduate days to have encountered this paradox, it would have baffled me, and I might have mentally accused Jerome of hypocrisy.

Today, though, after thirty years of teaching, I would not be inclined to do so. For Jerome, I think, can be seen as an archetype for the way in which teaching eventually requires all of us to contradict ourselves. Like Jerome, most teachers bring to their work ingrained assumptions about people. One teacher I know, for instance, who suffered through a less-than-happy secondary school experience, once admitted to me that if she were not careful she would find herself assuming that the conventionally pretty, perky cheerleader types in her classes were airheads; another, who was a rebellious intellectual in his youth, admitted that he had to fight his tendency to underrate student athletes. Our prejudices can be triggered by the most trivial things: I myself—with my messy penmanship, my aim being to get ideas down as quickly as possible—admit to being put off by big, round, preternaturally neat cursive handwriting, the sign of an absolutely conventional thinker, I'm tempted to assume. Students older (or younger) than we are used to encountering, students who dress a particular way (all of those bare tummies that young women sported a few years ago, or tongue rings, or super-expensive preppie clothes), even those who speak too slowly or too quickly can engage our prejudices.

As all teachers know, however, the strangest things can happen to prejudgments when we get to know actual people. Real people, observed individually and with attention, inevitably confound stereotypes. As students respond to the subject matter and to us, they reveal all sorts of quirky complications and endearing traits. A student who seemed least likely to possess the diligence or the faith or the creativity that we hope for may on closer observation be the embodiment of those qualities. Before long, we'll find ourselves talking with that student and not even noticing the off-putting traits anymore, just the potential.

To our astonishment, sometimes those students even become our "disciples," as the women became Jerome's. For all teachers—we might as well admit it—have an inner circle of students who seek out their tutelage, their advice, and their presence long after class is over. They are the people who, as one of my best friends says, are "members of our tribe" in ways difficult to explain, human beings whose minds and hearts are in tune with ours from the start. These are the students who naturally understand our purposes, our tastes, our faith, and our ways of thinking. They need to be convinced of nothing; all they want to do is learn from us. They help explain why we are alive, and their gaze helps keep us honest with ourselves.

They are not always, however, the people we expected to love. After years in the profession, we may find ourselves counting up a list of dearest, best students little less incongruous than Jerome's. Mine includes a female ex-private eye who was also once a hard-living, working-class single mother; a starchy, prim and proper MBA student who actually wears dress-for-success suits; several ranchers with decided twangs; a Mormon matron who, despite my repeated urging, continues to believe that the word "special" is a high and particular compliment; even some students with big round handwriting. What links us is that we all love words and love a certain kind of laughter; we love imagining the minds of other human beings. We all know how to work. No one ever had to teach us any of these things. When we are together, we're home.

And so I don't wonder about the paradox of Jerome's words and his deeds anymore. Kindred spirits come in many shapes. It's the spirit that matters.

For Further Reading

Elizabeth Clark and Herbert Richardson, *Women and Religion: A Feminist Sourcebook of Christian Thought* (New York: Harper & Row, 1977), 53–68.

J. N. D. Kelly, *Jerome: His Life, Writings, and Controversies* (New York: Harper & Row, 1975).

Eugene F. Rice, Jr., *Saint Jerome in the Renaissance* (Baltimore: Johns Hopkins University Press, 1985).

Jean Steinmann, *Saint Jerome and His Times*, trans. Ronald Matthews (Notre Dame, IN: Fides Publishers, 1959).

David S. Wiesen, *St. Jerome as a Satirist: A Study in Christian Latin Thought and Letters* (Ithaca, NY: Cornell University Press, 1964).

Butler's, 3:686–93.

Oxford, 270–72.

40

St. Thérèse of Lisieux

1873–1897 ~ France ~ Feast: October 1

S t. Thérèse of Lisieux is one of Catholicism's most beloved saints, cele-brated for her "Little Way," which is detailed in the spiritual auto-biography she was instructed to write before her death from tuberculosis at age twenty-four. Thérèse was born into the devout French middle-class Martin family in 1873, one of five surviving children. Thérèse was a pre-cocious, high-strung, and impulsive child, and she became an emotion-ally needy one when her mother died in 1877, adopting her sister Pauline as "Maman." Thérèse was a beautiful child with long curly blonde hair, her father's darling and a "little queen" in her family. She took to religion with great enthusiasm, becoming "voracious for communion" and full of scruples, but found that her seriousness set her apart from her peers at school, where she was isolated and unhappy.

Pauline entered a Carmelite convent when Thérèse was nine, plung-ing the child into emotional agony at this second separation. To com-fort Thérèse and encourage self-discipline, her older sister gave her a little book and told her to list the "flowers" she gave Christ. In just three months, the enthusiastic Thérèse filled it with more than eight hundred sacrifices and 2,800 acts of love. When another sister, Marie, entered the same convent just three years later, Thérèse broke down again. At Pentecost of 1887, she announced that she wanted to enter the Carmelite convent. Though postulants had to be twenty-one, Thérèse petitioned the pope for permission to enter at age fifteen, working through a local priest who was deeply touched by her determination. Thérèse became a postulant after Lent in 1888.

The convent's austere life suited Thérèse's ideas of self-sacrifice. The women slept on straw mattresses placed on trestle boards in tiny rooms, arose at 5:00 a.m., performed at least five hours of manual labor each day, kept silence at meals, and wore hemp sandals. This was not enough for Thérèse, who deliberately sought out additional trials. She chose a defective lamp for her room and ill-fitting shoes, and she delighted in the most humble housekeeping duties. Even after she took her final vows, Thérèse sought out jobs that were not sought after by her peers.

But Thérèse was troubled during her early years in the convent by "aridity": she could not pray, and she doubted her vocation. A series of spiritual events reassured her: a retreat during which she was told of God's pleasure with her; an epiphany telling her that she was called to pray for priests; a Trinity Sunday "Act of Oblation to the Merciful Love of God" indicative of martyrdom and espousal to Jesus. Though Thérèse dreamed of missionary service in Hanoi, she came to understand that her primary calling was "the vocation of love." She was to serve God by prayer, not great works in the world, and to surrender completely to his will. On Good Friday, 1896, Thérèse suffered a hemorrhage, and it became clear that she was suffering from tuberculosis. Over the next eighteen months, Thérèse endured a slow, painful deterioration; the Carmelites were amazed by her heroic acceptance of suffering.

During Thérèse's illness, Pauline and the convent's mother superior instructed her to write her spiritual autobiography, which became *Story of A Soul*. This work details her "Little Way," her insight that humbling oneself and doing small things could constitute appropriate service to God. Along with *The Last Conversations* recorded by Thérèse's sisters, *Story of a Soul* also reveals the hidden drama of Thérèse's longtime determination to be Christ's bride, her sense that "My vocation is love!" Her own sufferings, she said, reflected Christ's, and they were helping to redeem souls.

During the last few months of Thérèse's life, she was assailed by spiritual doubt, calling on Christ to pity his "little child." Though she remained confident of God's existence and love, she was unable to have faith in her own eternal life. In the end, though, she died with transcendent peace on September 30, 1897. Thérèse's autobiography was soon printed and sent to all Carmelite convents; it was a sensation, reprinted for general distribution just six months later. Lisieux became a place of pilgrimage so popular that guards had to be stationed at Thérèse's grave in 1899. By 1915 a million copies of her autobiography were in print, and the convent received many letters every day which testified to miracles worked in her name. Thérèse was canonized in 1925 (the most prompt canonization in church history to that point) and declared a doctor of the church in 1997, only one of three women saints to be so honored for "extraordinary . . . spiritual knowledge and teaching."

BREAKING THE CHAINS OF PRIDE AND INSECURITY

In the past, Thérèse has not been among my favorite saints. Even the *Oxford Dictionary of the Saints* admits that her devotees have "rendered [her] somewhat saccharine," and the little that I knew about her made "saccharine" seem like an understatement. Thérèse has a reputation as the saint of otherworldly humility, a young woman whose lack of ego the Dalai Lama might envy. One of her most often-repeated pronouncements is that God needs violets and daisies as well as roses. She was happy, she said, to be a small, insignificant flower, "too little to perform great actions." Other saints, including Peter Claver, acted in similarly humble ways, but Thérèse proclaimed her own humility explicitly and repeatedly. I considered that dramatized self-abnegation cloying. The cult of Thérèse's beautiful suffering also seemed to me just a little morbidly kinky—those books of progressive photographs that celebrate her lovely, heroic wasting away from tuberculosis.

Thérèse is so widely beloved, though, that I knew readers would expect to find her in this book, and so I began to read modern biographies of her. While they made Thérèse more interesting, they also tempted me to wonder if she had been too good to be true. This self-proclaimed "zero" or plaything of Christ, I discovered, was given to grand gestures that suggest she wasn't unaware of the impression she was creating after all: she proclaimed conversion or re-conversion in public; she took the heroic part of Joan of Arc in theatricals that she composed; she proclaimed that she was happy to see blood coughed from her tuberculosis-ridden lungs on the pillow and transcribed the Apostles' Creed in that blood; she told Pauline that her writings would be so important that they had to be guarded from Satan before publication. These biographies suggest that Thérèse craved love with deep hunger. One particularly revisionist writer ventures to suggest that Thérèse was a pleaser, a petted child who always needed reassurance. As I read, it occurred to me that humility can be a competitive sport. Perhaps Thérèse had been a hypocrite, I thought—not a deliberate one, but a wounded girl not consciously aware that her "surrender" played as an act of self-aggrandizement.

But then I read her own words, and everything changed. Thérèse herself is open about her innate tendency to pride. "I was full of self-love," she writes of her childhood. She is also open about her insecurity, saying directly that she "expected . . . thanks from creatures" when she did favors for them and, "if unfortunately [they] did not seem surprised and grateful for my little services, I was not pleased, and tears rose to my eyes." As psychologists know, attempting to validate oneself by winning others' approval is a losing proposition, and all of her efforts to be the perfect "little queen" brought Thérèse no lasting peace. Alternating between moments of joyful security and crashes into self-doubt, she suffered a series of what seem to have been psychosomatic illnesses. "I made troubles out of everything," she writes.

The Little Way was Thérèse's escape from this anguish. "Our Lord made me understand that the only true glory is that which lasts forever; and that to attain it there is no necessity to do brilliant deeds, but rather to hide them from the eyes of others, and even from oneself, so that 'the left hand knows not what the right hand does.'" She no longer had to worry about demonstrating her worth, for "Heaven was full of people who loved me." She was also exempted from guilt about her own sense of giftedness. "I often asked myself why God had preferences, why all souls did not receive an equal measure of grace," she writes. Ultimately, she believed, one could not understand this mystery and should rest contented and unapologetic with the graces that one has received. "If a little flower could speak," she writes, "it would tell us quite simply all that God has done for it, without hiding any of its gifts."

As it turns out, Thérèse has a great deal to offer all of us who long to stand out so that we can silence our self-doubt as well as share our talents. A good many such people do gravitate to the teaching profession, for it offers many opportunities to reassure ourselves that we are worthwhile human beings. When we succeed with particular students, when our fellow teachers look up to us, when we win awards, we can hug our triumphs to our hearts. Soon enough, however, our insecurities will begin clamoring: "What have you done for me lately?" And so we seek a new triumph, and a new one, and a new one. Thérèse offers a way out of this self-perpetuating cycle: we can accept our gifts as part of God's plan and stop comparing ourselves anxiously to other people. We can be content when our work seems humble. Our obligations are to work with love and to accept God's direction for us. We have nothing to prove.

And yet even Thérèse could not break completely free from the struggle with self-doubt and pride. The aridity of her last months confirms her continuing insecurity. A prayer she wrote for a novice, "to obtain humility," suggests her ongoing pride, for it could only have come from an ongoing familiarity with such a conflict, even after Thérèse was a nun, even after she was practicing her Little Way:

> And yet, dear Lord, Thou knowst my weakness. Each morning I resolve to be humble, and in the evening I recognize that I have often been guilty of pride. The sight of these faults tempts me to discouragement; yet I know that discouragement is itself but a form of pride. I wish, therefore, O my God, to build all my trust upon Thee. . . I will often say to Thee, "Jesus, Meek and Humble of Heart, make my heart like unto Thine.

Thérèse was anything but a saccharine, perfectly self-abnegating "little flower." She might, in fact, be exactly the saint for us "little queens" (and "little kings"), we who haven't yet learned how to deal with the yoking of ego and fear, striving and self-doubt that plague us.

For Further Reading

Guy Gaucher, *The Story of a Life: St. Thérèse of Lisieux*, trans. Sister Anne Marie Brennan (San Francisco: Harper & Row, 1987).

Kathryn Harrison, *Saint Thérèse of Lisieux* (New York: Lipper/Viking, 2003).

Saint Thérèse de Lisieux, *Story of a Soul: The Autobiography of St. Thérèse of Lisieux* trans. John Clarke, 2nd ed. (Washington, DC: ICS Publications, 1976).

Frederick L. Miller, *The Trial of Faith of Saint Thérèse of Lisieux* (New York: Alba House, 1998).

Patricia O'Connor, *In Search of Thérèse* (London: Darton, Longman, & Todd, 1987).

Jean-Francois, *Light in the Night: The Last Eighteen Months in the Life of Thérèse of Lisieux*, trans. John Bowden (London: SCM Press, 1996).

41

THE PROFLIGATE

St. Pelagia the Penitent

Fourth or fifth century ~ Antioch ~ Feast: October 8

St. Pelagia is one of the converted prostitute saints, said to have lived in fourth- or fifth-century Antioch. Sources note that her legend overlaps with others, including St. Thais (another reformed courtesan) and St. Margaret Pelagia (a nun accused of immorality). At least three saintly Pelagias lived during her period. According to a biography attributed (probably falsely) to James, Deacon of Antioch, this St. Pelagia was the city's "chief actress, the first in the chorus in the theater"—a glamorous woman who had become rich in her trade. Other accounts directly term her a harlot.

Her tale gives her a dramatic entrance. The Bishop of Antioch convened a conference of eight bishops, and the most renowned of them, Bishop Nonnus, was addressing the group in the open air before a church door. Then, as James puts it, "lo, suddenly there came among us" Pelagia, riding a donkey, "dressed in the height of fantasy, wearing nothing but gold, pearls and precious stones, even her bare feet were covered with gold and pearls." She was bareheaded, and her arms and legs were "shamelessly exposed in . . . lavish display." She was accompanied by laughing boys and girls dressed in gold, by the smell of perfume, and by music.

Aghast, all of the bishops covered their eyes and hid their heads in their clothes—except Nonnus. He stared intently at Pelagia, then asked the bishops if they were delighted by her beauty. None responded. He asked then, weeping and sighing, "How many hours does this woman spend in her chamber giving all her mind and attention to adorning herself for the play, in order to lack nothing in beauty and adornment of the body?" She devoted such immense effort to pleasing her lovers, he said, that she was an epitome of concentrated devotion. In contrast, he told the bishops, "Here are we, who have an almighty Father in heaven offering us heavenly gifts," an "immortal Bridegroom. . . . Why do we not adorn ourselves and wash the dirt from our unhappy souls, why do we let ourselves lie so neglected?" He suggested that Pelagia had shamed them all with the example of her single-minded focus. Nonnus then retired to his chambers, and he spent many hours weeping.

The next day Nonnus preached a sermon on judgment and salvation at the cathedral, and Pelagia attended—the first time she had ever done so. Overcome with a sense of her sinfulness, she asked him for baptism, throwing herself at his feet, weeping. She needed a sponsor, he said, taken aback, someone who would vouch that she would sin no more. Tenaciously, Pelagia kept holding onto his feet, begging for salvation.

All of the bishops present were impressed by her determination, and finally, with a deaconess and Nonnus serving as godparents, Pelagia was baptized. Though the devil visited her during the next few days, blustering and threatening, she ordered him away. She sold her wealth to benefit widows and the poor, and she freed her slaves, admonishing them to reform.

Eight days after her baptism, Pelagia exchanged her white robe for a man's tunic and pants, and she left town in secret, her destination known only to Nonnus. It was a hermit's cell on the Mount of Olives, where she lived as Pelagius, a man and a eunuch, imposing such fierce discipline on herself that she became a legend for sanctity and holiness. A few years later, Nonnus advised his deacon James to visit Pelagius, saying "truly I think you will be helped by him." James was impressed with the monk's wisdom and did not recognize the emaciated Pelagia. Returning a few days later, he received no answer to repeated knocks at the cell and discovered Pelagius dead. In reverence for the hermit's holiness, the monks "carried out his sacred little body as if it had been gold and silver they were carrying"—only to find, when they began anointing the body with myrrh, that Pelagius was a she.

The funeral drew a huge crowd, and Pelagia's transformed life became the subject of sermons for centuries. She was posed as an emblem of hope for sinners; if she could be converted, anyone could. In church lore, Pelagia became a symbol of the grace of God working directly upon a human life, a prototype of God's dealings with Israel and the whole human race.

ACKNOWLEDGING OUR LIMITED POWER

How infuriating they are, those students who misdirect their energy with great enthusiasm! My friends who are elementary school teachers complain of fourth graders who know every character in every computer game from nightly hours of play. A friend who teaches high school, comfortably into her second glass of wine in my backyard on a Friday evening, shakes her head with laughter about the tenth-grade girls in her second-period history class. "I can't imagine how much time they take every morning on their hair and makeup," she says. "Every day, every hair is perfect. Eyeliner, mascara, eye shadow, lip liner. They get up—at what time?—to do that, would you imagine? But they can't find time to read the assignments the night before. If they spent half the time on their work . . ."

If only our students would focus that effort on what matters, we tell ourselves. So much potential, going nowhere.

Mine was an athlete, a varsity tennis player recruited from Australia, an English major—sort of. She was famous in my department for attending class for the first few weeks of each semester, then disappearing. During her brief appearances, however, when she'd bothered to do the reading, she sometimes said the most insightful, amazing things. "Valerie's paper is the best in the class," my husband said one September night. "I can't believe it."

Most of the time, though, she was a washout, even when she came to class. She'd sleep and couldn't answer the simplest questions because she hadn't read the assignment. She'd yawn or roll her eyes while others talked. She wouldn't turn in assignments, or she'd turn in dashed-off garbage. "You're wasting your time and mine," I wrote one semester on one of her papers, in fury. "And you're distracting other students in class with your attitude. This is college; you don't have to be here if you don't want to." She never returned to that class.

Pelagia was the consummate profligate, the one who can give teachers hope for such as Valerie. Her life offered the assurance that anyone can be struck with God's grace, so great is God's power. Whatever sorts of conversions we seek in our classrooms, we should be cheered by her example. The extremism of her character, however, is nothing we should wish on our students. From being the best actress-courtesan, she turned to being the best hermit: the best at starving herself, the best at prayer and mortification, the one with the most spectacular parade of mourners. Today we would diagnose her as an obsessive personality.

It is in Nonnus's example, actually, that Pelagia's story becomes most useful for teachers. Nonnus was the master-teacher of his time and place, and Pelagia would have offered the ultimate challenge. When he saw her in the square, he must have been tempted to harangue her, to show off a little for the others. How glorious to be the one who converted her! And yet he let her go.

It is inviting for us, too, to pursue our Valeries. We might badger them, singling them out to shame or complement them into seeing the light, pursuing them . . . until we become angry at them and at ourselves for not being able to reform them. *We should be able to do something about this*, we think. From this follows our nagging and their avoidance.

Nonnus did none of the above with Pelagia. The story does not suggest that she noticed him weeping after she passed by (how could she have heard, with all that laughter and that music?), and she certainly didn't stick around for his little homily. If his response influenced her decision to come to the cathedral the next morning, it was magic or grace—some empathy filtering through the air into her consciousness. He did nothing manipulative or overt. She came of her own accord.

That's one of the wonders of conversion—it happens in its own time. Though we're often called to intervene as teachers, to encourage, remind, and chide, Pelagia's story reminds us that sometimes we simply have to admit that our power is limited. "Conductor's disease," my husband used to call the confidence that one can do everything for one's students, and it's a seductive ailment. "I am making this happen," we tell ourselves when class discussion dances, when a student has a breakthrough. But two people are in this picture, a teacher and a learner, and we are heading for trouble if we believe that we have all the power.

Pelagia and Nonnus remind us that in some cases all we can do is offer the best example and back off—a lesson that my own experience confirms. Six years after Valerie limped to her BA, she was back, applying for graduate school in English. We all laughed. "Valerie?" we said. "Are you kidding?"

She'd married, and she had enough money to pay her own way, didn't really need our teaching assistantship. Still, she wanted one, because she longed to teach. Her MA course grades were good, but it took us two years (and the urging of a young faculty member who knew only the new Valerie) to believe her. She turned out to be a marvelous graduate student, and a marvelous teacher.

Ultimately, Pelagia's lesson may be one of the hardest for us altruists to learn: that we can't force people onto the road to Damascus—or to the Mount of Olives. We can notice—must notice—must empathize and demonstrate through our own lives the rewards of application. But, finally, we also need to acknowledge, sometimes, that all we can do is trust that students will find their way in their own good time . . . and God's.

For Further Reading

Diane Apostolas-Cappadona, *Encyclopedia of Women in Religious Art* (New York: Continuum, 1996).

Larissa Tracy, "Saint Pelagia," *Women of the Gilte Legende: A Selection of Middle English Saints Lives* (Cambridge: D.S. Brewer, 2003), 94–96.

Jacobus de Voragine, *The Golden Legend: Readings on the Saints*, trans. William Granger Ryan (Princeton, NJ: Princeton University Press, 1993), 230–32.

Benedicta Ward, *Harlots of the Desert: A Study of Repentance in Early Monastic Sources* (Kalamazoo, MI: Cistercian Publications, 1987).

Butler's, 4:59–61.

Oxford, 419–20.

42

THE REAL VS.
THE IDEAL

St. Teresa of Ávila

1515–82 ~ Spain ~ Feast: October 15

St. Teresa of Ávila has been termed "one of the greatest, most attractive, and widely appreciated women the world has ever known." A Carmelite reformer and mystic and the first woman named a doctor of the church, Teresa was born to a wealthy merchant and his wife in Castile in 1515; her forebears may have included Jewish converts to Christianity. A lively, intelligent child, she played at going on a crusade and being a hermit alongside her brother. Her mother died when Teresa was fourteen. Under the influence of more worldly cousins, the girl began to read chivalric romances, to become preoccupied with her (beautiful) physical appearance, and to flirt to an extent that at least one biographer has suggested her reputation was in danger.

Her father placed Teresa in a convent of Augustine nuns to help protect and educate her, but she fell sick after a year and was recalled home. During her convalescence, she read St. Jerome's letters and decided to become a nun, although her father forbade it. Teresa, however, entered the Carmelite Convent of the Incarnation, in which one of her friends lived. She fell ill again and nearly died.

The convent of the Incarnation was "irregular," as Butler says, in a way common in Spain at that time: visitors of both sexes could come and talk privately with the nuns in the parlor. Teresa was popular for her charm, wit, and beauty, and she neglected her spiritual duties until her father's confessor warned her of her danger. Then, although her practice was still irregular, she began to grow in faith. She took St. Mary Magdalene as her patron and an image of the suffering Christ as her meditative inspiration. Teresa began experiencing ecstatic states while in prayer, including visions of angels. She had the sense that her heart was pierced with an iron spear, causing her to experience pain, sweetness, revelation, and rapture. Several confessors warned her against these visions, calling them deceptions of the devil, but a series of Jesuit confessors, among them St. Peter of Alcántara, set Teresa's mind at rest: she was experiencing God's spirit, they said.

After twenty-five years as a Carmelite, Teresa was inspired to found a new, reformed order, the Discalced (barefoot) Carmelites. In 1562, she and thirteen other nuns took up residence in a house in Ávila, vowing themselves to poverty, strict enclosure, and prayer. They led austere lives, abstaining from meat, wearing coarse brown habits and leather sandals, and performing manual work. The citizens of Ávila were upset by this foundation, and Teresa was brought back to the Incarnation to face criticism. Eventually she convinced skeptics and was allowed to return.

Even in the midst of her struggle to establish her order, Teresa was a prolific writer. She composed *The Way of Perfection*, a book of instruction for her nuns. On the instructions of her confessor, she also wrote her autobiography, and later, *The Interior Castle*. These books chronicle the varieties of prayer she experienced, guide readers toward greater union with God, and present Teresa's account of her own life. Although Teresa was a mystic, her wit and forthrightness are evident in her books and letters. For example, she favored intelligent nuns who had good judgment rather than "stupid" ones, she said, since they were able to understand their faults and be corrected.

Teresa established more than a dozen daughter houses of Discalced Carmelites during her lifetime. Little money was available for these foundations, but she had faith. "Teresa and this money are indeed nothing," she said of the four or five ducats she possessed for one foundation. "But God, Teresa and these ducats suffice." Carmelite friars, including St. John of the Cross, established monasteries based on her principles. As Teresa's credibility grew, Pope Pius V charged her with reforming the Incarnation convent. While the nuns met Teresa with antagonism, she soon won them over. "Do not fear my rule," she said. "Though I have lived among and exercised authority over those Carmelites who are discalced, by God's mercy I know how to rule those who are not of their number." Italian Carmelites also distrusted Teresa and had her brought before religious tribunals, but she defended herself with energy and escaped censure.

St. Teresa of Ávila died in 1582 and was canonized in 1622. Several well-known representations picture her in ecstasy, including a sculpture by Gian Lorenzo Bernini, completed in the mid-seventeenth century for the Roman church of Santa Maria della Vittoria. In art, her emblems are a flaming arrow or a dove. Convents of her order exist around the world, still dedicated to contemplation.

STAYING GROUNDED WHILE OUR SPIRITS SOAR

Teresa of Ávila provides one of the most comprehensively practical saintly models for teachers imaginable because of her inspired balance. Like teachers, Teresa was pulled in many different directions every day—directions that could have threatened mental and spiritual chaos to a less adept person. Since Teresa was a mystic, she required private time for learning, reflecting, and praying. She was also enmeshed in a world of practicalities, and her position as mother of her order made her liable to be "pecked to death by ducks," as one of my friends used to say when he was assistant department chair, constantly called on to fix trivial problems caused by others' incompetence or lack of understanding.

While it may seem odd to call a woman *practical* when her most famous representations in art show her swooning in ecstasy, ravished by her visions of "His Majesty," any reading of her own works or of any reliable biography will suggest that practicality was an important aspect of her personality. Teresa managed everything handily, with a famously "good temper," establishing the Discalced Carmelites, a revolutionary order in its austerity, overseeing her own convent and daughter houses, answering charges by religious authorities, yet maintaining one of the most celebrated prayer lives in Christian history. She did all this, it appears, through faith, but it was a faith substantially enhanced by an amazing capacity for hard work, by a clear-eyed, unsentimental view of human beings, including herself, and by a delightful sense of humor. While Teresa's spirit was often in the heavens, her discalced feet, one might say, were always firmly on the ground.

Teresa's down-to-earth nature is clear in her books, for she demystifies mysticism, walking her reader through her experiences in prayer moment by moment. Unlike some spiritual athletes who kept their trade secrets to themselves, Teresa attempts to show her readers how mysticism feels. She uses metaphors to familiarize the experience: the third state of prayer, for instance, "is like the dying man with the candle in his hand, on the point of dying the death desired." She also employs rhythmic, incantational language to replicate her emotions:

> As soon as the soul has arrived thus far, it begins to lose the desire of earthly things, and no wonder; for it sees clearly that, even for a moment, this joy is not to be had on earth; that there are no riches, no dominion, no honours, no delights that can for one instant, even for the twinkling of an eye, minister such a joy; for it is a true satisfaction, and the soul sees that it really does satisfy. (*Autobiography*, chapter 14)

Despite such rhetorical flourishes, Teresa's mysticism retains a human presence. She admits that she sometimes responded inappropriately and that God was forced to correct her. "I used to think that, in order to obtain sweetness in prayer, it was necessary to hide myself in secret places, and so I scarcely dared to stir. Afterwards, I saw how little this was to the purpose; for the more I tried to distract myself, the more the Lord poured over me that sweetness and joy which seemed to me to be flowing around me, so that I could not in any way escape it." This is mysticism with candor.

Teresa also writes with candor about her life in the world. Her autobiography is frank about her failings, both as a young girl whose thoughtlessness and vanity led her into dangerous waters and as a mature woman still liable to error. She admits that she initially doubted whether requiring her Discalced nuns to stay in their convent (enclosure) was correct (though God promptly appeared and set her right, she reports). She speaks of temporary inability to pray and of sins that she was embarrassed to tell even to her confessors; she admits that she became "weary of myself, so at the time I hold myself literally in abhorrence." Without illusions about herself, this mystic becomes approachable to her readers.

Teresa also had few illusions about others. As long as I've known Teresa (and I took her for my patron when I joined the church two decades ago), I've always loved her frank appraisal of some of the religious with whom she worked. She set high standards for members of her order: "God preserve us from stupid nuns," she once proclaimed. (Try making that announcement in a hiring committee!) She was also choosy about her confessors. "It is of great consequence that the director should be prudent—I mean, of sound understanding—and a man of experience. If, in addition to this, he is a learned man, it is a very great matter," she wrote. Finding a good director was clearly a "very great matter" with her in practice, for she changed directors often—one does not have to wonder how she would respond to modern penance services where participants go to whichever priest is available. She had little patience with banal spiritual reflections: "From silly devotions,

God deliver us!" It is important to realize, though, that Teresa *was* good-humored about working with what she had. "There is always a great deal to put up with" in the conduct of new nuns, she wrote to the prioress of a Carmelite convent under her direction, who had expressed frustration. "Do what you can with her, my daughter. If she has a good soul, reflect that it is one of God's mercies."

We might say that Teresa was centered, a realist and an idealist at the same time. Any educator—anyone, for that matter—who finds himself or herself in a position where he or she seems to be the only reliably competent person in the picture, responsible for everything, would do well to follow her lead. Private time for reflection is nonnegotiable, she reminds us, no matter how important we are. Defending what we believe is desirable. Perhaps most important, however, is maintaining perspective. Teresa reminds us that leaders are allowed to smile with rueful candor at the imperfections that they see in others—and in themselves—so long as they then pick up their tools and go about their business, their heads in the clouds, perhaps, but their own feet firmly on the ground.

For Further Reading

Shirley Du Boulay, *Teresa of Ávila: An Extraordinary Life* (New York: BlueBridge, 2004).

Victoria Lincoln, *Teresa, A Woman: A Biography of Teresa of Ávila* (Albany, N.Y.: State University of New York Press, 1984).

Saint Teresa of Ávila, *The Collected Letters of St. Teresa of Ávila*, trans. Kieran Kavanaugh (Washington, DC: ICS Publications, 2001).

Saint Teresa of Ávila, *The Collected Works of Teresa of Ávila*, trans.Otilio Rodriquez and Kieran Kavanaugh (Washington DC: ICS Books, 1976).

Butler's, 4:111–21.

Oxford, 500–01.

43

St. Jude

First century ~ Palestine ~ Feast: October 28

St. Jude was one of the apostles; at the beginning of the short epistle of Jude, which comes immediately before Revelation in the *New American Bible*, he calls himself "a slave of Jesus Christ and brother of James." Almost nothing is known about Jude. Indeed, biblical scholars have considered the possibility that his letter is pseudonymous and/or that it was written in the second century, not the first. Its similarity to 2 Peter has also been noted.

According to Butler, Jude is "Judas, not the Iscariot" who asks Christ at the Last Supper why he has chosen to reveal himself to the disciples and not the world at large (John 14:22). Other sources are less certain of that identification. He is generally thought to be the brother of James the Lesser; some legends make him Christ's blood relative, the son of Cleophas and Mary Cleophas (cousin of the Virgin Mary), even a man "reported to look a lot like" Christ. The apocryphal *Gospel of Thomas* identifies Jude with Thomas, calling the figure "Jude Thomas." Jude has been credited with the ability to exorcize demons and cause pagan statues to crumble. At any rate, after Pentecost Jude preached the gospel in Persia and was martyred with Simon Thaddeus. In artistic renderings, Jude's attribute is a club, in keeping with the legend that he was killed with one.

Jude has acquired the patronage of lost causes and lost things. The *Oxford Dictionary of Saints* cites a common explanation for that attribution: "because nobody invoked him for anything" in the early centuries of the church, "since his name so closely resembled that of Judas who betrayed the Lord." Another often-cited cause is that his epistle urges the faithful to persevere in difficult circumstances.

After Jude acquired his patronage of lost causes and things, he became a popular, frequently-invoked saint, and his cult continues even today. A common novena to him goes as follows:

> To Saint Jude: Holy Saint Jude, Apostle and Martyr, great in virtue and rich in miracles, near kinsman of Jesus Christ, faithful intercessor of all who invoke your special patronage in time of need. To you I have recourse from the depths of my heart and humbly beg to whom God has given such great power to come to my assistance. Help me in my present and urgent petition, in return I promise to make your name known and cause you to be invoked. Saint Jude pray for us and all who invoke your aid. Amen.

DEMONSTRATING THE SPIRITUAL—AND PSYCHOLOGICAL—EFFICACY OF FAITH

During my Protestant childhood, St. Jude was one of the few saints whose name I knew. I recognized him because the town nearest my suburban Philadelphia home was heavily Catholic, and the classified section of the weekly local newspaper frequently included appeals to him and thanks for services rendered. *How weird and funny*, I used to think—as if a saint had to read the newspaper to find out what people were thinking! I've since learned that the notices served a publicity function, attempting to make others aware of St. Jude and to spread devotion to him. Even understanding that, however, I still smile when I see such notices in my diocesan paper—and I do often.

It makes sense to me, however, that St. Jude remains a prominent saint. He's the patron of lost articles and lost causes, after all, and we humans specialize in such things. Teachers are likely to encounter multiple occasions to invoke him every day. Some of these will be symptoms of our busy, scattered lives (Where are my car keys? Where did I park my *car*?), others of more consequence (Will Angela ever grow up enough to pay attention in class? Can't we make Marty see that his drinking is dangerous?). How nice it would be to trust that we could simply call on a specialist who could help us magically solve such problems!

That's been part of the appeal of saints for many centuries, and virtually any human problem or situation has its heavenly patron. Many dictionaries of saints index holy men and women by their principle patronages, and these indices make interesting, even entertaining reading in what they reveal about ongoing human concerns. Spiritual yellow pages, one might call them. Got a sore throat? Call Blaise. Thinking of emigrating? Frances Xavier Cabrini is your woman. Nervous about fulfilling your duties as an altar server? Tarsicius can help. It's all very charming, and very naive, one might think.

But it can also be quite efficacious. Leaving aside the question of whether St. Jude can directly lead a person to her car keys or inspire Marty with a sudden burning conviction that he must dry out, it's clear that invoking a saint has the potential at least to change the person doing the invoking. Invoking a saint focuses energy. It affirms conviction. If one believes that the saint can help, one might begin looking for signs of change. One might even begin helping change along a little bit by acting as if it is occurring. Everyone knows about the observer effect in science, that experimenters are prone to see what they expect to see. That effect definitely has implications for the teaching profession: under experimental conditions, educators consistently evaluate student work not according to the work itself but to descriptions of the students prior to the work being done—in other words, if we are told that someone is a poor student or a good student, we are much more likely to see them that way even if their work indicates otherwise. Furthermore, students who are treated as if they were strong tend to perform better, and students who are subject to lower expectations tend to lag. Research on positive visualization corroborates that people can actually improve their physical or mental performance, their reactions and relationships, if they begin to believe that they can. Our attitudes can change reality.

Throughout this book, I've been posing mentor saints as people whose lives can encourage teachers to reflect on their own experiences, who can model behavior for us in particular situations. St. Jude is a different kind of saint, famous for his after-death powers, not his this-world example—a folk saint for those whose faith is simpler and more literal, at least in the eyes of those of us who consider ourselves educated and sophisticated. I'd argue, though, that there should be room for such direct devotion in our lives, too. Though we might smile at ourselves when we say a novena or light a candle to him or to other saints whose particular help we need at a given moment, and though we might never put a thank-you notice in the classified ads, we're denying ourselves a longtime source of human comfort if we never directly invoke holy people who have gone before us. In St. Jude's particular case, if we fail to invoke him because we believe that an apparently unsolvable problem will never go away, we might be denying change itself.

For Further Reading

"Introduction" to the *Letter of Saint Jude, New American Bible.* Iowa City, IA: Catholic World Press, 1987).

www.catholic-forum.com/saints/saintj03.htm.

Butler's, 4:213–14.

Oxford, 292–93.

44

St. Charles Borromeo

1538–84 ~ Italy ~ Feast: November 4

Charles Borromeo was born in northern Italy in 1538 to an established and wealthy family. Trained in civil and canon law in Pavia, he was called to Rome as a young man by his uncle, Pope Pius IV, to be secretary of state at the Vatican. "Always clear and precise in his views, firm in his demeanor, and constant in the execution of his projects," as one biographer has remarked, he played an important role in convincing Pius to reconvene the Council of Trent, which sought to address corruption in a sixteenth-century church beleaguered by Protestantism. Under the auspices of that council, beginning in 1563 Borromeo supervised the writing of an accurate catechism, rewrote liturgical texts and music, and began enforcing clerical reform in Rome. Pope Pius IV named Borromeo archbishop of Milan but kept him in Rome performing a multitude of official functions. Eager to be true to the letter of the Council of Trent, Borromeo chafed until he was allowed to take up residence in his diocese in 1566.

When Borromeo arrived in Milan, he faced a daunting task. Milan was the largest archdiocese in Italy at the time, with more than three thousand clergy and eight hundred thousand people. Both its clergy and laity had drifted from church teaching. The selling of indulgences and ecclesiastical positions was prevalent; monasteries were "full of disorder"; many religious were "lazy, ignorant, and debauched," and some did not even understand how to properly administer the sacraments.

The city had seen no resident bishop for *eighty* years. Borromeo immediately called a synod of his bishops to inform them of the new decrees. Setting an example of personal frugality and order, Borromeo reduced his household staff, forbade his retainers to accept any presents, and sold some of his property to help feed the poor. He began preaching in churches and monasteries, combining "exhortation with intimidation." He also addressed the backsliding of laypeople, curtailing Sunday entertainments and requiring that all teachers profess the faith. He traveled around his vast archdiocese, even venturing into the mountains of Switzerland to meet his priests, though on one occasion a priest who resented his reforming zeal shut a church door against him. Always interested in religious education, Borromeo established the Confraternities of Christian Doctrine to teach religion to children, and the organization grew to include 740 schools, three thousand catechists, and forty thousand students in Sunday schools. For his work in training priests he has been called the "most active innovator of the Catholic seminary system."

Borromeo's rigor predictably made him enemies. Before Borromeo went to Milan, while he was overseeing reform in Rome, a nobleman remarked that the latter city was no longer a place to enjoy oneself or to make a fortune. "Carlo Borromeo has undertaken to remake the city from top to bottom," he said, predicting dryly that the reformer's enthusiasm "would lead him to correct the rest of the world once he has finished with Rome." Once Borromeo arrived in his own diocese, he was forced to excommunicate and imprison some Milanese nobles, including some civil authorities, for defying his new policies. Some Milanese complained to the pope about Borromeo's allegedly excessive rigor, but the archbishop was vindicated. When he ordered the reform of a wealthy and corrupt religious order, the Humiliati, foes attempted to assassinate him.

Borromeo also displayed a gentler aspect, however, and many of his people loved him. During a plague in 1576, he stayed in the city and cared for the sick, ordering that decorative church hangings be tailored into clothing for the destitute. During a famine he incurred great debts to feed more than sixty thousand people. In more ordinary times, he liked to wander the city praying with the people. He established hospitals, colleges, orphanages, and other charitable institutions.

An energetic reformer who took "always the most austere and stringent interpretation" of the dictates of the Council of Trent, Charles Borromeo was instrumental in helping reinvigorate the church during the Counter-Reformation. His work, it is said, "gave new confidence to a shaken church." He died in 1584, at age forty-six, tired from his labors. He was canonized in 1610 and is the patron saint of catechists.

BLENDING TOUGH LOVE AND PERSONAL INTEGRITY

"An austere, dedicated, humorless and uncompromising personality" is the way that a biographer—an *admiring* biographer—describes Charles Borromeo. Charged with implementing the reforms dictated by the Council of Trent, Borromeo had to be tough, and his toughness brought him into conflict with secular leaders, priests, and even the pope himself. A biographer of Philip Neri, Borromeo's contemporary and friend, makes much of the personality differences between the two, suggesting that Borromeo even tried to staunch Neri's irrepressible, attractive wackiness by urging him to greater decorum. Today, when "approachability" and "consensus building" are widely held to be desirable qualities for leaders, many people would certainly consider Borromeo's model of leadership outdated.

Those teachers and educational administrators who have had the experience of implementing unpopular reforms, however, are likely to be more empathetic. Sometimes, for the greater good of our parish or our school, we must oversee change. Our administrators or religious leaders may have seen that our organization needs to be reinvigorated and may have chosen us to translate the reforms to others. Students in catechism classes may not be receiving the information and inspiration that they need; colleagues may have become lazy and/or resentful about attending necessary training sessions, meeting with students, or preparing their classes. Curriculum requirements may be falling by the wayside.

If we supervise teachers, we will try, of course, to sway them first by cheerful encouragement that suggests optimism about their worth. But sometimes that is not enough. When our encouragement falls on deaf ears and change doesn't happen, we may find ourselves issuing ultimatums: "If you don't attend this training class, begin preparing lessons more thoroughly, use religious education time more to the purpose, etc., we'll have to replace you." When we must say such things, we will likely hear bitter criticism, may be called unreasonable, because drawing a line and demanding, say, that teachers attend a crucial training session can raise as many hackles as requiring monks to return to their cloisters. Being tough, even when necessary, can hurt the person who initiates reform.

In such situations, Borromeo can offer us crucial inspiration and some very specific advice about tough love. For the larger good of the church during a time when it was beleaguered, he knew that he had to sacrifice his own popularity. His example demonstrates that we must be brave in God's service. Ultimately, the catechists, the students we serve will thank us.

Borromeo also teaches crucial fairness. Evenhanded in his demands, he expected the same compliance with Council of Trent reforms from everyone. Bishops and priests alike had to dismiss their female relatives from their households; all schoolteachers—no exceptions—were required to make public professions of faith; every workingman who was apprehended in the street by one of the Archbishop's "fishers" on Sunday was escorted to catechism class. Borromeo reminds us that the rules must be the same for all, and that we will not succeed if we make exceptions and play favorites.

Above all, he reminds us that we must be the best embodiments of the rules we enforce. Borromeo lived as simply as he could, shocking others by his economies. At night, after he set his obligatory archbishop's regalia aside, he is said to have worn one old cassock repeatedly. He ate little on his travels, giving his portion to others. He worked harder than any priest or monk in his diocese, putting himself in harm's way repeatedly, as when he personally nursed the plague-stricken while other leaders fled the city. Most important, he prayed with an ecstasy of devotion—not only in his cathedral, but also with children in the streets before the crosses he had ordered set up there. "It was impossible . . . that the people should not be drawn to a sanctity so evident and so robust and not respond to a reform which he sought to impose on them more by example than by word," a biographer writes.

Borromeo's life reminds us teacher/administrators that we cannot be hypocrites. If we expect to reinvigorate our organization, we must model that reform in our own lives. While others may be displeased with us at first, and while we may face hard words, we must take courage and know that the larger cause for which we work is worth the effort, and the pain.

For Further Reading

John P. Kleinz, "Charles Borromeo," in *The Who's Who of Heaven: Saints for All Seasons* (Westminister, MD: Christian Classics, 1987), 136–38.

Cesare Orsenigo, *Life of St. Charles Borromeo*, trans. Rev. Rudolph Kraus (St. Louis, MO: B. Herder Book Co. 1943).

John B. Tomaro, "San Carlo Borromeo and the Implementation of the Council of Trent," in *San Carlo Borromeo: Catholic Reform and Ecclesiastical Politics in the Second Half of the Sixteenth Century,* eds. John M. Headley and John B. Tomaro (Washington: Folger Shakespeare Library, 1988), 67–84.

Butler's, 4:255–62.

Oxford, 70–71

45

St. Martin of Tours

c. 316–97 ~ Gaul ~ Feast: November 11

St. Martin of Tours was one of the most beloved saints of the Middle Ages, famous for his miracles and celebrated in folk tradition. Born in what is today Hungary to pagan parents about 316, Martin was attracted to Christianity and became a catechumen. As the son of a soldier, he was obliged to enter the Roman army and did so against his will. One night before a battle against barbarians, his commander distributed gifts to the troops, but Martin refused his, proclaiming that he was a soldier of Christ and could not fight for the emperor. Martin told his furious commander that he was willing to face the enemy unarmed to show Christ's power, and he was jailed overnight to insure his presence the next day. The barbarians surrendered before the battle took place, however, so Martin's claim was never tested.

The single most famous story told about him took place while he was a soldier. One winter night, Martin saw a beggar at the church door whom others were ignoring. Filled with pity and having no possessions but his weapons and military clothing, he cut his cloak in half and shared it with the beggar. Later, in his dreams, he saw Christ wearing half of his cloak.

Martin was finally baptized, and he was released from the army in 357. Under the patronage of St. Hilary of Poitiers, he became a solitary hermit at Ligugé, in Gaul. Soon other monks joined him, and he established the first monastery in Gaul. In 371, Martin was made Bishop of

Tours, despite his own reluctance and the disapproval of some church officials. According to Martin's biographer Sulpicious Severus, the officials complained that Martin's appearance "was contemptible. . . . A man so despicable, with dirty clothes and unkempt hair was unworthy to be a bishop." Martin was appointed anyway in recognition of his faith and character.

Martin was an unconventional bishop, widely beloved by his people and energetic in the practice of the faith. This former conscientious objector was famous for conducting a personal war on paganism. Using an ax, he wrecked pagan temples, smashed idols, and cut down sacred trees. In one legend, barbarians agreed to let Martin fell their tree if he would stand in the direction that it was leaning. He complied, making the sign of the cross as the tree started to fall on him. Suddenly, "like a spinning top," the tree reversed its course, almost crushing the pagans. "A shout went up to heaven," and thousands begged Martin to baptize them instantly. "On that day salvation came to that region," a commentator writes. In another legend, when an outraged pagan rushed at Martin, the latter bared his neck and knelt meekly. Suddenly, the assailant was "overwhelmed by the fear of God" and begged Martin for mercy. Martin is said to have cured lepers, healed those near death, and raised the dead (including a dead baby, whose resurrection occasioned another mass conversion in the countryside).

Martin promoted the establishment of rural monasteries, and he championed orthodoxy at a time when the Gnostic heresy was flourishing in Gaul, although he unsuccessfully pleaded for mercy when a Gnostic leader was about to be executed; Martin argued that the church, not civil authorities, should deal with matters of faith. Despite his eminence, he remained unkempt in his dress, incurring the disdain of his successor, Bishop Brice, whom Martin referred to as "my Judas." Once, due to Martin's disheveled appearance, a party of soldiers whom he met on the road did not recognize Martin and beat him; only after the soldiers' mules miraculously refused to move did they realize what they had done.

"It would be impossible to exaggerate the popularity enjoyed by St. Martin even in his lifetime throughout the whole of Gaul," writes Omer Englebert, and Martin became, after his death in 397, one of the most widely known saints. His fame was promoted in biographies by Sulpicius Severus, who met Martin during his lifetime and gathered stories of him afterward, and by Gregory of Tours. Martin's tomb was a major pilgrimage site during the Middle Ages. More than four thousand churches are named for him.

USING THE LONG-TERM EFFECTS OF INSTITUTIONAL FOLKLORE

Despite St. Martin's inclusion in one modern book of "neglected saints," for many centuries he was one of the most popular of Catholic saints—in some times and places, arguably the *most* popular. Martin's cult developed slowly at first because his "confrontational behavior and controversial claims had led to dissention" in Tours, but 150 years later his shrine was drawing hundreds of visitors a year, one of the four most venerated spots in Christendom. He even had two feast days (the other is on July 4). Legends made him a byword for energetic faith and episcopal care; he was also credited with extraordinary powers before and after his death: facing down demons, performing exorcisms, and the magical granting of wishes. Folk customs associated with him proliferated; in the popular mind, Martin became associated with the festival of carnival because of his eccentric, free-spirited behavior.

Many of the stories about Martin seem to be apocryphal, overlapping with traditional folk tales, and it's tempting to smile at the credulity of medieval believers who told these legends as fact. But to reject such folklore as lies is to miss considerable insight. Folklore, scholars of the genre have long insisted, embodies a culture's fundamental truths, although the events narrated in legend may not physically have taken place. Legends transmit a people's values, folklorists say; they present lessons about how one should behave and how one should not. They also embody cultural anxieties and present idealized portraits of leaders. A folklorist would insist that popular legends about figures such as Martin help transmit fundamental wisdom.

Legends about notable personalities are not just phenomena of distant bygone days—we also tell them today in all regions, sub-cultures, and institutions. As in the past, they typically serve "cautionary" and/or "regulatory" purposes, inviting us to compare our behavior to that depicted in the legends. Some legends that teachers tell involve past colleagues. Sometimes these are funny warnings against pride—remember Tim, the prophet of technology, and the PowerPoint that went crazy? Sometimes they chronicle epic misbehavior—remember Bob, who became so angry with his students that he once walked out, telling his class that he did not want them to return the next week, or ever, that he was going to fail them all? Sometimes, in contrast, they describe idealized actions that motivate us—Jane, whose kindness to catechumens inspired many of them to become kind catechists themselves.

While some of students' folklore about their teachers seems designed simply to blow off steam, their tales can also instruct us. One such legend from my student days has helped shape my own behavior for decades: the rumor of a student who ignored specifications for a paper topic offered by a usually rigid teacher. This young woman, the story went, used her paper, which was meant to be an explication of Thoreau's "Civil Disobedience," as a forum to discuss the Vietnam War. "Don't do it!" her dorm mates warned. "She *never* accepts anything that's not on the topic list. She'll flunk you!" But the student went ahead and wrote her paper—and received an A+, accompanied by warm and copious comments from our stern teacher.

None of us knew this student personally; none of us would have dared ask our teacher if this incident really happened. And none of us ever dared similarly to ignore a prompt and twist one of her assignments to our own devices. Still, knowing (we thought) that this professor had once bent her rigidness in the service of a student's serious, honest enthusiasm changed her for us, and changed the way we responded to her. We sometimes tried to expand our thinking in our papers (after we'd safely answered her questions), to take some risks, because we "knew" she liked that. Thus, our work became stronger.

That story's persistence in my memory has also made my own teaching practice stronger. Like the teacher in the story (who became my first mentor), I'm usually strict about my assignments, which I write deliberately so that students will practice specific skills or explore ideas in specific contexts. Every now and then, though, a free-spirited student will ask me if he or she can rethink an assignment, do something different with it—and, remembering the legend, I sometimes allow such transgression. In doing so, I'm acting as I believe my teacher once acted, keeping "faith with [my] dead teacher," as folklorist Henry Glassie has written on the effects of legend on behavior, "shaping [my] actions responsibly" in accordance with past practice. I'm embodying the efficacy of folklore.

Medieval believers drew on stories of Martin for guidance. His reported charity, bravery, and frankness modeled desirable conduct for everyone who heard the tales. Who can guess how many people consulted his example as they shaped their own behavior? That's actually a daunting thought for us as teachers, if we consider its implications. For, besides consulting stories about other teachers, we must remember that we in turn provide daily fodder for new stories for our colleagues and our students. Like it or not, our lives are public, and such stories will be told, legacies with their own persistence. Will we be the subject of inspirational tales or of cautionary tales, after we're gone?

For Further Reading

Raymond Van Dam, "Martin of Tours," in *Saints and Their Miracles in Late Antique Gaul* (Princeton, NJ: Princeton University Press, 1993), 13–27.

Omer Englebert, *Adventurous Saints*, trans. Donal O'Kelly (New York: P. J. Kenedy and Sons, 1956).

Sulpicius Severus, "Martin of Tours," Reprinted in *Medieval Saints: A Reader*, ed. Mary-Ann Stouck (Peterborough, Ont.: Broadview Press, 1999), 137–66.

Martin W. Walsh, "Martin of Tours: A Patron Saint of Medieval Comedy," in *Saints: Studies in Hagiography*, ed. Sandro Sticca (Binghamton, NY: Medieval & Renaissance Texts & Studies, 1996), 283–316.

E. I. Watkin, "Saint Martin of Tours," in *Neglected Saints* (New York: Sheed & Ward, 1955), 315–97.

Butler's, 4: 310–13.

Oxford, 350–52.

46

THE POWER OF

JOYFUL OPTIMISM

St. Gertrude the Great

1256–1302 ~ Germany ~ Feast: November 16

St. Gertrude the Great was a thirteenth-century scholar, writer, and mystic, one of the great religious women of the Middle Ages. She was born into a time and place of violence—Germany in 1256—yet she wrote about God's unconditional love. Gertrude's Germany was rocked by anarchy and by military conflict between the pope and the Holy Roman Emperor, between feudal lords and town leaders. The country did not have a formal ruler between 1250 and 1273. When Gertrude was still a toddler, she was given as a child oblate to the Cistercian monastery at Helfta overseen by Abbess Gertrude Hackeborn (with whom she has often been confused). No clear records have survived to indicate why the younger Gertrude came to Helfta: her parents may have died, or they may have designated her as an offering to the church. In her own writing she refers to herself as an orphan. The fact that she was made a choir nun—a woman whose primary responsibility was singing the divine office rather than manual labor—suggests that she was of noble background.

The child was a quick, articulate student who eagerly absorbed the learning for which the monastery was famous. With Mechtilde of Helfta she studied rhetoric, Latin grammar, dialectic, and the writings of the church fathers; she might also have learned music, geometry, arithmetic, and astronomy. She became a fine scholar; once she became

259

a teacher, she rewrote complicated Latin passages and prepared extracts from the fathers so that they would be accessible to beginners. Her Latin has been described as highly skilled and "strongly Latinate."

Gertrude took her vows but faced a period of drifting attention in her early twenties, a time when, as she later wrote, she made "lukewarm devotions," and "bore—[as] an empty boast—the name and habit of the religious life." When she was twenty-five, she had a vision in which a young man offered her freedom from her sorrow and guilt, telling her "do not fear." Though she saw an "endless" hedge crowned with thorns between them, in an instant he transported her effortlessly across, and she was consumed with a sense of God's unconditional, boundless love. Further visions followed; Gertrude became enthralled with the Sacred Heart of Jesus. She became convinced that God's welcoming arms were always open, proclaiming that God had reached out to her again and again though she continued to sin. "Gertrude is careful to teach us," her biographer Evangela Bossert argues, "that the work of salvation is not something that we earn; it is accomplished already. We are invited to unite with and participate in the human-divine union that already is." Sin, in this equation, is what we do that blunts our appreciation of this union and keeps us from reaching the freedom from fear that is our birthright.

Gertrude apparently did not become an abbess but spent her time in liturgical prayer, study, writing and copying, meditation, and teaching, along with some physical labor. She was in demand as a spiritual advisor. Gertrude was an advocate of learning, enhancing the monastery's library and composing several books of her own. One, a brief spiritual autobiography that details her visions, was expanded in a companion volume biography after her death, using stories from those who had known her, and became the five-part *The Herald of God's Loving-Kindess* (or *Herald of Divine Love*). Gertrude's own commentary forms Part Two of this work and was composed in 1289. Her other book is a set of spiritual exercises (the *Exercises of St. Gertrude*), a sequence of thematically arranged meditations and prayers.

After years of poor health, Gertrude died in 1302. Though her fame temporarily lapsed, Latin and French editions of her writings became popular during the sixteenth and seventeenth centuries. Among the many people influenced by her were Saints Philip Neri, Francis de Sales, and Teresa of Ávila. Although Gertrude was not formally canonized, she has appeared in dictionaries of saints since Rome approved a Liturgical Office of prayer, readings, and hymns honoring her in 1606, and Clement XII extended her feast to the whole church in 1738. In the twentieth century, scholars' interest in women mystics has made Gertrude more widely known; several English translations of her work and commentaries on her life have appeared in recent years.

TRUSTING THAT "ALL SHALL BE WELL"

"All shall be well," the choir of the Monastery of St. Gertrude in Cottonwood, Idaho, sings with great enthusiasm on Easter Sunday. "It's our favorite song," my friend Sister Michelle told me, beaming, during the first Triduum I ever spent in that beautiful, sacred place. That's fitting, for the hymn's message of comfort and joy so exactly parallels the message of the convent's patron saint that Gertrude herself might have written its text instead of its actual author, Julian of Norwich.

I like to think of that song and of Gertrude at the start of each new teaching year. Ever since I became a teacher, that day in August when the halls are suddenly full of people again has been my favorite day of the year—not excepting Christmas, my birthday, the first day of spring, or any other. I'm insufferable, I admit, buzzing around my department and announcing with a huge smile, "It's New Year's Day!" Colleagues who wish it were still summer hate me, but I can't help myself. Everything seems so clean that day, so full of possibility. I look over each new group of students, certain that I'm going to love all of them. *They have such bright eyes,* I think, *How can they not be eager to learn?* I also look at my syllabi with satisfaction, sure that I've gotten things right, this time. It's not that I believe I won't have to work, or that my students won't ever disappoint me, but I'm filled with crazy, irrational surety that my classes can't help but succeed in the term ahead.

Gertrude lived her entire life in such optimism, and hers was a great deal more solid than mine, for it was grounded in the assurance that "God shall be in all." Humans were assured of God's love, she believed, because God's love was in them from the beginning. "I shall free you and I shall deliver you, do not fear," her God says. "No embarrassment or scorn can turn [God] aside or stop [God] from acting unwearyingly to draw us to [God's] joy."

Gertrude's radical message of innate unity with God is not only uplifting in a theological way; it also makes sense in terms of psychology. Gertrude knew that if we can allow ourselves to trust, we can bring a confidence to our work that inspires others to confidence. She found her own confidence flowering in works of charity, in scholarship, and in writing that invited many generations of readers to "take delight in the sweetness of [God's] love." She helped inspire other saints by the example of her unshakable faith, even in difficult times.

Few teachers are saints, however, and though we might admire Gertrude, most of us find it difficult to maintain our optimism as the school year progresses—even perennially optimistic me. Too soon the honeymoon is over, and students begin to grumble and/or to have difficulties with the material, our teaching style, or their own motivations. Too soon we find that our beautiful lesson plans aren't working, or that students do not perform as we expected them to. We may begin to doubt our own capacity to teach or these particular students' capacity to learn. When that starts to happen, it's easy for everyone's attitudes to sag. We become grumpy as we begin to doubt; we get on each other's nerves and become dissatisfied with ourselves. We begin to fail because we believe that we will fail.

If we are able to invoke Gertrude as the school year continues, remembering her unshakable confidence in the ultimate rightness of things under a loving God, how different our work could be! Like Gertrude, we could approach our tasks with diligent confidence rather than imagining short-term problems to be the beginning of the end. We would believe, with Gertrude, that God means for us all to share his joy. With the eyes of this worldview, student difficulties would become temporary setbacks along the way to the success in which we have continued trust. Our own less-than-stellar performances would become problems capable of being solved. No panic in this scenario, no guilt, no fear. Just trust that God will help us "tender little shoots," as Gertrude puts it, teachers and students alike, to "blossom." We can't help ourselves, Gertrude says. We might as well get over our doubt, understanding that we are cradled by God's love.

If we were able to remember Gertrude every morning, how different our lives would be! Every morning would indeed be New Year's Day, and, like Gertrude, we would become joyful voices assuring others that, in the sweetness of God's love, all *will* ultimately be well, whatever this particular day might bring.

For Further Reading

Alexandra Barratt, "Introduction," in *Saint Gertrude the Great, The Herald of God's Loving-Kindness* (*Books 1–2*) (Kalamazoo, MI: Cistercian Publications, 1991).

Evangela Bossert, *Gertrude of Helfta: Companion for the Millennium* (Cottonwood, ID: Twin Towers, 1999).

Mary Jeremy Finnegan, *The Women of Helfta: Scholars and Mystics* (Athens, GA: University of Georgia Press, 1991).

Gertrude the Great of Helfta, *The Exercises of Saint Gertrude: Introduction, Commentary, and Translation by a Benedictine Nun of Regina Laudis* (Westminster, MD: The Newman Press, 1956).

Saint Gertrude the Great, *The Herald of Divine Love (Books 1–3)*, trans. and ed. Margaret Winkworth (New York: Paulist Press, 1993).

Maximilian Marnau, "Introduction," in *The Herald of Divine Love (Books 1–3)*, trans. and ed. Margaret Winkworth (New York: Paulist Press, 1993), 5–46.

Butler's, 4:351–53.

Oxford, 219.

47

THE LOST BATTLE

Blessed Miguel Pro

1891–1927 - Mexico - Feast: November 23

B lessed Miguel Pro, a modern Mexican martyr, was born in 1891 into a central Mexico mining engineer's family that valued social justice. A happy child given more to practical joking than to study, he worked in his father's office until he was eighteen, when he left home to join the Jesuits. Since the Mexican government was hostile toward the Catholic Church, however, and novices were forbidden to study in the country after 1914, Pro had to travel to the United States, Spain, and Belgium for his religious formation. He became a priest in Europe in 1925.

By then the "archpersecutor" Plutarco Elías Calles had assumed power in Mexico; churches were being destroyed, and the teaching of religion was forbidden. Though Pro loved studying theology, he knew that he must go home. He was also suffering from stomach trouble, and his superiors believed that familiar food would alleviate his condition. Somehow, even though his passport identified him as a priest and thus technically prohibited him from entering Mexico, Miguel was able to return in 1926 and began serving in Mexico City. Within a month of his arrival, the government banned all public worship and began arresting priests. An armed uprising of protest, the Cristero Rebellion, began in response, and violence escalated under a regime that sanctioned "one of the most serious and systematic violations of basic human rights of the century," according to historian Robert Royal. The dictator Calles was to brag that he personally executed fifty priests. Elderly people were shot for attending Mass; villagers were murdered by the thousands.

Through all of this disruption, Miguel Pro worked clandestinely. Traveling from parish to parish, he would begin hearing confessions at 5:00 a.m. and continue for fourteen hours with few breaks. He established "communion stations" where hundreds of people each week participated in the Eucharist. He also provided food for starving families. Pro was famous for his daring and his disguises. He posed as a manual laborer, a ladies' man, a beggar—even a police officer, so that he could hear confessions in jails. His narrow escapes were legendary, including one during which he jumped from a moving taxi to escape capture. His code name was *Barreterillo*, the "little miner," testifying to his continued empathy with the working class.

During the elections of November 1927, insurgents threw a bomb into a car in which Álvaro Obregón, a Calles crony, was riding, and police discovered that the assassin's car had once belonged to Miguel Pro's brother. Authorities found bomb-making materials in a house where Pro sometimes stayed, and an informer betrayed him. Although Miguel Pro and his brother both had alibis, they went to jail. Calles decided to execute Pro in front of television cameras and journalists, hoping that the world would witness a degraded priest begging for his life. Pro maintained quiet dignity, however, simply asking for time to pray; he forgave a police officer who asked his pardon. Then he spread his arms in the form of a cross and proclaimed in a loud, clear voice, but without great drama, "Viva Cristo Rey"—"Long live Christ the King"—as he was shot by a firing squad.

Though public demonstrations were forbidden, five hundred cars formed Pro's funeral procession, and tens of thousands of people gathered in the streets. "Pro won the immediate public relations contest," Royal declares. Conditions did not improve for a long time, however; the United States backed Calles, and hundreds of thousands of people were murdered over the next few decades. Only in the 1990s did the church regain its status in Mexico, bolstered by "the public witness of the martyrs and the private fidelity of many millions under harsh conditions." One of the most beloved of those martyrs, Miguel Pro, was beatified by Pope John Paul II on September 25, 1988.

FINDING POWER IN DIGNITY AND TRUST

It's been a long time since a teacher in the United States suffered literal martyrdom as did Miguel Pro (perhaps a brave integrationist?). Still, though most of us can't imagine ourselves before a firing squad, teachers take dangerous stands every day. We argue for new curricula, new textbooks, new procedures, and new faculty, when doing so shakes up our organizations and brands us as unrealistic or as troublemakers. We argue for justice for students whom the system oppresses, defending individual students or programs that serve them before our school boards or state legislatures. We argue for higher standards, or for mercy. Now and then, we even win.

More often, though, we lose. Occasionally teachers lose jobs over such things; more often we just lose our battles. While this kind of experience is a long way from what Miguel Pro suffered, it is painful nevertheless, for when one believes deeply in a cause, its failure can seem like a kind of death, and it is tempting to feel that our defeat betrays the young people we serve.

Teachers face the death of their hopes in all kinds of educational settings, as have three of my friends this past year. One, a director of religious education, found a new catechetical curriculum that she believed would much improve her parish's work with teenagers. When she presented it to her teachers, though, she met a wall of inertia. They liked the old one, they said. It was working fine. Changing would be a lot of trouble. And so, the parish still has the "good enough" curriculum. Another friend, who teaches third grade in a Catholic elementary school, argued for clemency for one of her students, a troubled boy who had broken the rules so often that he faced expulsion. She lost, too, her principal suggesting with a smile that she was "too kind," as usual, not facing the facts. Another friend, chair of a university department that trains school administrators, suggested to her faculty that, since so many doctoral students were failing their comprehensive exams, the solution was not to make the exam easier, but to make classes more substantive and rigorous. She is no longer chair.

It's happened to all of us, or will, if we keep teaching. We know we're right, but we're overruled. The bureaucracy around us, or our supervisors, or our colleagues believe we're unrealistic, too gentle or too idealistic or too demanding—or just plain wrong. The worst times are when we lose big public battles, after we've spoken our piece in a meeting, when everyone knows we've lost. It's tempting, at those times, to make our disappointment vividly public. We might tell the people who thwarted us what we think of them (or tell others, loudly enough to be overheard); we might sulk; we might nurse our grievance (sometimes for years) and bring it up as an I-told-you-so whenever we get the opportunity. Sometimes, we might even appeal to higher-ups, immersing our teaching community in extended, bitter controversy.

The most amazing thing about Miguel Pro, in this context, is how he died. He displayed such dignity and such peace. His work was over, and he knew it; the people who relied on him would now be without a priest. The men who had forbidden worship, the bad guys, had won. Calles was foolish to think that Pro would beg for mercy. But, before those television cameras, Pro might have made a scathing speech, adopting the level of invective his enemies used. Instead, he simply prayed and surrendered himself, proclaiming "Long live Christ the King."

He knew that he was right. But he let his life—and death—speak, trusting that Christ the King would indeed live long, long enough to see the dictatorship overruled and the right to worship restored. His death immediately contributed to that progress. "Far from being a pro-paganda triumph for the government, the photographs of Pro's execution became objects of Catholic devotion in Mexico and a government embarrassment throughout the world," writes Robert Royal. Pro's confident death demonstrated the depth of his faith, and it inspired others, although the seeds that he had sown took a long time to blossom.

Pro's martyrdom can inspire teachers, too, as we face our little daily deaths. His life does *not* instruct us to capitulate to injustice; indeed, his fight *was* his life. He can model bravery for us, reminding us to use all of our resources of inventiveness, energy, and undaunted good cheer as we work for what we believe is right. His life also demonstrates, however, that our conduct in loss can say as much as our position. If what we were defending *is* really right, is life-giving, we need to be true to its spirit and be life-giving, too. Rather than poisoning our organization—and our own hearts—with complaint, we must show others what it means to be a person of integrity. It's never easy to go to work the day after a loss; it's even harder to take a deep breath and let the resentment go. But that is what we must do, sometimes, when we are truly right, turning our faces in prayer to the future, forgiving those who trespassed against us. Like Miguel Pro, we must be confident that God's will *will* be done . . . though maybe not by us alone, and maybe not right now.

For Further Reading

Ann Ball, *Faces of Holiness: Modern Saints in Photos and Words* (Huntington, IN: Our Sunday Visitor, 1998).

Gerald F. Muller, *With Life and Laughter: The Life of Father Miguel Augustin Pro* (Boston: Pauline Books & Media, 1996).

Robert Royal, *The Catholic Martyrs of the Twentieth Century: A Comprehensive World History* (New York: Crossroad, 2000).

48

St. Catherine of Alexandria

Fourth century - North Africa - Feast: November 25 (traditionally)

St. Catherine of Alexandria is said to have lived and been martyred in the fourth century, but her cult became prominent only several hundred years later. She was a wealthy, beautiful, and well educated young woman who discovered Christianity during her philosophical studies. After a vision of the Madonna and Child, Catherine embraced the new faith, and she went to the Emperor Maxentius to protest his persecution of Christians. Maxentius summoned fifty philosophers to refute her charges against his gods, but Catherine so thoroughly answered the philosophers that she converted many of them, at which point a frustrated Maxentius put them to death.

The emperor then proposed to Catherine, hoping to shake her resolve, but she declared herself a bride of Christ and spurned his offer. She was beaten and thrown into prison. While Maxentius was away inspecting a military encampment, Catherine spoke to his wife and an officer, and converted them—along with two hundred prison guards. Upon the emperor's return, Catherine was strapped to a wheel for torture, but the wheel broke, killing bystanders. She was finally beheaded, and milk rather than blood is said to have flowed from her neck.

Catherine's relics were supposed to have been transported to the large monastery on Mount Sinai in the eighth or ninth century by "angels" (or monks, who at that time were sometimes called angels). She was a very popular saint with Crusaders; her story is told in *The*

Golden Legend, and she has been a frequent subject of artists. Many medieval churches were dedicated to her. She is the patron of students (especially female students), philosophers, preachers, nurses, and those who work with wheels.

OVERCOMING SILENCE

One of my favorite moments in Handel's *Messiah* comes when the contralto soloist sings the aria "Oh Thou That Tellest Good Tidings to Zion." "Lift up thy voice with strength, lift it up, be not afraid!" she proclaims as the notes literally lift. I've always considered that a delightfully self-reflexive moment, as the soloist seems to give *herself* courage for her performance.

That might be Catherine of Alexandria's theme song. She certainly wasn't afraid to speak up. Debate fifty philosophers? No problem. Change the mind of the emperor's wife? Certainly. Convert two hundred hardened prison guards? Sure. No wonder Maxentius cut off her head. It must have seemed like the only way to stop her fervent, silver tongue.

A decade ago, it was the fashion in composition studies to talk about giving students "voice." Our job, theorists said, was to help students understand that they had something distinctive to say, and to help them discover what that might be by a great deal of explorative writing. I've never been completely in love with this theory. I believe that some of its practitioners ignore craft in the service of a vague notion of sincerity; others force every student to reinvent the wheel (forgive the Catherine pun) by not teaching organizational strategies, since such patterns are supposed to limit students' creative freedom. And yet I've had to concede that the "voice" philosophy has a good deal of relevance for a teacher of any topic. Whether we're teaching writing or religious education, history or science, we all know that our students learn best when they can articulate their own perspectives on subject matter. Articulating can literally *be* learning. The very act of putting ideas into words forces students to make choices in phrasing, and those choices bring students up against shades of meaning. As students frame, discuss, and debate ideas, they discover what they think. They make the concepts theirs.

This ideal of an engaged, vocal classroom isn't always met in practice, though, as all teachers know. We've encountered quiet students, passive groups of students, and groups of students who are quiet on particular days. There they sit, staring back at us, waiting to be fed the day's content. They do not volunteer to answer our questions, and, when we call on them, they may answer in monosyllables. They have no questions of their own. They're incredibly frustrating. Allowing such silence to continue sets a dangerous precedent, for once a class gets a teacher to accept that the teacher will do most of the talking, that pattern becomes increasingly difficult to break. Some days, however, it can seem as if we have no choice.

When silence threatens to take over our classrooms, Catherine is a good saint to remember, for she reminds us of the articulate possibilities of youth. She was eighteen when she spoke up and converted the philosophers, the emperor's wife, and the soldiers. Unlike our students, who keep silent because they fear to be wrong, because they don't understand the terms of the discussion, because they haven't prepared, or simply because speaking can be hard work, Catherine was energetic and confident. She was so confident, actually, that she accidentally initiated her own persecution when she sought out Maxentius to make a complaint. Catherine knew that learning involved more than merely taking in knowledge. Learning also had to do with bringing ideas into the world, forming them into vocal shapes distinctive with her own understanding.

Catherine challenges us to help our students unlock their own expressive potential. That might mean ascertaining why students are passive. Is the material too hard or too easy? Are they unprepared? Have we discouraged discussion somehow? Once we've corrected what needs to be corrected, however, if students still abstain because of reticence or laziness, Catherine's example insists that we must actively foster discussion. True, that work can consume a lot of planning time and classroom energy. We have to make sure that students have something to say, and that might mean inventing warm-up exercises and study questions and holding our students accountable for them. In class, we have to draw students into discussion. We might institute inclusive methods, such as working up and down the rows with easy, open questions, asking every student to give input. We might meet in reassuring conferences with shy students. We might need to change our teaching style, consciously blocking a tendency to snap back corrections or to coach students to say exactly what we want them to say. We must establish an atmosphere where thinking aloud is encouraged and where students are praised for taking chances, for having opinions.

Whatever we do, we can't take silence for an answer. We must undertake this work of encouraging students to express themselves aloud, difficult as it may be, because it has ramifications that go well beyond our classrooms. We're offering our students nothing less than self-respect. "Your voice matters," we're telling them implicitly when we assume that they will speak. "Your birthright as a human being is to have opinions that might change the world," we show them, every time we ask their opinion. The marvelous thing is that they *will* claim this birthright after a while, if we continue to insist that they speak up, for discussion fosters discussion just as silence fosters silence. We'll be able to watch them grow into people who believe that they have a right to be heard and who take that assurance with them after they leave our classrooms. What a gift for them—and for us!

As a young woman, Catherine was not expected to speak out, and yet she did, with astounding results. Her story reminds us that a young person can have a great deal to say; a young person can even be a leader in forming public opinion. But only if someone insists that the young person in question learns what his or her own voice sounds like. In lieu of a vision of the Virgin Mary, that someone is likely to be a teacher.

For Further Reading

Jacobus de Voragine, *The Golden Legend: Readings on the Saints*, trans. William Granger Ryan (Princeton, NJ: Princeton University Press, 1993), 334–41.

Butler's, 4:420–21.

Oxford, 95–96.

49

WHEN EVERYTHING CLICKS

Blessed Mary Kevin

1875–1957 ~ Ireland, England, Africa
Feast: December 3 (celebrated in Africa)

Mother Mary Kevin was born Teresa Kearney in County Wicklow, Ireland, in 1875. Her mother, widowed before Teresa was born, died when the girl was ten years old, and Teresa went to live with her beloved, devout grandmother. At fourteen, Teresa became a teacher for the Sisters of Mercy at Rathdrum. Just three years later, though, her grandmother died also, and Teresa found herself searching for direction at a new school in Essex. Teresa became engaged to a Dublin bank clerk but canceled her wedding after she dreamed for three nights of "a terrifying country and a dark people who needed her help." Looking into her heart and working with her spiritual director, Teresa decided to apply to the Franciscan Sisters of St. Mary's Abbey, Mill Hill, London, whose mission was working with people of African descent. In 1889 she took her vows as Sister Mary Kevin and began working as a teacher and nurse, adopting as her motto "For Thee, Lord."

In 1902, a bishop who was also a Mill Hill brother asked for nuns to support missions in Africa. African women especially were in great need, he reported; infant mortality was high. Answering the call, Sister Mary Kevin and five other women left for Uganda on December 3, 1902, and arrived five weeks later. They were met near Nsambya by "a tumultuous welcoming throng with jungle drums, pipes, and horns," which escorted them the last seven miles to their earthen-floor church and three-room convent decorated with golden flowers.

Despite the hearty welcome, conditions were rough at the mission. Water was miles away; the kitchen was a mud hut; insects (including malarial mosquitoes), snakes, and rats bothered the missionary nuns. They had no money. Still, the sisters persevered, with Sister Mary Kevin displaying particular energy and cheerfulness. When the sister who had been in charge stepped down, Sister Mary Kevin became the head of the mission. "Let us make the good God our banker," she proclaimed. Working with available resources, Mother Mary Kevin used the sandy ground for a blackboard, writing words in the sand so that her pupils could learn to read. She established a clinic to treat the sick and began to train African women as nurses. As time passed and the work of the mission prospered, Mother Mary Kevin also supervised the founding of secondary schools, a teacher training college, a formal hospital, home economics centers, and two leprosy clinics. Educating and empowering African women was one of the mission's primary goals, and Mother Mary Kevin taught the first East African women who served in the legislature, who earned their B.S. degrees, and who became doctors.

In 1923 she founded the Little Sisters of St. Francis, an African order. To insure a supply of British sisters to support this mission, Mother Mary Kevin established a "Uganda Novitiate" in Yorkshire in 1928, then a separate new congregation, the Franciscan Missionary Sisters for Africa, in 1952. Mother Mary Kevin served as its mother superior for several years, establishing new missions across Africa when she was in her late seventies, then "retired" to work as superior of a convent in Boston, where she enthusiastically raised funds for African missionary work. The American Cardinal Cushing called her "the greatest missionary nun I have ever met." She died peacefully in her sleep in October of 1957.

Though her body was flown to Ireland for burial, the Ugandans whom she had served insisted that she be brought "home" and quickly raised the expense money for transportation. Their wish was granted, and, on December 3, 1957, Mother Mary Kevin was laid to rest in her chapel at Nkokonjeru, fifty-five years to the day that she had set out for Uganda. There exists a memorial to her that is much greater than her headstone, however. As one biographer put it: "The African people have raised their own monument to Mother Kevin, the identification of great good of any kind with their Mama Kevina. A hospital, a school, any charitable institution, is a kevin or a kevina. To do a kevina is to perform some act of great generosity." During World War II, Ugandan soldiers even called the airplanes that dropped food to the troops in Burma *Mama Kevinas.*

Mother Mary Kevin was beatified on February 23, 1968. Her order, now more than five hundred strong, still carries out her goal: "to help empower the women and girls of Africa by offering health care, education, and developmental skills."

Cultivating Gratitude and Joy

So many saints faced such great discouragement at the start of their missionary work: hostile communities that did not want them, persecuting authorities, climates of fear and distrust. How delightful it is, then, to imagine the young Sister Mary Kevin and her companions coming upon a throng of laughing, singing, celebrating Ugandans who welcomed them with loud music and much gratitude. They must have been frightened at first, these Irish girls, by all the noise and strange harmony, but they would soon have realized that this parade was one of openhanded jubilation for their coming. No wonder, then, that despite the hardships—the lack of bread, the long walks for water, the mosquitoes and chiggers, the heat, the disease and poverty—Sister Mary Kevin embraced her work with so much energy. She had been bereft and drifting in Ireland; now she saw people who needed her, and who knew they needed her. The leader and her flock adored each other immediately.

Sometimes that will happen to us, too, as teachers. One adult catechetical teacher I know still talks about a group she led a few years ago that was so eager to discuss, so full of questions, that they asked her to extend their sessions, thanked her after every class, and still send her cards for Easter and her birthday. She's never taught better, she says, yet "teaching them was so easy. They were so hungry to learn." The memory of two students, in particular, warms her. One was a single mother of three, about thirty-five years old, who had been living a hard life with methamphetamines and incidental jobs and men, until a check-fraud charge landed her in jail. There, she met my friend the catechist, who was serving as a prison minister. After the former addict was released from jail, she cleaned up her life, found a real job, and began investigating Catholicism in this catechist's class. "Okay, God helped me listen," this student insists to my friend. "But you're the angel who showed me the way." This young woman always thought about the material ahead of time (sometimes even reading beyond the textbook) and brought questions that sparked lively discussion.

The other standout catechumen was a boy in his early twenties with Down syndrome. My friend admits that she was a little afraid of him at first, despite his gentleness, for she wondered whether he would have the patience to concentrate without frustration. He, too, threw himself into the class, and his most notable contribution was linking ideas to real-life situations, especially in ways that made others laugh. He'd always hug her, before and after every class, and his enthusiasm for learning was contagious.

Every teacher can remember times when teaching was similarly rewarding, joyful and seemingly effortless. Sometimes, as with my friend and Mother Mary Kevin, we find that the apparently toughest assignments can lead to the greatest rewards. The students whom others have neglected, whether for their backgrounds, level of previous learning, capacity, or reputations, are likely to be the most hungry for what we have to give. They, in turn, will feed our energy, make us better and happier teachers, more fulfilled than we have ever dreamed of being. Sometimes, though, even regular classes take off. We like the students on sight, and they like us. We work hard together, yet that work is a joy. These students tell everyone who will listen how wonderful our class is—even puzzled former students who did not find us quite so inspiring—and we sing their praises. We're all sorry when the class ends.

Blessed Mother Mary Kevin is a saint for such glorious intervals in our professional lives. We may not become bywords for goodness; we're almost certainly not going to be blessed with equally enthusiastic students the next term. Still, we need to let ourselves take unabashed pleasure in the times when life in a classroom soars. We must not sully these wonderful classes with false modesty or protestations that this is just an accident. Instead, we need to relax and enjoy the interval, quietly assuring ourselves that we've earned this through our hard work.

While we are taking deserved pride in our success, though, we need also to remember to give thanks to God for these shining students. Let us remember, too, that the best gratitude is *active* gratitude. Mother Mary Kevin knew that success creates momentum, and she went to work with untiring energy, riding the crest of her faith. We, too, when our professional lives are at their best, should try to multiply the goodness that we do, filling all of those baskets with an improbable wealth of loaves and fish, trusting in the power that moves us to be God's hands, beyond our former expectations.

For Further Reading

Mary Ryan D'Arcy, *The Saints of Ireland: A Chronological Account of the Lives and Works of Ireland's Saints and Missionaries at Home and Abroad* (St. Paul, MN: Irish American Cultural Institute, 1974), 225–26.

The Franciscan Missionary Sisters for Africa. http://fmsa.net/history.htm.

Sister M. Louis, *Love is the Answer: The Story of Mother Kevin* (Paterson, NJ: St. Anthony's Guild, 1964).

50

St. Lucy

c. 283–304 ~ Sicily ~ Feast: December 13

Very few records of Lucy's life exist, but she was among the most popular saints of the Middle Ages. Supposed to have lived in Syracuse, on the island of Sicily, she was born around 283 and martyred during Diocletian's persecutions in 304. Lucy's Roman father died, leaving her mother, Eutychia, with a substantial fortune. Though the family was not Christian and her mother had betrothed her to a young pagan man, Lucy took a secret vow to remain a virgin and live a life of poverty dedicated to God. Only after her mother was healed of a long illness at the shrine of St. Agatha, to which she had gone at Lucy's insistence, did Lucy dare to reveal her vow. Lucy then convinced her mother, after some resistance, to give their fortune to the poor.

When Lucy's betrothed learned that she was determined to remain a Christian virgin, he was outraged, both at the loss of Lucy and of her fortune. He denounced her as a Christian to the governor of Sicily, who ordered Lucy to sacrifice to pagan gods. When she refused, he asked her derisively if she were a god. Lucy declared that the Holy Ghost dwelt in her. Then the governor ordered her to be taken to a brothel, saying that the Holy Ghost would desert her soon enough when she was sullied. Lucy replied that, with her will uncompromised, she would still be pure. When soldiers tried to drag Lucy away, they found that she was immovable, standing "as if a mountain." Ropes could not budge her; magicians could not move her; even oxen could not drag her. The consul then had her sprinkled with pitch and oil and set afire, but she did not burn. "Furiously upset," the governor ordered Lucy's throat cut, and this wound eventually killed her. Lucy is supposed to have lost her eyes during these proceedings; some accounts say that they were put out during her torture, others that she maimed them to make herself less attractive and maintain her virginity. Butler notes that "in either case they were miraculously restored to her, more beautiful than before."

Some versions of the story say that, during her trial, Lucy foresaw that the governor was about to be relieved of his office, and this prophesy came true before she died, when he was led away to be killed, victim of a change in the Roman government and his own revealed corruption. Lucy herself lived to receive last rites. According to *The Golden Legend*, she lingered, testifying to God's power "as long as she wanted . . . to free the faithful from the fear of suffering," even though her entrails flowed out.

While Lucy's legend began as part of the literature supporting St. Agatha's cult, by the fifth century she was very popular in her own right. Both Latin and Greek texts of her life existed within a few centuries of her death, and she is one of the few women mentioned in the *Canon of St. Gregory I* (540–604). She was included in Bede's eighth-century martyrolgy. By 1100, she had been mentioned in at least forty-three litanies and twenty-one calendars; two pre-1700 English churches are dedicated to her. She is often portrayed as carrying her eyes on a platter.

St. Lucy's feast day, which fell on the winter solstice during the old calendar, was traditionally a festival to celebrate the year's turn to increasing light. The festival was particularly popular in northern countries and is kept in some places to this day. In Sweden, Lucy's day is "Little Yule," a feast of lights commemorating Lucy's association with eyes. Traditionally, one of the daughters of the household rises very early (in old times, at first cock-crow, well before dawn), dresses in white, and, wearing a crown of lighted candles, awakens her parents and others with coffee and food. She also carries food to household animals and later presides at a special breakfast in a well-lit room. Schools are brightly lit that day, also. In some smaller parishes, a girl is chosen to go to all of the homes and barns, dressed in white with a red sash and crowned with candles. This custom reveals the festival's accommodation of pagan solstice rites, argues Christina Hole, for Lucy is accompanied by a group of attendants, including masked demons and trolls, who represent winter "overcome and led captive by the power of the reviving sun." In Sicily, bonfires are lit. In central Europe, the night before Lucy's festival is regarded as the "true New Year's Day of nature," a time for seeing into the future.

REMEMBERING THE SPIRITUAL DIGNITY OF CHILDREN

When one is surrounded by young people all day, as teachers are, it is easy to begin to see them as ordinary. Teachers are confronted with children's squabbles and adolescents' sullenness every day; they face students' intellectual and spiritual laziness. Lucy's story might even make us grin, if we see how Fra Angelico depicted it: in his painting, Lucy stands stubbornly firm, her jaw set, defying oxen to drag her away. I must admit that, when I first encountered this image in a book of reproductions, I said aloud to myself the name of one of my own students. "I've seen that before," I murmured, shaking my head.

There are so many of them, these children in our classes and schools, and there will be more, with different faces, next year, and the year after that. We seem to have an inexhaustible supply of children, especially in those slack, mid-year times when we're tired of our students and they're tired of us and the next break is months away.

In such moods, it's easy to forget the essential sacredness of young people and the symbolism they have carried in so many cultures. Our culture celebrates them, all right, but not often in ways that evoke the sacred. Every day, we see children's images selling things; every day, advertisements urge us to indulge our children as little princes and princesses. Child beauty contests, talent shows, and athletic competitions ("endless soccer," as one mother I know calls it) celebrate their achievements. Sentimental movies and television programs sometimes depict children as helping their parents stop and smell the roses, but that's about as thoughtful as we usually become in considering children's significance.

"St. Lucy's presence drives out evil spirits and misfortunes; her candles typify the returning light of spring; her food and coffee are symbols of new life in which humans and animals must share," writes Christina Hole. If the girl playing Lucy omitted a village house during her rounds, that was considered bad luck for all of the coming year—serious bad luck, not pretend bad luck. The child playing Lucy, in this tradition, became sacred. An embodiment of fundamental truths, she participated in creating belief in renewal for those around her. Adults would certainly look at that child, and others, differently after St. Lucy's day. Such moments must also have been resonant symbols for the children involved, reminding them that they were not just small adults, but presences that could inspire those around them to new hope. Bringing the light in—what a marvelous responsibility!

Teachers today should not overlook the potential of Lucy's festival as an occasion to see children with new eyes, to remember that they can inspire adults and embody fundamental truths, as she did. Young as she was—perhaps *because* she was young, idealistic, even stubborn—Lucy not only stood fast in her faith, but also willed herself to live until others could be sustained by her example. Remembering Lucy, we might vow to remind our students that children have mattered in the past in ways far beyond those our culture trumpets, that they have the power to influence the larger human community. We want them to have easy, happy childhoods, not to take on adult responsibilities too early. But childhood is not a frivolous stage in a person's life, and children are not negligible people. They can inspire their parents; they can sustain hope in times of trouble; they can remind those around them what idealism looks like. They can be people of great courage.

To help our students share in the dignity and the wholesome power that children in other cultures have claimed, we might, at this Christmas season and at other times, invite them to participate in rituals such as St. Lucy's day, being sure to explain the symbolism of their involvement. Children in the traditional age range of "Lucia Queens" or "Lucia Brides" are surprisingly eager for such celebrations of the sacred. I imagine that, like me, you've seen the littlest altar servers standing wide-eyed; the tiny kindergarten Marys solemn in their blue dresses. Sometimes children even manufacture rituals themselves: one Christmas Eve, I caught a friend's five-year-old standing in a candlelit hallway, looking out at the stars, self-crowned by strands of tinsel in her hair.

The Catholic tradition includes many opportunities for children to be involved in rituals; teachers of catechism classes and parochial school classes might directly invite families to keep saints' days whose traditional festivals involve children as symbols of new hope. Even for non-Catholics, though, Lucy's day has an archetypal enough message that it can be widely appealing—in fact, Unitarian friends of mine had their daughter dress as Lucy when she was young.

Our children deserve such reassurances of who they are, and so do teachers. Especially in dark December days, our spirits can soar if we remember that these "ordinary" children whom we nurture are in fact bright—and sacred—sparks of possibility.

For Further Reading

Leslie A. Donovan, "Lucy," in *Women Saints Lives in Old English Prose* (Rochester, NY: D.S. Brewer, 2000), 91–95.

Christina Hole, *Saints in Folklore* (New York: M. Barrows, 1965), 122–27.

Eliza Allen Starr, *Patron Saints* (Baltimore: John B. Piet and Co., 1983), 365–71.

Jacobus de Voragine, *The Golden Legend: Readings on the Saints*, trans. William Granger Ryan (Princeton, NJ: Princeton University Press, 1993), 334–41.

Butler's, 4:548–49.

Oxford, 328.

51

When the Plan Changes

St. Frances Xavier Cabrini

1850–1917 ~ Italy, USA, South America ~ Feast: December 22

F rances Xavier Cabrini is the patron of immigrants. She was born in northern Italy in 1850, the youngest of thirteen children of a prosperous, religious family. As a child, she dreamed of being a missionary to China, and she dressed her dolls as nuns and floated them down streams in boats to mimic the journey to the Orient. She also gave up sweets, proclaiming that there were no sweets in China, "so she'd better get used to it." Trained as a teacher, she applied to a religious community but was turned down on account of poor health; she applied to another and again was rejected.

In 1874, her parish priest recognized her capabilities and assigned her to help in an orphanage that was being mismanaged. Although Cabrini's efforts at reform were opposed by the women in charge, she was determined to put the institution on a stronger footing and believed that directing it under the auspices of a religious order was the answer. She took vows along with seven other women she had recruited in the effort. When it became clear that even her work was not going to solve the problems at the orphanage, the bishop invited her to found an order of missionary sisters. With joy, Cabrini drew up orders and with her companions established the Missionary Sisters of the Sacred Heart. Within a few years the new order was overseeing multiple daughter houses, including several in Rome, along with schools and children's homes.

Though her work in Italy was expanding, Cabrini longed to become a missionary herself. In keeping with her lifelong dreams (and the surname she had taken because of her admiration for the great Jesuit missionary to China, Francis Xavier), she requested assignment to China. Instead, she was invited to go to the United States. The bishop of Piacenza was behind this call, for he was deeply concerned about the plight of Italian immigrants in the United States. When he asked Cabrini to consider serving in the United States, however, she refused, still insisting that her mission lay in China. Then the archbishop of New York, Michael Corrigan, sent a formal invitation noting that the city had received a pledge of $5,000 from a private donor to construct a home for Italian orphans, but that no religious were available to staff such a facility. Italian immigrants in New York badly needed the church's help, he wrote. Few of the fifty thousand Italians in the city ever attended Mass, and they lived with poverty and discrimination. "We are like mere animals. We live and die without priests, without teachers, without doctors," he quoted one as saying.

Cabrini refused again, insisting that she would go to China. Then, after a dream, she agreed to consult Pope Leo XIII, who said, "Not to the East, but to the West." Finally convinced, she traveled to America with six of her sisters, landing in New York in 1889. The nuns faced initial discouragement. After a rainy landing, when they had to shelter for the night in a cellar full of bedbugs, Archbishop Corrigan met them and said that the money promised for the home had been withdrawn. He needed priests, not nuns, he said, and they had better get back on the ship and go home. Undaunted, Cabrini insisted, "I have a letter from the Pope!" and stayed in New York. Soon Cabrini made friends with the wealthy Italian woman who had promised the money for the orphanage and learned that a disagreement over the site was all that had halted the project. With Cabrini's mediation, a modest orphanage soon opened as the Asylum of the Angels, and within a year the facility was housed in a larger building on the Hudson River.

As the Missionary Sisters' work prospered in New York, Cabrini extended the order's reach nationally and internationally. Cabrini visited New Orleans, where Italians had been lynched, and began a foundation; she established an orphanage in Nicaragua. Over the years, she came to oversee daughter houses across the United States, from Seattle to Denver to Chicago to Pittsburgh, along with foundations in South America and Europe. She was a tireless traveler, voyaging across the Atlantic nine times during her life to raise funds and expand her order's work in Italy, Spain, France, Switzerland, and England. By the time she died, she had established more than sixty foundations on three continents, and the Missionary Sisters of the Sacred Heart had more than a thousand members. They staffed free elementary schools and high schools, hospitals (including Columbus Hospital in Chicago), and orphanages; they worked with prisoners on death row.

Frances Xavier Cabrini became an American citizen in 1911. Though age slowed her, it did not curtail her energy, and when she died in 1917, at the age of sixty-one, she was wrapping Christmas presents for school children. Her body is enshrined in the chapel of Mother Cabrini High School in New York City. She was canonized in 1946, the first American to be so recognized.

SEEING DETOURS AS BLESSINGS

"I can't believe it," my friend said. "Why me?" Caught up in the enthusiasm of our parish's "sign-up Sunday," she had volunteered to work in religious education, stipulating that she wanted to work with adults in faith formation. Now, though, she had received her assignment, and it was with junior high school youth. "I don't know anything about kids that age!" she wailed to me. "I was looking forward to doing something substantive, to really talking about faith with people who wanted to listen. I don't want to be a babysitter. I don't want to deal with bored kids. Can I quit before I even start?"

Teaching assignments, as all of us teachers know, can be surprising things. We believe that those who supervise us know our strengths. We establish credentials working with a particular age group; we study hard to keep up-to-date on particular subjects. We let those in charge know what we'd like to teach. Then, for some reason, the powers that be give us assignments we consider uncongenial or for which we're unprepared—a new grade or age group, a different school or teaching situation, a new subject, a new committee or administrative assignment. It *is* tempting to want to quit when this happens, or at least to dream about quitting. It's discouraging to feel that our preferences and gifts have been dismissed.

To me, one of the many endearing things about Frances Xavier Cabrini is that—saint though she was—she initially dug in her heels when it seemed as if her dream of going to China was doomed. "No!" she said, several times, when she was asked to serve in New York. All of us who have ever said, "No" or "Are you kidding?" or "But I asked to teach *adults*!" can take comfort in the fact that even this holy woman was human enough to whine a little, at first, when those above her disregarded her wishes. Where Cabrini becomes a mentor, though, is in what she did next: she ascertained God's will (through the pope in her case, though it might have been also through prayer, or by consulting loving but truthful advisors) and, when she realized that she *would* have to do something other than what she'd wanted, she threw herself into the new work with good will and almost superhuman energy. No whining now; no looking back. If this were to be her path, she would follow it with all the dedication of which she was capable.

Frances Xavier Cabrini's letters show just how concrete her dedication was. Besides providing spiritual advice to her nuns (advice emphasizing obedience and humility, virtues that she herself had had to practice), she also offers very practical management instructions for the dozens of convents under her direction. She chides one sister for paying too much for coal; she advises another to make sure that wine is good before she buys it. She laments that one convent has incurred a huge repair debt without money to pay it, noting that she is transferring the sisters responsible; she asks nuns at another convent to pray especially hard that a novice's problems will be overcome because they need her to teach music and languages. "Who knows what the Sacred Heart wants! Surely I did not expect what I see," she laments of a boarding-school project that had become very complicated. She also did very basic hands-on work, literally pick-and-shovel work. Once, when sisters in San Francisco were beginning a building project, Mother Cabrini was on hand to demonstrate the use of construction tools. "A missionary must be able to do any kind of work," she proclaimed.

Despite the daunting task of overseeing the Missionary Sisters' work on three continents, Cabrini never lost her zest for expanding her order's reach. Though she had been afraid of water travel as a child, she went back and forth across the ocean, to Europe, to South America, crossing wild and dangerous territory. She knew the importance of personal contact in procuring funds and goodwill; had she lived today, she would have been a queen of frequent flyer miles. Because she was so energetic, her life brought hope, health, education, and spiritual gifts not simply to the Italian immigrants whom she was called at first to serve, but to people across the world. Through it all, she kept her individual touch, ministering to people one by one with great love: she is the internationally renowned mother superior who died wrapping a child's Christmas present. For all of this, she was deeply loved and universally honored.

Being thwarted in our expectations—short– or long-term—is difficult. But sometimes, as Frances Xavier Cabrini's life suggests, apparent detours can be blessings. If we can firmly bid our preconceptions good-bye, then turn to the work we have been asked to do, determined to make the best of it, we might even find, as she did, that we have come to the place we were supposed to be all along.

For Further Reading

A Benedictine of Stanbrook, *Frances Xavier Cabrini: A Saint of the Immigrants* (n.p.: Catholic Book Club, 1946).

Frances Xavier Cabrini, *The Letters of Frances Xavier Cabrini*, trans. Ursula Infante (Chicago: Office of the Archbishop, 1970).

Kathleen Jones, "Frances Xavier Cabrini," in *Women Saints: Lives of Faith and Courage* (Maryknoll, NY: Orbis Books, 1999), 259–67.

Theodore Maynard, *Too Small a World; The Life of Francesca Cabrini* (Milwaukee: The Bruce Publishing Company, 1945).

Butler's, 4:593–97.

Oxford, 82.

52

The Importance of
Meeting Fundamental Needs

St. Albert Chmielowski

1845–1916 ~ Poland ~ Feast: December 25

S t. Albert Chmielowski was born in Poland in 1845. Though he lost his father at the age of eight, he came from a comfortable family and was well educated, studying in Saint Petersburg and Warsaw. He also displayed a strong sense of social justice. Like so many Poles in his period, Chmielowski resented Russian rule of his country. He fought in the unsuccessful insurrection of 1863 but escaped sentencing to a firing squad because he had lost his leg and government mercy was extended to those who suffered grievous wounds. Disillusioned by the failure of the freedom fighters, he left Poland to study in Paris and Munich, completing his education as a painter.

In 1880, when he was thirty-five, Chmielowski entered the Society of Jesus at Stara-Wies, but poor health caused him to abandon his formation after six months. He found himself strongly called to an alternate vocation, however, which gave his life the direction for which he had yearned. He became an apostle of the Third Order of St. Francis in 1881, and, after meeting Blessed Raphael Jozef Kalinowski, decided to dedicate his life to serving God by serving the poor. As Brother Albert, he recruited for the order and gave practical aid to the homeless. One of his first acts, using funds he had saved through his own frugal life, was to provide a heated room where the poor could warm themselves during the bitter Polish winters. By begging for the homeless, he founded hostels and workshops, accumulating enough money to establish emergency lodging for hundreds.

In 1888, Brother Albert took formal vows of poverty and chastity and founded the religious congregation known today as the Albertine Brothers and Sisters (the "Grey Brothers" and "Grey Sisters"), dedicated to ministering to the physical needs of the poor. Brother Albert served as a model for the order, living as a poor man and fraternizing with the homeless. "Let us be bread," he instructed his followers, reminding them of Christ's words, "I was homeless, and you sheltered me." Christ is present, he would say, in those whom the order served. He was noted for his sympathy and respect for everyone who needed him and for his energy in reaching out to them.

Brother Albert died in 1916 in one of his own refuges in Kraków. Today brothers of his order continue to staff eight hostels. Pope John Paul II canonized him in 1989, "for the consolation of all homeless people, for whom this Polish saint can be a powerful intercessor, just as he was a generous helper to them while on earth." Praised for his "tireless, heroic service on behalf of the marginalized and the poor," Brother Albert Chmielowski serves as an inspiration for all who work with those in need.

BEING BREAD FOR OUR STUDENTS

By giving his life to the homeless people of Poland, Albert Chmielowski embodied a truth that also applies in teachers' work: before one can hope to influence people's souls and minds, one must make sure that people are not anxious about their most basic needs. Warmth in times of cold; food in times of hunger; friendship in times of loneliness—when people do not have these physical and emotional necessities, their ability to grow spiritually and intellectually is hampered. Brother Albert, the political revolutionary manqué, became a hero of *Christian* revolution when he established his hospices and became an active friend of the poor. "Be good, like the nourishing bread that's ready on the table for all who may be hungry," he proclaimed as his motto, and he was "bread" in all senses for his poor.

Like Brother Albert, teachers every day see young people entrusted to their care who need "bread" of some kind, and we must address their fundamental hungers if we hope to touch their minds and spirits. In almost any community, we may see children who are physically hungry or without adequate warm clothing. Taking Brother Albert as a mentor, we can help those children and their families take advantage of social services about which they might be uninformed, especially if they are new to our community. It feels risky to reach out to such families—what if we have misread their circumstances, and we insult them?—but the good that we may do exponentially outweighs such a risk. We might recommend a child for a subsidized lunch program; we might meet with the child's parents and offer them a list of contact names and numbers; we might even, if the parents are timid, offer to accompany them to a social service agency. Won't this impose on our time? We may already feel a little resentful at working so hard for a low salary compared to what other professionals are paid, or may feel that we are already being exploited in our calling as volunteers. But can we do less, if we take Brother Albert as our mentor?

Another kind of bread that children often lack is a feeling of belonging. Less visible, this hunger nevertheless hampers students' development. Even children who appear to have everything going for them can find themselves lonely, shunned, and mocked by their peers in the cruel system of childhood cliques. Sometimes these children are stigmatized by their weight, looks, or clothes; sometimes they are shunned for being smarter, less intelligent, more introspective, even more cooperative with adults than others; sometimes they simply don't have good relational skills. While adults might be tempted to shrug off clique behavior ("kids are just like that—what can you do?"), a recent book, *Odd Girl Out: The Hidden Culture of Aggression in Girls*, by

Rachel Simmons, discusses the serious effects such shunning can have on children's psychological health. One of the saddest things Simmons reveals is that teachers often seem oblivious to children's cruelty toward one another. Emotionally devastated by peers' behavior, shunned children may find their self-doubt and sorrow compounded when teachers appear complicit. *There must be something wrong with me,* they think, *if even the teacher thinks that they're right.*

Reaching out to such children is as risky as addressing children's physical needs. We may think it's not our business to intervene in their quarrels or their pecking order. *It will blow over,* we tell ourselves. But shunning often does not blow over, and we are dodging our fundamental responsibilities if we turn a blind eye. We must find ways to involve the outsider student with peers, to help that child shine in ways that other children will admire. Simply praising the student usually won't do, for others may resent a teacher's pet. We are challenged, in such situations, to be actively creative, drawing the student into relationships with others from which others will benefit. At the very least, we can offer lonely students our friendship: recommend books, offer to be a sounding board, share our wisdom about making friends. If we do such things, we are bread indeed.

When Pope John Paul canonized Brother Albert in 1989, he praised him for his "tireless, heroic service on behalf of the marginalized and the poor." As teachers, we can also perform such service—but only if we open our eyes and see all the varieties of poverty that come between our students and what we hope to teach them.

For Further Reading

Ferdinand Holböck, "Albert Chimielowski," in *New Saints and Blesseds of the Catholic Church: Blesseds and Saints Canonized by Pope John Paul II during the Years 1979–1983,* trans. Michael J. Miller (San Francisco: Ignatius Press, 2000), 162–67.

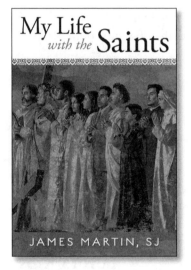

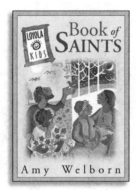
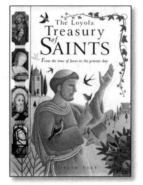

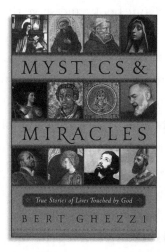

A Special Invitation

Loyola Press invites you to become one of our Loyola Press Advisors! Join our unique online community of people willing to share with us their thoughts and ideas about Catholic life and faith. By sharing your perspective, you will help us improve our books and serve the greater Catholic community.

From time to time, registered advisors are invited to participate in online surveys and discussion groups. Most surveys will take less than ten minutes to complete. Loyola Press will recognize your time and efforts with gift certificates and prizes. Your personal information will be held in strict confidence. Your participation will be for research purposes only, and at no time will we try to sell you anything.

Please consider this opportunity to help Loyola Press improve our products and better serve you and the Catholic community. To learn more or to join, visit **www.SpiritedTalk.org** and register today.

—THE LOYOLA PRESS ADVISORY TEAM